THE
PRACTICE
OF
RESPONSE:

STRATEGIES
FOR COMMENTING
ON STUDENT WRITING

Richard Straub
Florida State University

Printed in the United States of America

Library of Congress Cataloging-in-Publication Data

Straub, Richard.
    The practice of response : strategies for commenting on student writing / Richard Straub.
       p. cm.
    Includes bibliographical references and index.
    ISBN 1-57273-335-7 (pb)
    1. English language--Rhetoric--Study and teaching. 2. Report writing--Study and teaching. 3. Grading and marking (Students) 4. College prose--Evaluation. I. Title.

PE1404.S8368 2000
808'.042'0711--dc21

00-056705

Hampton Press, Inc.
23 Broadway
Cresskill, NJ 07605

To the teachers who responded with such involvement and care
to my work as a student, and, in responding as they did,
made a difference:

Joan Bobbitt
Helen Hogan
Paul Bradigan
Sam Incavido
Barnett Gutenberg
Frank Wills
Ronald F. Lunsford
Joan Bobbitt
James Phelan
Frank O'Hare

You set some example.

Contents

Acknowledgments

Once again, I'd like to thank the twelve teachers who contributed to the original study and whose work I examine again here: Chris Anson, Peter Elbow, Anne Gere, Glynda Hull, Richard Larson, Ben McClelland, Frank O'Hare, Jane Peterson, the late Donald Stewart, Patricia Stock, Tilly Warnock, and Edward White. Just how much I've made of their sample responses across the years indicates how valuable I think they are. I'd also like to thank the teachers who contributed materials from their classrooms to this project: Simone Billings, Ron DePeter, Christine Helfers, Margaret Lindgren, Peggy O'Neill, Summer Smith, and Tom Thompson. It has been refreshing working with them. Finally, I'd like to thank the readers who reviewed this project in its early stages and offered such rich responses: Peter Elbow, Richard Fulkerson, Susan Taylor, and Edward White. Their comments helped me envision the possibilities in this book and make it far better than it would have been without their help, their presence. And, once again, I'd like to thank Barbara Bernstein, for once again trusting in the value of this kind of work with teacher response—and trusting generally in the value of books that help teachers reflect on their teaching and make themselves better teachers.

I appreciate all your help.

(Note: Chapter 7 is a revision of an article that first appeared in *Research in the Teaching of English* 31 (February 1997).

Introduction

You sit down to a stack of 25 student papers, your legs curled under the chair, your whole body leaning into the table. The third assignment in the class. This time, you think, I'm going to be more focused. More decisive, more disciplined, more efficient. No going back and forth about what to comment on or how much to say. No getting bogged down.

The first paper goes by fast. And the second. Good papers more or less, with something to say and some wherewithal of form. You're sticking to your agenda and happy with what you say. You do just a bit more than planned with the third and it takes a little longer. Half way through the fourth you're pausing more than you read, wondering how this narrative of a friend's wedding goes with the opening paragraphs about the writer's relationship with her father. And then, by the fifth or sixth paper, one a maelstrom of words and ideas, the other a meticulous ordering of the obvious, you find yourself puzzling over every other line. Should you help the writer see how to clarify these sentences? Should you suggest ways of complicating those commonplace claims? You're getting off track, falling behind schedule, needing to make up ground.

You sit back in the chair and take a breath. Glance furtively at the still-tall stack of papers. Quell a ping of anxiety. Rock back to the paper in front of you, read faster, pause less, write more quickly. A couple more papers and you're counting how many papers you've got left, thinking there's got to be a better way to do this, wondering whether all this commenting will make any difference, a voice in the back of your mind saying no, it won't, just get them done, another voice saying yes, it might, just give it a try. And so it goes, paper by paper, until it seems your whole attention is given to just getting through that last response.

Writing teachers probably spend as much time and effort responding to student writing as they do teaching and preparing for class. It is the most demanding, work-intensive part of the job, and I would argue that there is no more important task that writing teachers take on. Response is at the heart of writing instruction. Here on the pages of your students' writing you find the most telling signs of what they are getting from the course. You have the best opportunity to give substance to the principles you've been advocating in class. You can see what is taking root and what needs more water or light. Here, you can help students work on what they most need to work on individually as writers. But it is difficult. Difficult because it calls on everything you are about in the class and sets in motion a universe of concerns you've got to keep in mind: the words on the page, the assignment and genre, the audience and rhetorical situation, the point in the course, the work in class, the student, the student's earlier work, and the work of other students. What do you look for? How much do you comment? Do you mark whatever you see or, if you get more selective, how do you decide what to addresss and what to pass by? What roles should you assume? Editor? Critic? Adviser? Collaborator? Coach? Difficult because so much in response depends on your goals for commenting. Are you looking to assess the quality of the writing? Identify areas to work on? Make improvements in the text? Lead the student back into the writing, back into revision, and perhaps even help him develop his sense as a writer? Difficult because so much depends, in turn, on your course goals. Are you trying to clarify and clean up students' prose? Make their writing more rhetorically effective? Help them develop and share their thoughts more productively with others? Initiate them into the conventions of academic discourse? Give students practice in discovering, drafting, and revising? Help them develop as writers over time? Are you looking to prepare them for the writing they'll do in the second-semester writing class? Their writing in other courses? Their work to come after graduation? Are you looking (simply?) to help them express themselves better? Discover the uses that writing may have in their lives? Help them become critical citizens? All of these goals? Some of them? Response to student writing can be only as successful as it works within this universe of goals. To respond well, you have to know what you want to accomplish in your comments—and you have to know what you want to accomplish in this assignment and through the class as a whole. No wonder all the difficulty, all the anxiety, all the time.

This book tries to give order to this complexity by defining certain ways of looking at response and offering strategies for pursuing your own purposes as a writing teacher. It tries to provide a manageable list of principles and practices that might guide your attempts to develop your own ways of responding. It does so by:

1. displaying samples of how experienced teachers respond to student writing;

2. analyzing the strategies these teachers use in their responses;

3. considering methods of response in terms of the larger context of instruction.

The book follows up on research I have done with Ronald F. Lunsford and published in *Twelve Readers Reading: Responding to College Student Writing* (Hampton 1995), a study of the ways that 12 well-recognized compositionists respond to a common sampling of student writings. It is also a companion to another guide I have put together on response, *A Sourcebook on Responding to Student Writing* (Hampton 1999), which presents 36 sample teacher responses—free of any analysis—and an anthology of key articles by frontliners in research on response. *The Practice of Response: Strategies for Commenting on Student Writing* provides plenty of sample teacher comments, but, in addition, it offers detailed analyses of these comments, formulates these responders' practices into a set of principles, and situates response in relation to the overall work of the writing class.

Chapter 1 presents 13 sets of responses on a sampling of three student papers. The responses are made according to hypothetical classroom situations and written by nine recognized teacher-theorists: Edward White, Anne Gere, Ben McClelland, Peter Elbow, Glynda Hull, Chris Anson, Richard Larson, Frank O'Hare, and Patricia Stock. Each of the papers is presented with a hypothetical context—a scenario including the writing assignment, the stage of drafting, the point in the course, some information about the work in class, and a short profile of the student writer. I present short analyses of each set of responses, examining what these teachers focus on and how they shape their comments. Chapter 2 presents a method for analyzing comments and demonstrates how teachers may use it to define their methods of response and make strategic adjustments in their own responding styles.

Chapter 3 moves the study of response into real classroom settings. I present six case studies of teacher response: six sets of responses made by six different teachers to students in their own classrooms. The six teachers are all new composition specialists who have recently published work on responding to student writing: Simone Billings, Ron DePeter, Margaret Lindgren, Peggy O'Neill, Summer Smith, and Tom Thompson. Each case includes a description of the course, presents the writing assignment, recreates the circumstances that inform the writing, and provides a brief profile of the student writer. I analyze these responses and look at them in relation to the larger work of the class and use the cases to raise questions about responding to student writing. In Chapter 4, I go one step further into examining response in the full context of an actual course. Instead of studying isolated cases of response—comments to one student, on one paper, at one point in the course—I study a series of responses to several students over a series of assignments. This time, the cases come from my own first-year writing classroom. I use these cases to show how the responses we make on a given paper, to a particular student, are influenced not only by the larger work of the class but also by the work of other students and by the individual student's ongoing work as a writer. Through the three chapters of case studies—from model responses, to actual classroom responses in isolation, to actual responses in the fuller context of a class—I aim to provide readers with a profile of the principles, methods, and goals that animate well-informed teachers' ways of responding to student writing, with the hope of helping them develop their own ways of talking with students about their work as writers.

The next three chapters present a series of short essays on practical matters of response. Chapter 5, "Guidelines for Responding to Student Writing," presents an overview of strategies for commenting. Chapter 6, "Managing the Paper Load, Or Making Good Use of Time," offers tips for cutting back on the time it takes to respond and, at the same time, making better responses. Chapter 7, "Students' Perceptions of Teacher Comments," reviews the results of a survey of how students viewed teacher commentary and rated different types of responses. Chapter 8 presents a selected bibliography on teacher response. The final chapter offers several additional student essays and classroom contexts without any comments, to give teachers a chance to experiment with their own (evolving) response styles, unencumbered by the anxiety of immediate influence.

All of the comments have been refitted into a common format. I have accepted the loss in the original appearance of the comments for a gain in space and readability. The only resulting change in format I regret is the loss of displaying the marks and comments that these teachers made, as they made them, between the lines of a student's text. All the comments they made on the papers are now displayed in a common area in an extended right-hand margin, which sometimes makes a page look busier than it was (or sometimes not as busy as it was) in the original and sometimes does not capture graphically how much or little a teacher marked up a text. I tried as best I could to replicate the responders' use of lines and arrows to identify passages they were addressing and indicate changes they proposed. I inserted a caret (^) where the responder layered her own words or corrections between the lines of the student's text, and I underlined words that the teacher underlined or circled. (All underlinings and boldface markings in the students' texts, in fact, are by the teachers, not by the student writers.) I standardized all end comments and letters to the student. In my own writing, I alternate the uses of "her" and "his" to avoid sexist language.

This book is predicated on the belief that there is no single best way of teaching writing and no single best way of responding to student writing. Different teachers, in different settings, with different students, different kinds of writing, different course goals, and with different time constraints may do substantially different things with their comments, and do them well. Ultimately it comes down to what works best for us as individual teachers, given our own inclinations and aims, and what can be made to work best for this particular student, with this paper, in this setting, at this time. This is not to say that anything goes. Or that whatever we come up with in a set of comments will do. There are some principles and practices that I think should be part of every teacher's response style—and some practices that have no place at all in teacher response. The book sets out to show a range of informed teachers about the task of responding to student writing, define an array of responding strategies, examine response in the context of the larger work of teaching writing, help new and experienced teachers find ways to develop their own methods of response, and inspire a positive attitude about responding to student writing.

Response is not just one of the things we do as writing teachers, just another task that comes with the territory. Response is integral to the teaching of writing and to improvement in writing. Getting responses from others helps writers see how their writing is experienced by readers, where it is and is not working, and how it might be made to work better. It helps them revisit what they think and envision how they might shape their texts in ways that more aptly instantiate their intentions and share their ideas and experience with others. In the long term, getting responses from others helps writers develop their sense of how texts work and how their own texts can be made to do more, to work better. Responding to student writing, properly pursued, takes time. It involves an enormous effort, a deep belief in the power of language and the possibilities of writing. But there is no more effective way to teach writing or help students learn to write better. If this book helps teachers reflect on their ways of commenting, expand their repertoire of response strategies, tie their comments more tightly to their course goals and the needs of individual students, and see how they may make good use of their time as responders, it will have done plenty.

1

Models of Response: How Recognized Teachers Respond to Student Writing

There is no single best way to respond to student writing. Different teachers, assuming different styles and different classroom goals, can make very different kinds of comments yet make them effectively. Different students will find some kinds of comments more or less useful than others. Nevertheless, some ways of responding are better than others, and some kinds of responses it is hard to imagine being of any use at all. In this chapter I present 13 sets of teacher responses to a sampling of three student essays and use them as cases for examining effective strategies of commentary. The comments were written by well-recognized composition theorists on a common sampling of essays written by first-year college writers. The papers were presented with hypothetical contexts—scenarios that included the writing assignment, the stage of drafting, the point in the course, information about the work in class, and, as often as not, a short profile of the student writer. The teachers were asked to respond to the essays, according to these hypothetical contexts, in ways that would illustrate their best responding style.

Taken together, the comments form a test site for teacher response, providing examples of how well-informed teachers read texts and talk with students about their writing. What do these teachers address in their comments? Do they concentrate more on form or content? On the writer's ideas and purposes or on sentence structure and wording? How much do they deal with the larger contexts of writing: the rhetorical context, the classroom context, and the larger academic and social setting? How much do they deal with errors in mechanics, spelling, and punctuation? How many issues do they attempt to deal with in a given set of comments? How many comments do they make on each paper? Do they make more comments on rough drafts or final drafts? On immature drafts or mature drafts? What roles do they assume as responders and how do they talk with students about their writing? Do they come straight out and point to errors and make corrections? Do they offer advice and indirectly lead students to make certain changes? Or do they encourage students to decide themselves what changes to make and how to make them? To what extent do they direct students' revisions? To what extent do they allow students to retain control over their own writing choices?

I'll take up these questions incrementally in three groups, using sample responses on each essay as cases for studying a different set of issues. I'll present four sets of comments on "What If Drugs Were Legal?," an argument written in response to a *New York Times* column calling on Americans to think about legalizing drugs like marijuana and cocaine, and I'll consider issues about the focus and scope of teacher commentary. I'll present four sets of comments on "The Four Seasons," a descriptive essay about the writer's views on the seasons in Syracuse, New York, and consider the number, length, and specificity of these teachers' comments. Then I'll present five sets of comments on a third student paper, an expressive essay entitled "Street Gangs: One Point of View," and consider the various modes of response and the issue of control in teacher commentary. Here is a listing of the responders and issues I'll take up for each sample essay:

"What If Drugs Were Legal?": Focus and Scope of Comments

> Edward White
> Anne Gere
> Ben McClelland
> Peter Elbow

"The Four Seasons": Length and Specificity of Comments

> Anne Gere
> Edward White
> Glynda Hull
> Chris Anson

"Street Gangs": Modes of Commentary and Teacher Control

> Richard Larson
> Frank O'Hare
> Glynda Hull
> Patricia Stock
> Peter Elbow

In order to make possible a more fruitful study of responding styles, I'll present two sets of comments by four teachers with markedly different styles: Edward White, Anne Gere, Glynda Hull, and Peter Elbow. Through this analysis, I hope to provide a language and a method for helping teachers reflect on their strategies of commentary and develop their own style of response.

What If Drugs Were Legal?
Context

BACKGROUND

This is the first rough draft of an argumentative response essay. Through the first several weeks of the course, the class has focused on various kinds of expressive writing, and students have been writing essays mostly from their personal experience. Now the class is moving into transactional writing on topics which may include, but which must extend beyond, their firsthand experience. As a bridge into the second half of the course, students are to write a response essay in which they express their views on what another writer has to say about an issue. In anticipation of this assignment, students have been given practice in summarizing and paraphrasing the ideas of others. Although they have written several essays up to this point, this is the first paper that they will take through several drafts and receive another's comments on before they hand in the final draft.

This particular student, Nancy, sees herself as a "good writer." As she has told you a few times already (both verbally and in her course journal), she "has always gotten A's in English." Evidently, she is confused, or even put off, by your view of writing and, particularly, your assessment of her work thus far in the course. She has been somewhat resistant to changing her style and process of writing, and has not been very responsive to your comments on the four previous course papers.

ASSIGNMENT

Select from a journal, magazine, or newspaper, a recent article on an issue you are interested in, one that presents a view you disagree with or that you find some problem with. In an essay intended for the same publication, write a response to the article. You may respond to the article as a whole or to parts of it. Your task is not to review the article for its own sake but to express your views on what this writer has to say. Your final draft should identify the author, title, and publication information somewhere in the opening, define the topic or issue you are responding to and summarize what the author says about it, and then present your response.

We'll take this essay through two rough drafts before the final draft is due, two weeks from today. I will respond to both the first rough draft and the second rough draft.

Legalize Drugs

By John LeMoult

As a trial lawyer with some 20 years' experience, I have followed the battle against drugs with a keen interest. Month after month, we have read stories of how the Government has made a major seizure of drugs and cracked an important drug ring. It is reassuring to know that for more than 20 years our Federal, state and local governments have been making such headway against drugs. It reminds me of the body counts during the Vietnam War, when every week we heard of large numbers of North Vietnamese and Vietcong soldiers killed in battle. Somehow, they kept coming, and they finally forced us out and overwhelmed their enemies.

Every elected official from President Reagan on down goes through the ritual of calling for stiffer enforcement of drug and trafficking laws. The laws get stricter, and more and more billions of dollars are spent on the police, courts, judges, jails, customs inspectors and informants. But the drugs keep coming, keep growing, leaking into this country through thousands of little holes. Traffic is funded by huge financial combines and small entrepreneurs. Drugs are carried by organized crime figures and ordinary people. The truth is, the stricter the enforcement, the more money there is in smuggling.

Legalization is not a new idea. But perhaps it is time to recognize that vigorous drug enforcement will not plug the holes. Perhaps it is time to think the unthinkable. What would happen if we legalized heroin, cocaine, marijuana and other drugs? What if they were regulated like liquor and with the protections provided for over-the-counter drugs? Would we turn into a nation of spaced-out drug addicts?

Drugs have been a part of our society for some time. The first antidrug laws in the United States were passed in 1914. They were really anti-Chinese laws, because people on the West Coast were alarmed at the rise of opium dens among Chinese immigrants. Before that, there were plenty of opium addicts in the United States, but they were mostly white middle-class women who took laudanum (then available over the counter) because it was considered unacceptable for women to to drink alcohol.

After the first laws were passed, and more drugs added to the forbidden list, the sale of heroin and other drugs shifted to the ghettos, where men desperate for money were willing to risk prison to make a sale. Middle-class addicts switched to alcohol. Today, one in 10 Americans is an alcohol addict.

It is accepted. The number of addicts of heroin and other drugs is tiny compared with the number of alcoholics. But these drugs cause 10 times the amount of crime caused by alcohol.

What would happen if the other drugs were legal? Many experts believe there would be no increase in the number of drug addicts. They speak of an addictive personality and say that if such a person cannot easily obtain one drug he will become addicted to another. Many feel that the legalization of heroin and other drugs would mean that such addictive types would change from alcohol to other drugs. A 1972 Ford Foundation study showed that addiction to these other drugs is no more harmful than addiction to alcohol.

But what about crime? Overnight it would, be dealt a shattering blow. Legal heroin and cocaine sold in drugstores, only to people over 21, and protected by our pure food and drug laws, would sell at a very small fraction of its current street value. The adulterated and dangerous heroin concoctions available today for $20 from your friendly pusher would, in clean form with proper dosage on the package, sell for about 50 cents in a drugstore. There would be no need for crime.

With addicts no longer desperate for money to buy drugs, mugging and robbery in our major cities would be more than cut in half. The streets would be safer. There would be no more importers, sellers and buyers on the black market. It would become uneconomical. Huge crime rings would go out of business.

More than half the crime in America is drug related. But drugs themselves do not cause crime. Crime is caused by the laws against drugs and the need of addicts to steal money for their purchase. Overnight the cost of law enforcement, courts, judges, jails and convict rehabilitation would be cut in half. The savings in taxes would be mom than $50 billion a year.

We may not be ready for a radical step of this kind. Perhaps we are willing to spend $50 billion a year and suffer the unsafe streets to express our moral opposition to drugs. But we should at least examine the benefits of legalization. We should try to find out whether drug use would dramatically increase, what the tax savings would be. I do not suggest that we legalize drugs immediately. I ask only that we give it some thought.

— *New York Times 1984*

What If Drugs Were Legal?
Rough Draft

Nancy S.
First Rough Draft

What If Drugs Were Legal?

What if drugs were legal? Could you imagine what it would do to our society? Well according to John E. LeMoult, a lawyer with twenty years of experience on the subject, feels we should at least consider it. I would like to comment on his article "Legalize Drugs" in the June 15, 1984, issue of the *New York Times*. I disagree with LeMoult's idea of legalizing drugs to cut the cost of crime.

LeMoult's article was short and sweet. He gives the background of the legalization of drugs. For example, the first antidrug laws of the United States were passed in 1914. The laws were put in effect because of the threat of the Chinese imagrants. In addition, he explains how women were the first to use laudanun, an over the counter drug, as a substitute for drinking; it was unacceptable for women to drink. By explaining this he made the reader feel that society was the cause of women using the substitute, laudanun, for drinking. LeMoult proceeded from there to explain how the money to buy drugs comes from us as society. Since drug addicts turn to crime to get money we become a corrupt society. Due to this we spend unnecessary money protecting inocent citizens by means of law enforcment, jails, and ect. LeMoult says that if we legalize drugs that "Overnight the cost of law enforcement, courts, judges, jails and convict rehabilitation would be cut in half. The savings in tax would be more than $50 billion a year."

LeMoult might be correct by saying that our cost of living in society would be cut in half if drugs were legalized, however, he is justifying a wrong to save money. In my opinion legalizing drugs is the easy man's way out. Just because crime is high due to the fact that the cost of drugs is unbeleivable it doesn't make legalizing them right. We all know drugs are dangerous to the body and society without any explanation, therefore, you shouldn't legalize something that is dangerous.

My only and most important argument to LeMoult is the physical harm it would bring by legalizing drugs. People abuse their right to use alcoholic beverages because they are legal. For example, LeMoult himself says the amount of drug addicts is small compared to alcoholics. Why?—of course it is because of the legalization of alcohol. When you make something legal it can and will be done with little hassel. Why allow something to be done with ease when it is wrong? LeMoult's points are good and true but I believe he is approaching the subject in the wrong manner. Drugs are wrong, therefore, should not be legal!

What If Drugs Were Legal?
Edward White's Comments

Nancy S.
First Rough Draft

What If Drugs Were Legal?

What if drugs were legal? Could you imagine what it would do to our society? Well according to John E. LeMoult, a lawyer with twenty years of experience on the subject, feels we should at least consider it. I would like to comment on his article "Legalize Drugs" in the June 15, 1984, issue of the *New York Times*. I disagree with LeMoult's idea of legalizing drugs to cut the cost of crime.

Now that you are clear on what you have to say (see your last prgh), revise the opening to begin your argument.

LeMoult's article was short and sweet. He gives the background of the legalization of drugs. For example, the first antidrug laws of the United States were passed in 1914. The laws were put in effect because of the threat of the Chinese imagrants. In addition, he explains how women were the first to use laudanun, an over the counter drug, as a substitute for drinking; it was unacceptable for women to drink. By explaining this he made the reader feel that society was the cause of women using the substitute, laudanun, for drinking. LeMoult proceeded from there to explain how the money to buy drugs comes from us as society. Since drug addicts turn to crime to get money we become a corrupt society. Due to this we spend unnecessary money protecting inocent citizens by means of law enforcment, jails, and ect. LeMoult says that if we legalize drugs that "Overnight the cost of law enforcement, courts, judges, jails and convict rehabilitation would be cut in half. The savings in tax would be more than $50 billion a year."

Select the parts of LeMoult's article that are appropriate for your paper and omit the rest. Be sure to quote accurately.

LeMoult might be correct by saying that our cost of living in society would be cut in half if drugs were legalized, however, he is justifying a wrong to save money. In my opinion legalizing drugs is the easy <u>man's</u> way out. Just because crime is high due to the fact that the cost of drugs is unbel<u>e</u>ivable it doesn't make legalizing them right. We all know drugs are dangerous to the body and society without any explanation, therefore, you shouldn't legalize something that is dangerous.

Your first argument: the financial reasons are not good enough for legalization. Focus this prgh on this argument and develop your case.

<u>My only and most important argument</u> to LeMoult is the physical harm it would bring by legalizing drugs. People abuse their right to use alcoholic beverages because they are legal. For example, LeMoult himself says the amount of drug addicts is small compared to alcoholics. Why?—of course it is because of the legalization of alcohol. When you make something legal it can and will be done with little hassle. Why allow something to be done with ease when it is wrong? LeMoult's points are good and true but I believe he is approaching the subject in the wrong manner. Drugs are wrong, therefore, should not be legal!

Not so. Look at the previous prgh.

Second argument. Now develop this one.

Make this into a full closing prgh.

The paper is a good discovery draft that could become a good paper. As you revise, be sure you focus each prgh on its central idea. I enjoy the energy of your style.

What If Drugs Were Legal?
Anne Gere's Comments

Nancy S.
First Rough Draft

What If Drugs Were Legal?

What if drugs were legal? Could you imagine what it would do to our society? Well according to John E. LeMoult, a lawyer with twenty years of experience on the subject, feels we should at least consider it. I would like to comment on his article "Legalize Drugs" in the June 15, 1984, issue of the *New York Times*. I disagree with LeMoult's idea of legalizing drugs to cut the cost of crime.

What about starting with this point?

LeMoult's article was short and sweet. He gives the background of the legalization of drugs. For example, the first antidrug laws of the United States were passed in 1914. The laws were put in effect because of the threat of the Chinese imagrants. In addition, he explains how women were the first to use laudanun, an over the counter drug, as a substitute for drinking; it was unacceptable for women to drink. By explaining this he made the reader feel that society was the cause of women using the substitute, laudanun, for drinking. LeMoult proceeded from there to explain how the money to buy drugs comes from us as society. Since drug addicts turn to crime to get money we become a corrupt society. Due to this we spend unnecessary money protecting inocent citizens by means of law enforcment, jails, and ect. LeMoult says that if we legalize drugs that "Overnight the cost of law enforcement, courts, judges, jails and convict rehabilitation would be cut in half. The savings in tax would be more than $50 billion a year."

How does this advance LeMoult's argument for legalizing drugs?

LeMoult might be correct by saying that our cost of living in society would be cut in half if drugs were legalized, however, he is justifying a wrong to save money. In my opinion legalizing drugs is the easy man's way out. Just because crime is high due to the fact that the cost of drugs is unbeleivable it doesn't make legalizing them right. We all know drugs are dangerous to the body and society without any explanation, therefore, you shouldn't legalize something that is dangerous.

How can you be sure we all know "without any explanation"?

My only and most important argument to LeMoult is the physical harm it would bring by legalizing drugs. People abuse their right to use alcoholic beverages because they are legal. For example, LeMoult himself says the amount of drug addicts is small compared to alcoholics. Why?—of course it is because of the legalization of alcohol. When you make something legal it can and will be done with little hassel. Why allow something to be done with ease when it is wrong? LeMoult's points are good and true but I believe he is approaching the subject in the wrong manner. Drugs are wrong, therefore, should not be legal!

Can you develop this argument?

Nancy—

You have done a good job of summarizing much of LeMoult's article. I think you have overlooked a couple of important points, however. Reread the section where he traces the history of drugs in this country, and look again at his distinction between drugs and alcohol.

I find your argument against legalizing drugs the most convincing when you compare the number of alcoholics with the number of drug addicts. Perhaps you can develop this idea further. In contrast, I find the statements that we all know drugs are wrong less than convincing. Just exactly why is legalizing drugs the easy way out? If danger is the issue, how do you respond to the idea that cars are dangerous? (Think about how many people are killed and maimed in automobile accidents every year.) In your next draft try to focus on developing more convincing arguments against legalized drugs.

When you have completed your next draft, try reading it aloud before you turn it in. I think you will find a number of places where your ears will help you express your ideas more effectively.

What If Drugs Were Legal?
Ben McClelland's Comments

What is it that you want me most to know about your position on LeMoult's article, "Legalize Drugs," Nancy? Try stating that point in a sentence or two. In order to understand your position on LeMoult's article then, just what do I need to know about his article? That is, what specific points do you need to summarize from his article and which ones may you disregard? I ask you to work out these two matters because, as I read your draft, I need a clearer sense of both. Before reading further in my comments, please jot down a list of items on them.

First, with regard to your position, did you say that you were against legalizing drugs because they were physically harmful and, therefore, morally wrong? Those are the points that I gleaned from your last two paragraphs. However, you say, "We all know drugs are dangerous to the body and society *without any explanation* . . ." [my emphasis]. Given the nature of LeMoult's radical proposal (which I also have read), I think some further explanation is due us readers. Of course, you do give somewhat of one in the last paragraph, don't you? But your causal linking of illegal drugs and their relatively few addicts and legal alcohol and its relatively many addicts fails to convince me. But perhaps there is something that you could use to your advantage in the behavior of other sorts of addicts: smokers, gamblers, shoppers? What else could you say in favor of your position?

Second, with regard to what you summarize from LeMoult, what main point of his do you want to focus on? In a sentence, what is his major reason for suggesting that we consider legalizing drugs? At two points (paragraph 2 & 3) you indicate that it has to do with crime and the cost of enforcement of drug laws. Why do you include the points on the first antidrug laws and on women's use of laudanum when you don't refer to them later? Do they relate to your argument with LeMoult over legalizing drugs? Moreover, when you say, "LeMoult's points are good and true," to what specific points are you referring? Sometimes it's useful to make a concession to an opponent, but it must be qualified or limited to some specific point that does not detract from your main objection to the opponent's position.

If I were pressed to say what your argument with LeMoult came down to, I would say that you stacked some general point about the harm of drugs against his proposition that legalizing drugs would cut crime and law enforcement costs dramatically. Is that what you attempted? Look again at his data and his logic. Search for ways of composing a more effective argument by (1) calling his conclusions into question and (2) making your case more detailed and convincing.

What If Drugs Were Legal?
Peter Elbow's Comments

Dear Nancy,

It's fine not to worry about mechanics or correctness or nice sentences on a rough draft (I don't either); a way to put all attention on your train of thought; but remember that you'll need to get mechanics up to snuff for the final draft.

Seems like you've tried to build yourself a good framework and foundation—to build on for future drafts. You do an OK job of introducing the article. You don't give a full summary, but weren't asked to. And it strikes me that you move fairly quickly to one of your best arguments: alcohol. The widespread abuse is so undeniable.

My reactions. I don't disagree with your *position*, but somehow I find myself fighting you as I read. I'm trying to figure out why. I don't want to legalize drugs, but somehow I want to *listen* more to that writer. After all, he has a delicate thesis: not that we should do it but think about doing it. There's nothing wrong with you picking on part of his argument (legalizing) and ignoring the other part ("let's just think about it")—but the effect is somehow to make it seem as though you are having a closed mind and saying "Let's not even think about it." I guess I feel that the drug situation is so terrible that we have to let ourselves think about more things; I'm feeling stuck. So I think (self-centeredly) that the question for your next draft is this: what can you do to get a reader like me not to fight you so much? Try thinking about that; see what you can come up with.

I'd be happy to talk more about this in a conference.

Best,

Peter

The Focus and Scope of Comments

The most important decisions we make as responders are concerned with what we comment on, the areas or features of writing we address. Because it is not practical or productive to try to deal with every issue that may come up in student writing, we are left as teachers to decide on the areas that are most important. The focus of our comments reveals what we most value in student writing and helps establish what students will look to accomplish in their subsequent work. Once we decide *what* we are going to attend to, we have to confront another closely related question: *how much* are we going to address in a given set of responses? Do we deal with whatever comes up, as it comes up? Or do we read with an eye to certain concerns—for this assignment, this particular writing, or this particular writer? How many issues do we take up, and how many comments do we make?

"What If Drugs Were Legal?" is, to be sure, a rough draft. Nancy has strong views on her subject, and she has no problem getting her feelings out on the page. The writing is animated by her voice and the energy of her style. But the essay, in spite (or maybe because) of the passion behind it, gets blown off course. Her summary of LeMoult's article is not shaped to her own purposes as a writer. Her arguments against LeMoult's position are muddled and undeveloped. Across the essay the writing is vexed by problems in sentence structure, usage, mechanics, and spelling. It has a long way to go.

The teacher-theorists recognize this range of problems, but they limit the number of concerns they address in their comments to the student, according to a tacit set of priorities. Edward White calls on Nancy to sharpen the focus of her essay, tells her to cut back on her summary of LeMoult's argument, points out her main arguments, and directs her to develop them. His brief end note acknowledges the paper's potential, reiterates his call to unify each paragraph, and praises her voice and style. He writes 15 comments—roughly 15 statements—on the paper. Three of them deal with the focus and organization of the essay. Eight deal with the arguments themselves and their development. White does not get involved in pointing out every problem raised by her arguments. He doesn't respond, for instance, to the claim that "we all know drugs are dangerous to the body" or the related claim that "you shouldn't legalize something that is dangerous." He is looking at the broad picture here, and he is content to let Nancy first work out these arguments on her own. He also foregoes making any comments about sentence structure, usage, or correctness (though he does mark the paper with a few editorial symbols). It is a rough draft with ample work remaining on its overall content and shape. There will be time for refining her claims and cleaning up the paper.

Anne Gere makes a similar number of comments, about a similarly limited number of concerns. She wonders about the shape of the opening paragraph, considers the amount of information Nancy needs to summarize from LeMoult's article, and calls on her to develop her arguments. She also questions her bold claim that we all know drugs are dangerous "without any explanation." But whereas White presents most of his responses in the margins, next to the specific concerns, Gere streamlines her marginal comments to a few representative questions and then deals with the issues in greater detail in her end note. She also questions Nancy's second argument, her claim that legalizing drugs is the easy man's way out, and in a series of follow-up comments challenges her to refine it: "Just exactly why is legalizing drugs the easy way out? If danger is the issue, how do you respond to the idea that cars are dangerous? (Think of how many people are killed and maimed in automobile accidents every year)." Thirteen of Gere's 16 comments are focused on Nancy's summary, her own arguments, and the development of her arguments. She adds, at the close of her end note, a suggestion about reading the paper for sentence-level concerns (importantly, to be done *after* she completes her next draft), but she refrains from going further into these issues. For Gere, as for White, the priority is clear. Nancy needs first of all to deal with developing and ordering her arguments. There's no need at this time to dwell on local matters.

Ben McClelland may be more exacting in his comments than White or Gere, but he covers no more ground in his response. Although he writes significantly more comments, he concentrates his response to Nancy on the same concerns: the focus of the essay, the purposiveness of her summary of LeMoult's article, and the strength of her arguments. McClelland makes no marginal comments. He writes 26 comments in his letter of response, the format he typically uses in his commentary. He makes three comments about sharpening the focus of the paper, 10 about Nancy's summary of LeMoult's argument, and 11 about her own arguments. He doesn't even mention any other problems, choosing to keep Nancy's attention focused on the content and shape of the next draft.

Elbow's response is distinctive among the group—for many reasons, not the least of which is his even sharper focus of attention. White, Gere, and McClelland concentrate their comments on the focus, shape, and arguments in the paper. Elbow deals with these areas too. In his first nine comments, he gives rapid treatment to mechanics, organization, her summary of LeMoult's article, and her argument comparing drugs and alcohol. Like Gere, he even notes that it's okay to hold off on addressing problems with correctness. But he deals with all these matters quickly, at the start of the response, so that he can get to the real focus of his commentary: the attitude or stance that Nancy brings to her writing as a writer. The rest of his response—a total of 11 comments—is devoted to one issue that Elbow sees as more important than, and perhaps behind, all the others: the way Nancy positions herself in relation both to her arguments against LeMoult and to her audience. Elbow dramatizes the effect the writing may have on readers by foregrounding his own reactions as an individual reader: "somehow I find myself fighting you as I read"; "somehow I want to listen more to that writer"; "I feel that the drug situation is so terrible that we have to let ourselves think about more things; I'm feeling stuck." The entire second half of his response focuses on this one issue. He leaves it up to Nancy to decide how she will address this problem with her voice and tone—and trusts that by working on this area of her writing she will also improve her arguments.

These teachers privilege global matters of content, organization, context, and purpose over local matters of paragraphing, sentence structure, wording, and error—especially on drafts that are not yet maturely developed. All four responders also limit the scope of concerns they take up. Rather than address every area of writing on each paper, they concentrate on two or three concerns. At times, they focus their comments even more tightly on only one or two concerns. They also limit the number of items they address. Rather than deal with every instance of a given concern, they deal with only selected cases. Their comments seem to suggest that they believe students do best when they have a limited number of issues to deal with when they look back on their writing and engage in revision. If, however, these teachers are determined to restrict how many issues they address, they are not stingy with the number of comments they make. Even for this short essay, they write between 15 and 24 comments, an average of 19 comments per response. As we will see later, they are also not stingy with the number of words they give to each comment or the number of comments they devote to a given passage or concern.

The Four Seasons
Context

BACKGROUND

This is the final draft of the fourth essay of the course. You have not responded to previous draftings of this paper.

Students have already written a personal narrative, a thesis-support essay, and a comparison-contrast essay. The class has emphasized writing as a process and has worked on those composing strategies and features of discourse that you would typically emphasize in the first half of Freshman Composition.

You may assume that students have the option of rewriting, for a change in grade, one of their course papers by the end of the term.

David, is a confident, perhaps even a cocky, student who comes across as someone who thinks he is a better writer than (in your view) he is. However, his confidence is by no means groundless. You have been both taken with and disappointed by aspects of his previous writings, and now you receive this paper.

ASSIGNMENT

Most of you are off at school and in a new place, away from the people and settings you have become accustomed to and attached to. Similarly, those of you who are from Tallahassee have likely not had the time or the opportunity to visit some of the old places that are special to you.

Choose some place, atmosphere, or situation that you miss from home—or, if you *are* at home, that you have not had the chance to experience for some time, and miss. Depict this scene, mood, or setting in a way that will allow your reader—someone who does not know about it—to see the significance it has for you.

Remember that since your aim is to give readers a sense of place, you will do well to use specific details.

The Four Seasons
Final Draft

David B.
Final Draft

The Four Seasons

I like Tallahassee very much. The heat and sunshine almost everyday makes each day very pleasant. I intend to spend my next four and one half years here, but I miss my other home, Syracuse, New York. One thing that I truly miss about Syracuse is the four seasons. Each season is distinct and clear in its own way. I will do my best to describe each season to you, but remember that my description cannot compare to experiencing each season for itself.

In the Spring the ground is soft from the melting snow. You can feel the moist ground wanting to seep into your shoes. As the ground begins to dry, the trees begin to blossom and the faint smell of pollen lingers in the air. The flowers work their way out of the ground and bloom for another year. The familiar sound of geese is heard overhead as you look into the sky and see a "V" formation travelling north for the summer. A long winter's nap has ended for the bears, squirrels, rabbits and other hibernating animals. After they awake, their chattering conversations ramble through the forest.

Not only do the animals come out of their shelter in the springtime, but also people. Many people have a tendency to "hole up" in the wintertime. All your neighbors, that you thought had died, open up their houses to allow the spring breeze to come along and carry away that musty air that built up during winter. You can hear voices and

lawnmowers everywhere as people are outside doing their springtime yard work. Wives are planting new flowers while husbands are raking and mowing the lawn. Spring is the season of awakening where everything becomes refreshing.

Following Spring is the season that most people look forward to, that is Summer. Summer is the time of the year when kids are everywhere, because school has been let out. You can hear their voices and giggles fill the atmosphere. People are always outside in the summertime because the sun beats down onto the earth and warms everything up. There are enormous amounts of families going to the beach for the weekend or going on vacation for a week. As you look down the road, you can see heat waves resting on the pavement. The foliage is green and spirits are high. There is a feeling of warmth amongst neighbors, friends, and family.

Fall is my favorite season. I do not care for the way Fall strolls into Tallahassee, the way the leaves and flowers just shrivel away. In Syracuse you can tell when Fall has arrived, because the leaves turn rustic, auburn, garnet, and gold. They fall from the trees onto your lawn, where you spend hours raking the leaves into a pile. After the leaves are sitting neatly in a humongous pile, you may get this crazed feeling. This feeling might just cause you to run and dive into that neat pile. As you are sitting in a natural mattress an aroma of the dried leaves stimulates your olfactories. This aroma gives you a feeling that you are secure.

When you wake up on a typical fall morning you can look out the window and see the ground lightly dusted with frost. So when you get dressed you may put on a sweater. The fall weather is sometimes referred to as

"sweater-weather", because you are able to wear a sweater and be perfectly comfortable. The sweater is just enough to keep the chill off of you. This is a sign that winter is just around the corner.

Winter is the last season of the year. It ranks a close second to Fall in my opinion. Many people complain about snow, but I love it. There is nothing that can compare to the feeling of taking a walk in the winter at night, when the sky is clear and everything is placid. The moon glistens off the snow. While you stroll along, you can hear the soft scrunching of that magical white carpet underneath your feet. You can "feel Jack Frost nipping at your nose" and the rosiness in your cheeks. Yet you stay warm, nestled underneath your winter garb. The atmosphere that surrounds you is serene. It is as though you could disrobe yourself and still stay warm.

After your walk, in the "winter wonderland", you return to the homestead. After hanging up your coat, hat, gloves, and scarf, you shake off the cold and sit by the fire. That burning wood, that has been seasoned since the summer, smells so wonderful and the heat it radiates could lull a person to sleep. Winter nights are great to cuddle up with that special person, by the fire, and listen to the wind blowing outside or watch the snow fall to the ground. That snow gives you a refreshing feeling.

These were my brief descriptions of the four seasons in Syracuse. Of course I only told of the good things about each season. I enjoy the changing seasons and when school is through, I intend to move back up north. The weather down here may be fine for some people, but it was not meant for me. The only real way to understand what I was trying to describe is to experience the four seasons for yourself.

The Four Seasons
Anne Gere's Comments

David B.
Final Draft

The Four Seasons

I like Tallahassee very much. The heat and sunshine almost everyday makes each day very pleasant. I intend to spend my next four and one half years here, but I miss my other home, Syracuse, New York. One thing that I truly miss about Syracuse is the four seasons. Each season is distinct and clear in its own way. I will do my best to describe each season to you, but remember that my description cannot compare to experiencing each season for itself.

In the Spring the ground is soft from the melting snow. You can feel the moist ground wanting to seep into your shoes. As the ground begins to dry, the trees begin to blossom and the faint smell of pollen lingers in the air. The flowers work their way out of the ground and bloom *Good description.* for another year. The familiar sound of geese is heard overhead as you look into the sky and see a "V" formation travelling north for the summer. A long winter's nap has ended for the bears, squirrels, rabbits and other hibernating animals. After they awake, their chattering conversations ramble through the forest.

Do conversations ramble?

Not only do the animals come out of their shelter in the springtime, but also people. Many people have a tendency to "hole up" in the wintertime. All your neighbors, that you thought had died, open up their houses to allow the spring breeze to come along and carry away that musty air that built up during winter. You can hear voices and

lawnmowers everywhere as people are outside doing their springtime yard work. Wives are planting new flowers while husbands are raking and mowing the lawn. Spring is the season of awakening where everything becomes refreshing.

Can women rake and men plant?

Following Spring is the season that most people look forward to, that is Summer. Summer is the time of the year when kids are everywhere, because school has been let out. You can hear their voices and giggles fill the atmosphere. People are always outside in the summertime because the sun beats down onto the earth and warms everything up. There are enormous amounts of families going to the beach for the weekend or going on vacation for a week. As you look down the road, you can see heat waves resting on the pavement. The foliage is green and spirits are high. There is a feeling of warmth amongst neighbors, friends, and family.

How does this warmth show itself?

Fall is my favorite season. I do not care for the way Fall strolls into Tallahassee, the way the leaves and flowers just shrivel away. In Syracuse you can tell when Fall has arrived, because the leaves turn rustic, auburn, garnet, and gold. They fall from the trees onto your lawn, where you spend hours raking the leaves into a pile. After the leaves are sitting neatly in a humongous pile, you may get this crazed feeling. This feeling might just cause you to run and dive into that neat pile. As you are sitting in a natural mattress an aroma of the dried leaves stimulates your olfactories. This aroma gives you a feeling that you are secure.

How could you combine these sentences?

When you wake up on a typical fall morning you can look out the window and see the ground lightly dusted with frost. So when you get dressed you may put on a sweater. The fall weather is sometimes referred to as

"sweater-weather", because you are able to wear a sweater
and be perfectly comfortable. The sweater is just enough
to keep the chill off of you. This is a sign that winter is
just around the corner.

Winter is the last season of the year. It ranks a close
second to Fall in my opinion. Many people complain
about snow, but I love it. There is nothing that can compare to the feeling of taking a walk in the winter at night,
when the sky is clear and everything is placid. The moon
glistens off the snow. While you stroll along, you can hear
the soft scrunching of that magical white carpet underneath your feet. You can "feel Jack Frost nipping at your
nose" and the rosiness in your cheeks. Yet you stay warm,
nestled underneath your winter garb. The atmosphere that
surrounds you is serene. It is as though you could disrobe
yourself and still stay warm.

After your walk, in the "winter wonderland", you
return to the homestead. After hanging up your coat, hat,
gloves, and scarf, you shake off the cold and sit by the fire.
That burning wood, that has been seasoned since the summer, smells so wonderful and the heat it radiates could lull
a person to sleep. Winter nights are great to cuddle up
with that special person, by the fire, and listen to the wind
blowing outside or watch the snow fall to the ground.
That snow gives you a refreshing feeling.

These were my brief descriptions of the four
seasons in Syracuse. Of course I only told of the good
things about each season. I enjoy the changing seasons
and when school is through, I intend to move back up
north. The weather down here may be fine for some   *Why is this weather not
people, but it was not meant for me. The only real way to   meant for you?*
understand what I was trying to describe is to experience
the four seasons for yourself.

David—

This paper is filled with excellent descriptions. You have done a very good job of conveying to your audience the "feel" of the seasons. Phrases like "V formation," "heat waves resting on the pavement," "auburn, garnet and gold," and "soft scrunching" make your descriptions particularly vivid. I come away from this paper with a clear sense of place. Your use of the second person (you) is also effective because it draws the reader into your account. The significance of the four seasons for you remains somewhat vague. Although I understand that you take pleasure in each of the four seasons, I'm still not sure if they have any other meaning for you.

As noted in the margins, there are several usage problems in this paper. Please check each one and see me if you have questions about any of them.

The Four Seasons
Edward White's Comments

David B.
Final Draft

The Four Seasons

I like Tallahassee very much. The <u>heat</u> and <u>sunshine</u> almost everyday make[s] each day very pleasant. I intend to spend my next four and one half years here, but I miss my other home, Syracuse, New York. One thing that I truly miss about Syracuse is the four seasons. Each season is distinct and clear in its own way. I will do my best to describe each season to you, but remember that my description cannot compare to experiencing each season for itself.

In the Spring the ground is soft from the melting snow. You can feel the moist ground wanting to seep into your shoes. As the ground begins to dry, the trees begin to blossom and the faint smell of pollen lingers in the air. The <u>flowers</u> work their way out of the ground and bloom for another year. The familiar sound of geese is heard overhead as you look into the sky and see a "V" formation travelling north for the summer. A long winter's nap has ended for the bears, squirrels, rabbits and other hibernating animals. After they awake, their chattering conversations ramble through the forest.

Not only do the animals come out of their shelter in the springtime, but also people. Many people have a tendency to "hole up" in the wintertime. All your neighbors, <u>that you thought had died</u>, open up their houses to allow the spring breeze to come along and carry away that musty air that built up during winter. You can hear voices and

Good detail, well observed

Which flower is the first to appear?

Tone suddenly becomes flip.

lawnmowers everywhere as people are outside doing their
springtime yard work. Wives are planting <u>new flowers</u>   *Detail needed. Names?*
while husbands are raking and mowing the lawn. Spring
is the season of awakening where everything becomes
<u>refreshing</u>. *Notice you use the same term for snow on the next page.*

Following Spring is the season that most people look   *This prgh needs detail*
forward to, that is Summer. Summer is the time of the   *and clarity, as well as a*
                                                                                              distinction (or connection)
year when kids are everywhere, because school has been   *between <u>nature</u> and <u>people</u>.*
let out. You can hear their voices and giggles ^ <u>fill the</u>   *Detail needed: "in the*
                                                                                              parks, playgrounds,
<u>atmosphere</u>. People are always <u>outside in the summertime</u>   *beaches, and ball parks."*
because the sun beats down onto the earth and warms
everything up. [There are enormous amounts of] families
go<del>ing</del> to the beach for the weekend or go<del>ing</del> on vacation
for a week. As you look down the road, you can see heat
waves resting on the pavement. The ^ [<u>foliage</u> is] green   *^ "scrub oaks and pines are"*
and spirits are high. There is a feeling of warmth amongst
<u>neighbors, friends, and family</u>.

Fall is my favorite season. I do not care for the way   *Good detail here*
Fall strolls into Tallahassee, the way the leaves and flowers
just shrivel away. In Syracuse you can tell when Fall has
arrived, because the leaves turn rustic, auburn, garnet, and
gold. They fall from the trees onto your lawn, where you
spend hours raking the leaves into a pile. After the leaves
are sitting neatly in a <u>humongous</u> pile, you may get this   *Oral tone*
crazed feeling. This feeling might just cause you to run
and dive into that neat pile. As you are sitting in a natural
mattress an aroma of the dried leaves <u>stimulates your</u>   *Artificial tone*
<u>olfactories</u>. This aroma gives you a feeling that you are
secure.

When you wake up on a typical fall morning you can
look out the window and see the ground lightly dusted
with frost. So when you get dressed you may put on a
sweater. The fall weather is sometimes referred to as

"sweater-weather", because you are able to wear a sweater and be perfectly comfortable. The sweater is just enough to keep the chill off of you. This is a sign that winter is just around the corner.

Winter is the last season of the year. It ranks a close second to Fall in my opinion. Many people complain about snow, but I love it. There is nothing that can compare to the feeling of taking a walk in the winter at night, when the sky is clear and everything is placid. The moon glistens off the snow. While you stroll along, you can hear the soft scrunching of that magical white carpet underneath your feet. You can "feel Jack Frost nipping at your nose" and the rosiness in your cheeks. Yet you stay warm, nestled underneath your winter garb. The atmosphere that surrounds you is serene. It is as though you could disrobe yourself and still stay warm.

I don't get your meaning here.

After your walk, in the "winter wonderland", you return [to the] home[stead]. After hanging up your coat, hat, gloves, and scarf, you shake off the cold and sit by the fire. That burning wood, that has been seasoned since the summer, smells so wonderful and the heat it radiates could lull a person to sleep. Winter nights are great to cuddle up with that special person, by the fire, and listen to the wind blowing outside or watch the snow fall to the ground. That snow [gives you a refreshing feeling].

Detail?

You mean something here about watching snow from indoors. What do you mean precisely?

[These were my brief descriptions of the four seasons in Syracuse.] Of course I ^ only told of the good things about each season. I enjoy the changing seasons and when school is through, I intend to move back up north. The weather down here may be fine for some people, but it was not meant for me. The only real way to understand what I was trying to describe is to experience the four seasons for yourself.

^ "have"

Are there "not good" things to put in here, as you suggest?

WHITE

Parts of this paper are very fine, rich with detail and emotion. But sometimes your language gets very general, as if from a greeting card: "Jack Frost nipping at your nose," "that special person," "long winter's nap," and so on. Look closely at the top prgh on p. 2 for an example of ways to revise, to make your language more clear and detailed.

Your revision should keep the good organization and concept, but show careful attention to making the memories _yours_, by detail, rather than just anyone's.

The Four Seasons
Glynda Hull's Comments

David B.
Final Draft

The Four Seasons

I like Tallahassee very much. The heat and sunshine almost everyday makes each day very pleasant. I intend to spend my next four and one half years here, but I miss my other home, Syracuse, New York. One thing that I truly miss about Syracuse is the four seasons. Each season is distinct and clear in its own way. I will do my best to describe each season to you, but remember that my description cannot compare to experiencing each season for itself.

This sentence and its sibling at the end could be seen as an author providing an escape-hatch. Is this tactic okay?

In the Spring the ground is soft from the melting snow. You can feel the moist ground wanting to seep into your shoes. As the ground begins to dry, the trees begin to blossom and the faint smell of pollen lingers in the air. The flowers work their way out of the ground and bloom for another year. The familiar sound of geese is heard overhead as you look into the sky and see a "V" formation travelling north for the summer. A long winter's nap has ended for the bears, squirrels, rabbits and other hibernating animals. After they awake, their chattering conversations ramble through the forest.

A vivid image

Not only do the animals come out of their shelter in the springtime, but also people. Many people have a tendency to "hole up" in the wintertime. All your neighbors, that you thought had died, open up their houses to allow the spring breeze to come along and carry away that musty air that built up during winter. You can hear voices and

I hadn't thought of people hibernating too — this is a neat comparison.

lawnmowers everywhere as people are outside doing their springtime yard work. Wives are planting new flowers while husbands are raking and mowing the lawn. Spring is the season of awakening where everything becomes refreshing.

Following Spring is the season that most people look forward to, that is Summer. Summer is the time of the year when kids are everywhere, because school has been let out. You can hear their voices and giggles fill the atmosphere. People are always outside in the summertime because the sun beats down onto the earth and warms everything up. There are enormous amounts of families going to the beach for the weekend or going on vacation for a week. As you look down the road, you can see heat waves resting on the pavement. The foliage is green and spirits are high. There is a feeling of warmth amongst neighbors, friends, and family.

Fall is my favorite season. I do not care for <u>the way Fall strolls into Tallahassee</u>, the way the leaves and flowers just shrivel away. In Syracuse you can tell when Fall has arrived, because the leaves turn rustic, auburn, garnet, and gold. They fall from the trees onto your lawn, where you spend hours raking the leaves into a pile. After the leaves are sitting neatly in a humongous pile, you may get this crazed feeling. This feeling might just cause you to run and dive into that neat pile. As you are sitting in a natural mattress an aroma of the dried leaves stimulates your olfactories. <u>This aroma gives you a feeling that you are secure.</u>

Another neat image—but I don't get how "strolling" is a way of "shrivelling."

When you wake up on a typical fall morning you can look out the window and see the ground lightly dusted with frost. So when you get dressed you may put on a sweater. The fall weather is sometimes referred to as

Wow—the smell of dried leaves must conjure up powerful associations for you. I bet you could write an interesting paper just about this.

"sweater-weather", because you are able to wear a sweater and be perfectly comfortable. The sweater is just enough to keep the chill off of you. This is a sign that winter is just around the corner.

Winter is the last season of the year. It ranks a close second to Fall in my opinion. Many people complain about snow, but I love it. There is nothing that can compare to the feeling of taking a walk in the winter at night, when the sky is clear and everything is <u>placid</u>. The moon glistens off the snow. While you stroll along, you can hear the soft scrunching of that magical white carpet underneath your feet. You can "feel Jack Frost nipping at your nose" and the rosiness in your cheeks. Yet you stay warm, nestled underneath your winter garb. The atmosphere that surrounds you is serene. It is as though you could disrobe yourself and still stay warm.

This word seems just right.

After your walk, in the "winter wonderland", you return to the homestead. After hanging up your coat, hat, gloves, and scarf, you shake off the cold and sit by the fire. That burning wood, that has been seasoned since the summer, smells so wonderful and the heat it radiates could lull a person to sleep. Winter nights are great to cuddle up with that special person, by the fire, and listen to the wind blowing outside or watch the snow fall to the ground. That snow gives you a refreshing feeling.

These were my brief descriptions of the four seasons in Syracuse. Of course I only told of the good things about each season. I enjoy the changing seasons and when school is through, I intend to move back up north. The weather down here may be fine for some people, but it was not meant for me. The only real way to understand what I was trying to describe is to experience the four seasons for yourself.

David—

You've got an unusual paper here in that some readers will love it and some will feel just as strongly in the opposite direction. What I want you to do is figure out what it is about your paper, and about different readers, that could produce such different reactions. For example,

(1) Your seasonal portraits could have, with a few exceptions, been written by someone who grew up in Tallahassee. What will some readers like about this quality; what will others dislike?

(2) You say at the end of your paper that you've told only the good things about the seasons. Why might this be pleasant to some readers but offensive to others?

(3) You use a lot of phrases that are often used in conjunction with the seasons. Again, what will some readers like about this, others dislike, and why?

Given your consideration of these questions, would you now make any changes in your paper? Why or why not?

The Four Seasons
Chris Anson's Taperecorded Comments

Hi, Dave. Well, having grown up in New England, I share a lot of your feelings about the beauty of the different seasons in the northern part of the country. (In fact, I spoke to my mother yesterday and she said they'd gotten nine inches of snow over the weekend!)

First let me talk about structure. A paper with the topic of the four seasons has a real natural structure; it's hard to see an alternative to, uh, to one section on each of the seasons. It's interesting that you chose to start with spring. That's obviously one way to do it because it's the, traditionally the first season of the year when everything comes to life again, and that forces you to end with winter, which has a kind of serenity, not quite the sense of ending and death that fall conveys but certainly not a feeling of life. Now essentially, if you're sticking to one chunk on each season, you've got four alternatives. One possibility would be to begin with summer, then work your way through to spring, which has, um, gives you the advantage of ending on a note of rebirth and rejuvenation. The one you chose is fine, but you didn't say anything about it in your revision plans following the conference group, and we'd really spent some time talking about these various possibilities.

Uh, I guess my strongest reaction has to do with the question of credibility. Because what you're trying to do here is presumably describe something so that people who haven't experienced it can do so through your words. And in this case, if you romanticize too much, and if it's clear that you're romanticizing, um, your reader may question the credi- . . . well, let me put it this way, your reader may be less prone to accepting the case you make for the beauty of the seasons, especially if you're separating yourself from your readers by implying, you know, "you haven't experienced this, so let me tell you how wonderful it is." Part of the problem, for me anyway, stems from two things—a tendency to exaggerate without providing specific, realistic details, and a tendency to interpret the, uh, the phenomenon you're describing very subjectively, so that *your* impressions, *your* sensations and feelings are at the center of the piece.

The exaggeration problem is pretty quickly remedied. Bruce talked about how he was bothered by the image of bears and squirrels and rabbits all carrying on a kind of woodland conversation, and I think I agree, but you really didn't rethink that much. Along those lines, some specific expressions we questioned in the conference group were things like, um, "enormous amounts of families" (by the way, if you're going to say that, it should be "numbers," and we've talked already about that mass vs. count noun business), and "humongous pile," and "stimulating your olfactories," and the cliché about Jack Frost. And Jody also objected to the sex-role stereotyping of wives planting flowers while husbands rake leaves and mow the lawn. Anyway, all this is a matter of a few stylistic revisions which are easily done.

The other problem is harder to describe, but it concerns, um, how much we as readers depend on your feelings to capture the essence of the seasons. Giving impressions and personal responses is perfectly fine to do, but I think it needs to be balanced with some very descriptive details. And, um, what gives me the sense that you haven't really pushed this piece much from the rough draft we talked about comes in your last line, when you say [flipping through paper], when you say here, um, "The only real way to understand what I was trying to describe is to experience the four seasons for yourself." I think we all said to scrap the entire last paragraph because it doesn't do anything, and I even recall that you put a line through it, so what happened? The point of the essay is essentially to give the reader an experience through words, but here it's as if you've told us, "well, you've wasted your time reading this, because I can't capture it in language." And then the whole essay sort of collapses in on itself.

Anyway, I think you get the point here, and I don't want to repeat what we talked about last week. So, what I'd encourage you to do here, Dave, is to spend a lot more time thinking through your drafts before turning them in. Remember that that's where most of the learning comes in; if you, um, if you shortchange yourself at this stage, you'll be giving up that chance to think of alternative strategies, tones, styles, words, and so on.

All in all, this project is about a solid C. OK, Dave, see you in class.

The Length and Specificity of Comments

Another distinguishing feature of these composition theorists' responses lies in the detail and fullness of their comments. The three teachers who make written comments on "The Four Seasons" average 10 words per comment: 6 words per marginal comment, 14 words per comment in their end notes. These teachers are not only selective about what they comment on, they are also careful to define what they are referring to in the student's writing and elaborate on what they have to say. As their comments on "The Four Seasons" illustrate, they focus their comments on certain key issues *and* they go the extra mile to communicate their responses clearly to students.

"The Four Seasons" is the work of a writer who has clearly achieved a certain fluency. David has a keen eye for rendering a description with feeling and comes up with several sharp descriptions of the seasons: "You can feel the moist ground wanting to seep into your shoes," "the smell of pollen lingers in the air," "I do not care for the way Fall strolls into Tallahassee, the way the leaves and flowers just shrivel away," "you can look out the window and see the ground lightly dusted with frost," "The moon glistens off the snow," "the soft scrunching of that magical white carpet underneath your feet." He has something to say, and from time to time he discovers just the way to say it. But more often than not, as these teachers note, he is all too content to accept the commonplace idea, to go with the easy turn of phrase. He is only moderately successful at capturing the distinctiveness of the four seasons in Syracuse and defining his own feelings for the place, as the assignment calls for.

Anne Gere gives some attention to problems of usage, but she devotes most of her comments to praising the writer's descriptions and calling on David to say more about the significance the seasons have for him. What makes the response work is the way that Gere goes out of her way to make her comments clear to the student. Nearly every comment she makes is written out in a full sentence and, more than this, tied directly to words from the student's text. In response to David's saying that animal conversations "ramble" through the forest, she doesn't say, "Word choice?" or "Imprecise"; she says more fully, "Do conversations ramble?" Instead of responding with a blunt "How?" to his claim that in summer there is a feeling of warmth in the neighborhood, she takes her time and writes out: "How does this warmth show itself?" At the end his paper, instead of saying simply "Why not?" she asks: "Why is this weather not meant for you?" These comments are what Nancy Sommers has aptly dubbed "text-specific" because they make the student's own words part of the comment and show the responder dealing specifically with the text in front of her, not relying on stock responses that may be "rubber stamped" on essay after essay.

Edward White scatters comments across the essay about the writer's ideas, organization, sentence structure, and usage. But he concentrates on two areas: problems with stilted language ("enormous amounts of families," "humongous," and "stimulates your olfactories") and the detail in the descriptions. He praises instances where the student provides sharp detail, but where David is content to rely on broad, general descriptions, he looks for him to get more concrete. If White takes on a variety of concerns in his interlinear comments, in his end note he focuses on what he sees as the real issue of the essay: inadequate detail. A number of White's comments are presented in terse, general comments: "Detail needed. Names?" "Detail?" Some seem vague: "Oral tone," "Artificial tone." But more often than not, White writes out his comments in full statements, tying his comments directly to the words of the student's text:

> Notice that you use the same term for snow on the next page.

> You mean something here about watching snow from indoors. What do you mean precisely?

> Are there "not good" things to put in here, as you suggest?

Notably, whereas Gere, who is more pleased with the writing, elaborates on what she likes about the paper in her end note, White elaborates on his main criticism: that the language "gets very general." He also writes a number of his responses in the form of combination comments, a technique that the next responder, Glynda Hull, uses extensively.

Hull's commentary is more tightly focused than either White's or Gere's. All but three of her comments are devoted to the writer's descriptions and the ways they may be taken by prospective readers. In addition to writing out her comments in full statements that invoke the language of the student's text, Hull presents almost every one of her points as a combination comment. That is, she presents a base comment first—praise, criticism, reader-response, or interpretation—and then immediately follows it up with another comment on the same subject. The heart of her end comment provides three good examples:

> Your seasonal portraits could have, with a few exceptions, been written by someone who grew up in Tallahassee. What will some readers like about this quality what will others dislike?

> You say at the end of your paper that you've told only the good things about the seasons. Why might this be pleasant to some readers but offensive to others?

> You use a lot of phrases that are often used in conjunction with the seasons. Again, what will some readers like about this, others dislike, and why?

In each of these combination comments, Hull provides an interpretation of the writing and then follows it with a question for the writer to consider. The initial comment identifies a concern—getting her and the writer on the same wavelength—and the second comment presents her main response. At other times Hull combines other types of comments, to achieve the same kind of layering:

> Wow—the smell of dried leaves must conjure up powerful associations for you. I bet you could write an interesting paper just about this.

> This sentence and its sibling at the end could be seen as an author providing an escape-hatch. Is this tactic okay?

In both cases, the first comment provides a context for the second and influences the way it is read. Notice how different the comments would be without the opening comment:

> I bet you could write an interesting paper just about this.

> Is this escape-hatch tactic okay?

Without the opening reader's response, the first example would come across as a suggestion more than an exhortation. Without the opening explanation, the second example might well confuse the student writer: What escape hatch? What is she talking about? To be sure, a great deal of the effectiveness of Hull's comments comes from the constructive attitude she brings to her responses and the casual voice she assumes in her commentary. But it derives just as much from the detail, specificity, and fullness she gives to each of her main comments.

Chris Anson's comments on "The Four Seasons" offer a similar case study of the benefits of doing more with less. In his taperecorded response to David, Anson concentrates on just a couple of issues and offers detailed commentary on each. Like Hull, he also gives added dimension to his response by looking at the writing in relation to the larger rhetorical and classroom contexts. Across the 800 words and 34 comments of his response, Anson takes up only four concerns. He wonders about the ordering of the seasonal portraits. He notes the problems with the exaggerated language and stereotyped descriptions. He criticizes David's failure to balance his highly subjective impressions with more realistic, concrete descriptions. And he frames both of these problems with description in terms of David's lack of credibility, that is, his questionable ethos as a writer. Essentially, he could present these concerns in four comments:

1. Think about ordering your seasonal portraits in a way that best serves your purpose.

2. Try to do less exaggerating and rely less on clichéd descriptions.

3. Try to balance your personal impressions with some concrete descriptions that will help readers get a sense of the seasons. Don't cop out by saying you can't describe these seasons in words—that's the very task you are called to take on as a descriptive writer.

4. Work at giving more to, and getting more out of, your drafting and revising in future writing.

But instead of presenting only these comments, in this general way, Anson offers a detailed, layered response: he defines a problem, identifies where he sees it coming up in the text, explains it, and offers advice about how it might be resolved. In commenting about David's problem with credibility, for instance, Anson doesn't simply say, as he easily might have, "Your last paragraph reveals your willingness to settle for easy descriptions and hurts your credibility." He presents a detailed response, one layer on top of another:

> What gives me the sense that you haven't really pushed this piece much from the rough draft we talked about comes in your last line,
>
>> when you say . . . "The only real way to understand what I was trying to describe is to experience the four seasons for yourself."
>>
>>> I think we all said to scrap the entire last paragraph because it doesn't do anything, and I even recall that you put a line through it, so what happened?
>>>
>>>> The point of the essay is essentially to give the reader an experience through words, but here it's as if you've told us, "Well, you've wasted your time reading this, because I can't capture it in language." And then the whole essay sort of collapses in on itself.

First he identifies the problem, David's failure to push himself as a writer. Then he points to an instance of the problem in the last sentence of the essay. Only then does he point to what is presumably his main response: Why didn't you scrap the last paragraph? It ruins your credibility. He closes by offering a detailed explanation about why resorting to this maneuver creates such a problem. At each break, Anson might easily have brought his response to a close, but instead he goes back over the ground of the earlier statements and adds commentary that is intended to clarify the problem for the writer.

This detail and recursiveness, of course, is more readily accomplished in spoken commentary, where words come as quickly as they can be voiced, but it is manageable—and no less desirable—in written commentary. To achieve such a textured style, you have to limit yourself to only a few issues per paper, deal specifically with the words of the student's text, and explain your ways of reading the text and your calls for revision. If the responses you make are only as valuable as they communicate your concerns to the student, it makes sense to elaborate your key responses. It makes sense to spend a little extra time writing your comments out fully, in detail. In teacher commentary, less is more—especially if you do a lot with the little that you do take up.

Street Gangs: One Point of View
Context

BACKGROUND

This informative paper is the third paper of the course, the third time students have taken an assignment through several drafts with in-draft commentary. The class has been studying the principles of informative writing and paying special attention to the use of examples. Students have already completed invention activities and a first rough draft toward this paper, neither of which you have made written responses to. They will take the assignment through two more drafts.

Rusty is the kind of student who comes into writing classes apprehensive and expecting not to do well, largely because, as he wrote in his journal at the beginning of the course, his "grammar and structure are not too good." He keeps to himself in class, and he has not talked with you after class or in conference about his writing or his performance in the class, even though your written responses on his first two papers indicated that you expected more from him—in substance and correctness—in his future papers. Now he hands in this paper.

ASSIGNMENT

For your third paper, I'd like you to write about a hobby or activity in which you regularly engage and in which you have some level of authority or proficiency. In an informative essay of 600-900 words, inform or advise a general audience (say, the members of this class) about an aspect of this hobby or activity. As you write, try to say as best you can what precisely you mean, in a way that will spark your readers' interest in the subject. In our work on this paper, we will pay special attention to the *use*, as distinct from the mere *citation*, of examples to examine and illustrate a point. As you write, keep this objective in mind.

We will take this paper through four drafts. The first is an exploratory draft, a place where you should try to get some words and ideas produced and begin to get them into some general shape. It may well be sketchy and rough. Do what you can to make it a place where you think through and discover what you want to say. You need not concern yourself with being neat and orderly—this is not a draft for readers, but for you as a writer at work. The second and third drafts are working drafts, places where you begin to do more careful shaping and crafting, and perhaps some more discovering and producing, some more experimenting. The fourth is a "final draft"—not in the sense that it is complete and forever done with, but in the sense that you can "finally" let it go now that your writing is ready for readers.

Street Gangs: One Point of View
Rough Draft

Rusty S.
Second Rough Draft

Street Gangs: One Point of View

I'm writing this paper on street gangs because I was once part of one, and I feel that this gives me some authority to write a legitimate opinion.

I never asked or set out to join a gang, it just happened by association. I knew some guys who were members of the Cripps and by hanging around them I was sort of "taken in" by the gang and generally thought to be a part of them by everyone else.

Unlike some members I tried to maintain a low profile. I didn't provoke fights or do destructive things on purpose, but we had a strong bond. If one person was in trouble, no matter who or what kind it was, everyone was there regardless.

This sticking together almost always occured in a physical sense. If one of our guys were to be beaten up, the rest of us would take a revenge of some sort, whether it be by beating someone up or vandalizing someones property, we always got even. That was a basic rule, nobody could "be one up on us", we always had to get even.

Except for this one occasion, I can't really remember us actually going out and starting trouble for no "reason". We were at the pool, and what we did was single out one person at a time. Once we had a target, one of us would go up to that certain someone and "sucker punch" him and before he could retaliate the rest of the gang would break it up.

Being a member had its ups and downs. The worst part was being paranoid about something happening to you. It wasn't a frightening feeling, but more like a burden. You knew something, somehow, somewhere would eventually happen, either to you or the gang. Many times I paid the price for being part of the Cripps with black eyes or broken noses. I even had my windshield busted once.

The good side was the family type atmosphere between us, we were more than friends, almost like cousins or even brothers. That sense of support that I got from being part of that gang was unmeasurable. Walking down the halls of school and having everyone know that your in this gang was great, almost like an "ego-trip". For it did make some of the guys cocky. This over-all feeling is hard to explain, it deals a lot with acceptance and friendship. I guess these two things were what kept me in the gang so long. I liked the feeling of being part of something that (where I come from) is almost like a status symbol. My parents called this insecurity, this may be, but more importantly it gave me a purpose and an identity.

During the time I spent in the gang, we were more a "party" gang. We got into trouble and fights, but not with other gangs. Gangs at the time were more friendly and were only gangs by name. I mean everyone knew each other and it was only the name of the gang and their symbols that separated us.

Our symbols were one, a blue and red hankerchief worn around the right ankle, a diamond stud earring in the left ear and most important the thin white cane each member had. This was in relation with our name: "THE CRIPPS".

I left the gang last year because it started getting to violent, especially the growing conflicts between gangs. Many gang fights started to break out in the streets, schools and school related events. I just couldn't handle this, somebody could get really hurt or killed. I also felt I didn't need the ego boost anymore. I felt I could be my own person, with my own traits and characteristics. To sum it up, I grew up.

Street Gangs: One Point of View
Richard Larson's Comments

Rusty S.
Second Rough Draft

Street Gangs: One Point of View

I'm writing this paper on street gangs because I was once part of one, and I feel that this gives me some authority to write a legitimate opinion.

I'm not sure I see your "opinion" in the paper.

I never asked or set out to join a gang, it just happened by association. I knew some guys who were members of the Cripps and by hanging around them I was sort of "taken in" by the gang and generally thought to be a part of them by everyone else.

Unlike some members I tried to maintain a low profile. I didn't provoke fights or do destructive things on purpose, but we had a strong bond. If one person was in trouble, no matter who or what kind it was, everyone was there regardless. *Where? At a police station? A hospital?*

This sticking together almost always occured in a physical sense. If one of our guys were to be beaten up, the rest of us would take a revenge of some sort, whether it be by beating someone up or vandalizing someones property, we always got even. That was a basic rule, nobody could "be one up on us", we always had to get even.

Except for this one occasion, I can't really remember us actually going out and starting trouble for no "reason". We were at the pool, and what we did was single out one person at a time. Once we had a target, one of us would go up to that certain someone and "sucker punch" him and before he could retaliate the rest of the gang would break it up. ⟶ *The attack?*

Being a member had its ups and downs. The worst part was being paranoid about something happening to you. It wasn't a frightening feeling, but more like a burden. You knew something, somehow, somewhere would eventually happen, either to you or the gang. Many times I paid the price for being part of the Cripps with black eyes or broken noses. I even had my windshield busted once.

Might be useful to say more on these experiences.

The good side was the family type atmosphere between us, we were more than friends, almost like cousins or even brothers. That sense of support that I got from being part of that gang was unmeasurable. Walking down the halls of school and having everyone know that your in this gang was great, almost like an "ego-trip". For it did make some of the guys cocky. This over-all feeling is hard to explain, it deals a lot with acceptance and friendship. I guess these two things were what kept me in the gang so long. I liked the feeling of being part of something that (where I come from) is almost like a status symbol. My parents called this insecurity, this may be, but more importantly it gave me a purpose and an identity.

During the time I spent in the gang, we were more a "party" gang. We got into trouble and fights, but not with other gangs. Gangs at the time were more friendly and were only gangs by name. I mean everyone knew each other and it was only the name of the gang and their symbols that separated us. *Word needed?*

Our symbols were [one,] a blue and red hankerchief worn around the right ankle, a diamond stud earring in the left ear and most important the thin white cane each member had. This was in relation with our name: "THE CRIPPS".

I left the gang last year because it started getting to violent, especially the growing conflicts between gangs. Many gang fights started to break out in the streets, schools and school related events. I just couldn't handle this, somebody could get really hurt or killed. I also felt I didn't need the ego boost anymore. I felt I could be my own person, with my own traits and characteristics. To sum it up, I grew up.

Say more about the incidents that led you to get out.

In many respects this is an interesting draft—its story told with apparent honesty. There is useful detail here, though, as I hope the notes will suggest, the details could be extended some, and a few of the experiences you have in mind could have been rendered more vividly.

But as this piece stands it is essentially an account of a period in your life: how you got into a gang, what you did, why you stopped. The assignment asked, on the other hand, to discuss an activity in which you "regularly" engage and on which you can speak from some authority. Clearly you can speak with authority on street gangs, but your focus, for this paper, might be on letting readers know how street gangs operate, what they do, why they do it, rather than on the chronology of your experiences as a gang member. Your goal here is to enlarge the reader's knowledge of a subject that the reader might find important and might genuinely want to know more about. I think you've got such a subject (I surely would be glad to learn more about gangs, which I hear a great deal about). But I'd like to know a bit more about gangs in general than you tell me. Maybe you could use your experiences to illustrate more general observations (observations that might cover many gangs, of different sorts). In using your experiences so, you might give a few more details about some of the experiences. In the next draft, try to accomplish some of the steps I've suggested. The result probably will be a longer paper, but that should cause no difficulty; the present draft is a trifle short.

I've underlined some places where I think you should reconsider the punctuation of sentences.

If you need to discuss my suggestions, please come in and do so.

Street Gangs: One Point of View
Frank O'Hare's Comments

Rusty—

I get the feeling that you are still thinking through your experiences with the gang and that you haven't yet decided the significance of this experience.

In the first paragraph, you seem hesitant about your right to write about this subject. Of course, your opinion about this subject is of value. Your opinion will be not only legitimate but authoritative.

This hesitancy has, I think, caused you to neglect focusing on your purpose in this paper. It would probably be useful for you to sketch quickly an informal outline of your draft. What major points do you want to establish?

Why did you talk about keeping a low profile?

You seem to be combining the bonding issue with "starting trouble."

You claim that your gang didn't look for trouble, and yet the fifth paragraph discusses the only time you did.

Paragraph six needs specifics. What incident or incidents led you to use the terms "paranoia" and "burden"? You suffered black eyes and broken noses and yet weren't afraid. Please explain.

Paragraph seven does a good job of establishing your sense of identity.

Paragraph eight is confused and confusing. Are you saying that gang rivalries weren't as nasty as they appear to be? If so, the point is interesting and well worth explaining to your readers.

Paragraph nine: what point are you establishing here?

This subject is well worth writing about, but you must decide what your major points will be.

Two comments about code:

1. The level of your vocabulary is just a little too informal.

2. I have marked six places where you failed to recognize sentence boundaries. Please examine these examples and see if you can rewrite them correctly. Please come in for a conference and we'll discuss this problem. All six are, in reality, examples of just one problem.

Street Gangs: One Point of View
Glynda Hull's Comments

Rusty S.
Second Rough Draft

Street Gangs: One Point of View

I'm writing this paper on street gangs because I was once part of one, and I feel that this gives me some authority to write a legitimate opinion.

I never asked or set out to join a gang, it just happened by association. I knew some guys who were members of the Cripps and by hanging around them I was sort of "taken in" by the gang and generally thought to be a part of them by everyone else.

This is interesting. Somehow I always thought joining a gang involved initiations and so forth.

Unlike some members I tried to maintain a low profile. I didn't provoke fights or do destructive things on purpose, but we had a strong bond. If one person was in trouble, no matter who or what kind it was, everyone was there regardless.

(See my comments at the end.)

This sticking together almost always occured in a physical sense. If one of our guys were to be beaten up, the rest of us would take a revenge of some sort, whether it be by beating someone up or vandalizing someones property, we always got even. That was a basic rule, nobody could "be one up on us", we always had to get even.

Except for this one occasion, I can't really remember us actually going out and starting trouble for no "reason". We were at the pool, and what we did was single out one person at a time. Once we had a target, one of us would go up to that certain someone and "sucker punch" him and before he could retaliate the rest of the gang would break it up.

Oh, my—were you ever the one to do the punching?

Being a member had its ups and downs. The worst part was being paranoid about something happening to you. <u>It wasn't a frightening feeling, but more like a burden.</u> You knew something, somehow, somewhere would eventually happen, either to you or the gang. Many times I paid the price for being part of the Cripps with black eyes or broken noses. I even had my windshield busted once.*

This is a great way to describe the paranoid feeling.

The good side was the family type atmosphere between us, we were more than friends, almost like cousins or even brothers. That sense of support that I got from being part of that gang was unmeasurable. Walking down the halls of school and having everyone know that your in this gang was great, almost like an "ego-trip". For it did make some of the guys cocky. This over-all feeling is hard to explain, it deals a lot with acceptance and friendship. I guess these two things were what kept me in the gang so long. I liked the feeling of being part of something that (where I come from) is almost like a status symbol. <u>My parents called this insecurity, this may be, but more importantly it gave me a purpose and an identity.</u>

This is interesting too. I don't think most people recognize the family-like attraction of being in a gang.

I admire the way you're able to acknowledge your parents' view but go on to give your own.

During the time I spent in the gang, we were more a "party" gang. We got into trouble and fights, but not with other gangs. Gangs at the time were more friendly and were only gangs by name. I mean everyone knew each other and it was only the name of the gang and their symbols that separated us.

Our symbols were one, a blue and red hankerchief worn around the right ankle, a diamond stud earring in the left ear and most important the thin white cane each member had. This was in relation with our name: "THE CRIPPS".

This is interesting—is it common for gangs to choose names and symbols that could be associated with disability or weakness?

I left the gang last year because it started getting to

I left the gang last year because it started getting to violent, especially the growing conflicts between gangs. Many gang fights started to break out in the streets, schools and school related events. I just couldn't handle this, somebody could get really hurt or killed. I also felt I didn't need the ego boost anymore. I felt I could be my own person, with my own traits and characteristics. To sum it up, I grew up.

Rusty--

You have the makings of a very interesting paper here. Here are two suggestions for your next draft:

(1) I want you to add some more extended examples—not just one sentence or two, but whole paragraphs. I've marked several places you could make some additions with an asterisk (*). On the first page, for example, you might tell specifically about a time when someone got in trouble and everyone was there. Give details: what time, when, what situation, where. These long examples should be used to illustrate and provide evidence for points you're making.

(2) After you've added the examples, get some scissors and tape, and cut your paper up—one paragraph per strip of paper. Experiment with putting these paragraphs in different orders. Which ones seem like beginning material? Which ones come next? And so on. If there isn't any order that seems better than another, then try to imagine what you would need to do to your paper to connect up the paragraphs. Then tape your draft together again.

Street Gangs: One Point of View
Patricia Stock's Comments

Rusty S.
Second Rough Draft

Street Gangs: One Point of View

I'm writing this paper on street gangs because I was once part of one, and I feel that this gives me some authority to write a legitimate opinion.

I never asked or set out to join a gang, it just happened by association. I knew some guys who were   members of the Cripps and by <u>hanging around</u> them I was sort of "taken in" by the gang and generally thought to be a part of them by everyone else. *I'd like an illustrative anecdote.*

Unlike some members I tried to maintain a low profile. I didn't provoke fights or do destructive things on purpose, but we had a strong bond. If one person was in trouble, no matter who or what kind it was, everyone was there regardless.

This sticking together almost always occured in a physical sense. If one of our guys were to be beaten up, the rest of us would take a revenge of some sort, whether it be by beating someone up or vandalizing someones property, we always got even. That was a basic rule, nobody could "be one up on us", we always had to get even.

Except for this one occasion, I can't really remember us actually going out and starting trouble for no "reason". We were at the pool, and what we did was single out one person at a time. Once we had a target, one of us would go up to that certain someone and "sucker punch" him and before he could retaliate the rest of the gang would break it up.

Rusty, maybe as you are moving from these first two exploratory drafts to more finished ones, you might want to think about revising your introduction.

This usage works for me. I feel as if you are lending an informal-appropriate tone to an essay about street gangs. When you use it elsewhere, I don't think you need to put it in quotations because you're making it the working usage of the essay.

These two paragraphs (2 and 3) read like one to me.

I'd like to see this scene in all its detail.

STOCK

Being a member had its ups and downs. The worst part was being paranoid about something happening to you. It wasn't a frightening feeling, but more like a burden. You knew something, somehow, somewhere would eventually happen, either to you or the gang. Many times I paid the price for being part of the Cripps with black eyes or broken noses. I even had my windshield busted once.

If you didn't start trouble, how come all the black eyes and broken noses?

The good side was the family type atmosphere between us, we were more than friends, almost like cousins or even brothers. That sense of support that I got from being part of that gang was unmeasurable. Walking down the halls of school and having everyone know that your in this gang was great, almost like an "ego-trip". For it did make some of the guys cocky. This over-all feeling is hard to explain, it deals a lot with acceptance and friendship. I guess these two things were what kept me in the gang so long. I liked the feeling of being part of something that (where I come from) is almost like a status symbol. My parents called this insecurity, this may be, but more importantly it gave me a purpose and an identity.

I'd like you to show me what the acceptance, the friendship, looks like.

During the time I spent in the gang, we were more a "party" gang. We got into trouble and fights, but not with other gangs. Gangs at the time were more friendly and were only gangs by name. I mean everyone knew each other and it was only the name of the gang and their symbols that separated us.

Who did you get into trouble and fights with?

Our symbols were one, a blue and red hankerchief worn around the right ankle, a diamond stud earring in the left ear and most important the thin white cane each member had. This was in relation with our name: "THE CRIPPS".

Oh, I'd like this up front. I wondered why CRIPPS. I thought it might be an acronym.

I left the gang last year because it started getting to violent, especially the growing conflicts between gangs. Many gang fights started to break out in the streets, schools and school related events. I just couldn't handle this, somebody could get really hurt or killed. I also felt I didn't need the ego boost anymore. I felt I could be my own person, with my own traits and characteristics. To sum it up, I grew up.

This really interests me. How did you grow up? How did you change? Is there some representative incident you can share with your reader to demonstrate your change?

Dear Rusty,

Your essay surprised me. I found it hard to think of you as a member of a street gang. Just this morning I heard about the tragic shooting of a seven-year-old girl in Detroit by a fifteen-year-old boy, a member of a street gang. You seem so kind to me, so completely incapable of violence. I understand that you mean for me to understand that your gang was more social, more like what I would call a club or a fraternity, but you did pick on kids at pools; you did get black eyes and broken noses.

I've been thinking about street gangs recently, not just because they fig-ure in the news, but because Shirley Brice Heath, who teaches anthropology and linguistics and English, and whom I admire very much, is interested in how children and young adults learn to make texts—spoken and written ones. She thinks that since participation in the customary institutions in which young people learned to build texts—the nuclear and extended family, the church, the Boy Scouts, and so on—are on the decline, since young people are substituting other institutions for them, institutions like street gangs, they are not learning to do the same things with language that they once did. Furthermore, she would argue they are not learning the moral values they once did.

Do you think Heath is right? When were you in a gang? junior high? high school? Was it because you didn't participate in other institutions such as church groups, sports? Was everyone you knew in a gang when you were? Was there a real difference between your gang and the gangs I read about in the papers? What exactly should I understand by the meaning of the word gang? Why do you not use the word club or clique or fraternity instead of gang to describe your group? You suggest that your parents disapproved of your being in a gang. Were you in it, in part, as the kind of rebellion against your parents that most teenagers express in one form or another? I am very interested in how you would respond to questions like the ones I have asked you. I've never known anyone who was a member of a gang before.

Rusty, I've noted on your essay some thoughts I had when I was reading it, and I'm attaching to this note "Apropos," an essay that another student of mine wrote because your essay reminded me of issues he was addressing in his essay. Was your gang like his group? Or different? I got a fairly good sense of his group and what being a member of it meant to him because he showed me some specific examples of how he acted in that group and how it affected his life. If you could provide me with several full blown examples of your activities as a member of your gang and some reflections on what impact your participation in the gang had on your thinking and understanding, I would learn from reading them.

When you have taken this essay through the revisions you want, may I please share it with my colleague, Shirley Brice Heath. I think she would be able to learn from you too because you are a young man who has been a member of a gang writing about his membership in that gang.

I'm really looking forward to reading your next draft of "Street Gangs: One Point of View."

Street Gangs: One Point of View
Peter Elbow's Comments

Dear Rusty,

This is interesting to read and sometimes has a strong impact on me.

What I noticed first are the places where you talk about your feelings while being in the gang: the oddly, interestingly, low-key "burden" as you put it. I would feel flat out *fear*. Also the feeling of comfort and support and family quality. Seems important. I would enjoy getting a bit more exploration here: but not just finding more words for it but more *examples*: what does all that look like in events or scenes?

At the bottom of 1 you give the example of picking on people at the pool. You tell it in a kind of deadpan way, but it's kind of horrifying for me. I think *I* was the kind of person who was picked on—or always felt I was about to be. There's something intriguing or even moving about your low key tone here, but I'm also curious to know a bit more how you actually felt–and feel. Something mysterious here: perhaps it's more interesting this way, despite my unsatisfied curiosity. But I do know I'd like you to flesh it out more as an example: it's a specific scene or incident, but you don't let us see any particulars.

The symbols of the gang are nice and concrete. I had the thought of somehow starting with them—or at least finding some way to start that has some zip to it; it's a little bit of a soggy opening as you have it. And the ending sentence is very sudden—though now I see you were building to it. I need some kind of help here; not sure what; don't want some abstract discussion of "growing up"—but somehow this important point (I really like it) needs something.

The heart and strength is your investment and relation; the weakness is need for more concretes and specifics.

Best,

Peter

The Modes of Commentary and Teacher Control

Two responders can focus on more or less the same concerns from paper to paper and even make their comments as lean or full, yet their responding styles can be remarkably different. The reason? Their modes of commentary. Read back over the four sets of comments on "Street Gangs" and you'll hear four different voices and construct four distinct images of these responders. The roles they assume as readers, responders, and teachers will vary and, with them, the relationships they implicitly establish with the student writer.

Teachers may assume any number of roles: editor, critic, judge, gatekeeper, trouble-shooter, guide, coach, adviser, ally, motivator, collaborator, mentor, fellow explorer, sounding board; they may take on the role of sympathetic reader, common reader, representative reader, questioning reader, challenging reader, or others. These roles, in turn, can be differentiated according to the relative control the teacher exerts over student writing: how much she directs the writer's work or, to look at it positively, how much she offers direction to the writer. Different ways of framing comments—different voices, different grammatical structures, different functions—instantiate different images of the writer and implicitly create different relationships between teacher and student. Comments presented in the form of corrections, evaluations, and imperatives—the forms of traditional teacher response—are the most controlling:

> Inappropriate word choice.
>
> Awkward sentence.
>
> Put this idea, your thesis, at the end of your first paragraph.
>
> S: This was ~~in relation with our name~~: the Cripps.
>
> T: This was a symbol for our gang: the Cripps.

Praise comments are arguably less controlling than these modes, if only because they don't expect anything more from students, but they are nevertheless authoritative and controlling inasmuch as they present firm judgments about the writing, judgments that will doubtlessly affect the student's way of viewing those passages. (How many times have you struggled over something a teacher has praised?)

Comments presented as qualified evaluations, reader reactions, and advice are typically less controlling than their authoritative counterparts:

> I'm not sure about the choice of words.
>
> I tripped over this sentence.
>
> Maybe this sentence would go better at the start of your paper.

Comments in the form of questions exert various degrees of control, depending, among other things, on whether they are open or closed, but they are usually less controlling than the modes listed above. Consider the following examples, arranged from more controlling to less controlling:

> Is this really a sentence?
>
> But didn't you just say that you didn't provoke fights??
>
> How old were you when you were in the gang?
>
> Is there anything else you can tell us about this bond?
>
> What did you like most about being in the gang?

Comments that are presented as interpretations, reader responses, lessons, and explanations are the least controlling modes:

> So this wasn't the kind of gang that we have in mind from the media.
>
> I think I'd get tired of this paranoia pretty quickly.
>
> A comma splice occurs when you "splice" together what could be two sentences with only a comma (instead of a comma followed by a conjunction such as "and").
>
> [I like this image.] It's really suggestive.

The last sample, an explanatory comment, suggests how the mode of a comment can be affected by the surrounding comments. In isolation, the comment, "This image is really suggestive," would be considered praise; however, when it follows a praise comment ("I like this image"), its function changes: it now serves to explain the earlier comment. Notice how the meaning and function of the following comment changes when it is preceded by different responses:

> This idea doesn't work. Is there anything else can you say?
>
> I like this idea about getting a sense of belonging from the gang. Is there anything else can you say?

While the criticism has the effect of making the follow-up comment come across as a closed question, a call for different material, the introductory praise makes it more open-ended, a genuine question.

A teacher's control is more than just a matter of the modes he employs. The number of comments he makes, the focus and range of those comments, and the agenda he brings to his reading, among other things, also make a teacher's comments more or less controlling. But his choice of mode is the dominant factor in the images he creates of himself on the page and the control he assumes over the student's writing, as the following analysis of the responses to "Street Gangs" will attempt to show.

"Street Gangs: One Point of View" is a rich rough draft. Rusty clearly has involved himself in the writing. He has a lot to say about his experience in a gang. He offers some interesting views about gang life. He ties his talk to specific activities and episodes. And he reflects in an engaging way on his motives for joining, and then leaving, the gang. The writing is more mature and more risky than his earlier writing in the course, and it catches Rusty on an upswing. Yet there is still much to do. He is not sure just where he wants to take the essay. Will it be more an informative article about gangs, a glimpse into what gangs do and how they work? Or will it be more about his own experience with this particular gang? What kind of voice or posture will be most appropriate for his aims? How can he shape the material that he already has down on the page according to one purpose or the other? Which areas does he need to cut or cut back on. Which does he need to develop? The key question for response: How much to direct Rusty in his work with revision?

Richard Larson has a clear sense of what he'd like to see in the revision of "Street Gangs," and he is fairly direct in laying out the changes he sees necessary. Larson is impressed with the honesty and detail of the writing, but he wants it fitted to the demands of the assignment, which calls for an informative essay. His comments cover a range of concerns, but he is most concerned with having Rusty refocus the paper on gangs themselves, rather than on his experience in a gang, and provide more information on how gangs in general operate. He acknowledges Rusty's accomplishments and sums up, in some detail, his reading of the draft as it stands. Then he reviews the aims of the assignment and indicates how Rusty might (or, more accurately, should) revise his material to suit these demands, again in some detail. His agenda for revision is set, his response style rather controlling. Nevertheless, he manages to temper his directiveness by pointing out the strengths of the draft and by casting his calls for revision as advice, his predominant mode of response.

> Your focus, for this paper, might be on letting readers know how street gangs operate, what they do, why they do it, rather than on the chronology of your experiences as a gang member.
>
> I'd like to know a bit more about gangs in general than you tell me. Maybe you could use your experience to <u>illustrate</u> more general observations.
>
> You might give a few more details about some of the experiences.
>
> On the next draft, try to accomplish some of the steps I've suggested.
>
> I've underlined some places where I think you should reconsider the punctuation of sentences.

These advisory comments are marked by the conditional mood and, when they are combined with other nondirective comments, implicitly allow the student leeway to decide whether to take them up. They would be more controlling if they were presented as commands:

> Change your focus to how street gangs operate, what they do, why they do it.
>
> Tell me more about gangs in general.
>
> Give more details about some of the experiences.
>
> Follow the steps I've outlined here.
>
> Fix the punctuation.

Larson also moderates his directiveness by avoiding blunt criticism. He doesn't say that the paper doesn't provide much information about gangs in general. He says, "I'd like to know a bit more about gangs in general than you tell me." He doesn't say the draft doesn't fit the assignment or isn't acceptable given its present focus. He provides a summary sketch of the writing and then juxtaposes it against the expectations of the assignment:

> But as this piece stands it is essentially an account of a period in your life: how you got into a gang, what you did, why you stopped. The assignment asked, on the other hand, to discuss an activity in which you "regularly engage" and on which you can speak from some authority.

Nevertheless, Larson establishes a clear agenda, and his response is clearly directive. The fact that he expects Rusty to recast the paper along certain lines has the effect of making the advice less open than it might be. Further, his two main pieces of advice are followed up with comments that reinforce his call for revision and make the advisory comments less open and more insistent:

> Your focus, for this paper, might be on letting readers know how street gangs operate, what they do, why they do it, rather than on the chronology of your experiences as a gang member. *Your goal here is to enlarge the reader's knowledge of a subject that the reader might find important and might genuinely want to know more about.*
>
> I'd like to know a bit more about gangs in general than you tell me. *Maybe you could use your experience to <u>illustrate</u> more general observations.*

The first follow-up comment, an explanation, presumes that the advice is to be followed and serves to reinforce it. The second follow-up comment, offering further advice about focusing the paper on gangs in general, provides help, to be sure, but it also sets a clear agenda for revision, especially in the absence of any alternatives. The advice would be more open if it were presented without the earlier criticism or followed by more than one possible path for revision. A study of Larson's modes of commentary, then, reveals how his comments look to direct Rusty toward a certain set of revisions even as they try to soften the edge of authority in the response.

Like Larson, Frank O'Hare finds a problem with the focus of the essay. But whereas Larson directs Rusty to bring the focus in line with the assignment and write about gangs in general, O'Hare points to different ideas that surface in the paper and calls on him, in the next draft, to decide what his focus will be. Instead of firm criticism or strong advice, he relies on more temperate modes of response. Most of his evaluations are qualified and filtered through his perspective as a single reader, not laid down as the objective criticisms of a judge:

> The level of your vocabulary is *just a little* too informal.
>
> *I get the feeling that* you are still thinking through your experiences with the gang and that you haven't yet decided the significance of this experience.
>
> This hesitancy has, *I think*, caused you to neglect focusing on your purpose in this paper.

Instead of falling into a judgmental role and either praising or criticizing the writing, on several occasions he simply offers an interpretation (or an interpretive question) about what Rusty is saying:

> In the first paragraph, you seem hesitant about your right to write about this subject.
>
> You seem to be combining the bonding issue with "starting trouble."
>
> Are you saying that gang rivalries weren't as nasty as they appear to be?

Several of his key comments about the focus and development of the paper are cast in the form of open questions:

> What major points do you want to establish?
>
> Why did you talk about keeping a low profile?
>
> What incident or incidents led you to use the terms "paranoia" and "burden"?
>
> Paragraph nine: what point are you establishing here?

This is not to say that O'Hare doesn't make sharp judgments about the writing or that he doesn't have a certain idea of how Rusty might go about revising the paper. He does. He points out what he sees as a contradiction between Rusty's claim that he did not provoke fights, in paragraph 3, and the "sucker punching" episode at the pool, in paragraph 5. He says that paragraph 6 "needs specifics." He says straight up that paragraph 8 "is confused and confusing." And he notes that he has marked six places where Rusty has "failed to recognize sentence boundaries." Yet in almost every one of these cases he attenuates his criticism. After noting the need for specifics in paragraph 6, he helps Rusty imagine what kind of specifics he might employ. After complaining of the confusion in paragraph 8, he wonders about what the main point might be and then exhorts Rusty to work it out. After he points to the problem with sentence-boundary errors, he calls on him to try to fix them on his own and then assures him that "All six are, in reality, examples of just one problem."

He also makes several calls for revision, but, significantly, all of them look to engage Rusty in certain composing processes, rather than elicit definite changes in the text:

> It would probably be useful for you to sketch quickly an informal outline of your draft.

> You must decide what your major points will be.

> Please examine these examples and see if you can rewrite them correctly. Please come in for a conference and we'll discuss this problem.

There is clear direction, even firm control, here and across O'Hare's comments, yet there's also a sense of openness, a clear attempt to put Rusty in the driver's seat of his revision.

Glynda Hull's response is less critical, more pointed, and more interactive than Larson's or O'Hare's. Hull tightly coordinates her marginal and end comments in order, first, to convince Rusty that the material he has come up with so far is interesting and promising and, second, to guide him through his work with revision. She writes 18 comments—nine in the margins and nine in her note at the end. All of her marginal comments focus on his ideas and (save for one) present a positive evaluation or her personal reactions to what he has said. In her end note she concentrates on just two issues: development and organization. Never mind about straightening out sentences or even settling on the focus. She has other priorities right now. Through two detailed clusters of comments, Hull looks to mark out a path for Rusty's revision while simultaneously leaving the work and the responsibility for those changes up to him. Each cluster starts with an imperative comment, a directive that somehow has the sound of a friendly suggestion. She doesn't say, "Add fuller examples. She says, "I want you to add some extended examples—not just one sentence or two, but whole paragraphs." She is urging him on, almost exhorting him through this call for revision. She doesn't say, "Reorganize the paragraphs." She suggests certain activities he might take up in order to play with the organization of the essay: "After you've added the examples, get some scissors and tape, and cut your paper up—one paragraph per strip of paper. Experiment with putting these paragraphs in different orders." Then, in each cluster, she adds commentary that is meant to clarify her suggestion and guide his work—in the first case, a series of examples and explanations, in the second, a series of questions and further advice. I'll set them out in layers of specificity to dramatize the rich texture of the comments:

> (1) I want you to add some extended examples–not just one sentence or two, but whole paragraphs.
>
>> I've marked several places you could make some additions with an asterisk (*).
>>
>>> On the first page, for example, you might tell specifically about a time when someone got in trouble and everyone was there.
>>>
>>>> Give details: what time, when, what situation, where. These long examples should be used to illustrate and provide evidence for points you're making.
>
> (2) After you've added the examples, get some scissors and tape, and cut your paper up–one paragraph per strip of paper. Experiment with putting these paragraphs in different orders.
>
>> Which ones seems like beginning material? Which ones come next? And so on.
>>
>> If there isn't any order that seems better than another, then try to imagine what you would need to do to your paper to connect up the paragraphs.
>
> Then tape your draft together again.

As she adds this information, applying layer on layer to her comments, she provides more direction and offers more help to Rusty, even as she leaves the work of adding examples and ordering the material wholly up to him. To be sure, much of the effect of Hull's response derives from the limited scope of her comments and from her casual voice: she comes across as a coach who, having diagnosed the strengths and weaknesses in a performance, has selected the most important issues to deal with right now and devised a set of exercises the player might work on to improve. But much of her effect is achieved through her choice of modes and her habit of doing a lot with the little she takes up. Her response establishes a clear direction for revision and at the same time allows Rusty to maintain control over the writing.

Patricia Stock has the same casual voice and supportive style as Glynda Hull. She has a similar way of using her comments to get into a give-and-take exchange with the student. But in her response to Rusty's essay Stock ups the ante. More than refining the ideas he already has down on the page, more than getting his materials shaped into a sharper focus, Stock looks to engage Rusty in an inquiry into his subject. More than the role of critic, guide, or mentor, she assumes the role of an interested reader, a fellow explorer—someone who is really interested in finding out more about the workings of gangs from a person who has first-hand experience with them. She writes 41 comments in the margins and end note. Almost 30 of them are focused on two areas of response: nine of them on the development of his ideas in the draft, another 18 on the nature of street gangs.

Stock challenges him to explore his experience as a gang member and use his writing as a way of learning. In her marginal comments, she writes one comment after another that expresses her interest in his involvement in the gang and her desire to know more about it. Some of these comments are cast in a form that blends reader response and advice:

> I'd like an illustrative anecdote here.
>
> I'd like to see this scene in all its detail.
>
> I'd like you to show me what the acceptance, the friendship, looks like.

Others are presented as open questions:

> Who did you get into trouble and fights with?
>
> This really interests me. How did you grow up? How did you change? Is there some representative incident you can share with your reader to demonstrate your change?

In the opening paragraphs of her end note, she construes Rusty's work as a real act of researching, discovering, and sharing knowledge. Then, in the third paragraph, she confronts him with a series of open-ended questions about street gangs—questions she seems genuinely interested in and that, she is convinced, Rusty has the wherewithal to take on. Why were you in a gang, she asks Rusty:

> Was it because you didn't participate in other institutions such as church groups, sports? Was everyone you knew in a gang when you were? Was there a real difference between your gang and the gangs I read about in the papers? What exactly should I understand by the meaning of the word gang? Why do you not

use the word club or clique or fraternity instead of gang to describe your group?

She keeps the bar high when she presents a former student's essay as a model to guide (and spur) his investigation and help him develop his own ideas in the text. These are pretty demanding comments. To be sure, they are also somewhat directive. Stock thinks that the paper would be improved, and, perhaps more importantly, that Rusty would most benefit as a learning writer, if he turns back into his thinking about his involvement in a gang and deals more fully with his own first-hand knowledge and views. She is not content simply to have him focus and arrange the information he has here. She is not interested simply to have him add details and examples. She wants him to push himself to figure out what he knows about gangs and what he can learn about his experience as a gang member—and then to share this knowledge with readers.

We might be inclined to think that Stock's expectations far outstrip the capabilities of the writer of this rough draft. Yet this is probably the defining characteristic of her response to Rusty. Her comments look to challenge him to think more about his subject, at a higher level, and say more in his writing, as a real act of communication, than he has likely ever been asked in school. The response construes Rusty as a more than capable student, or perhaps as an average student who might well be able to give much more if much more is expected of him. It challenges him to stretch himself as a writer and a thinker, and it offers support all along the way.

Elbow is after something different in his response, different from either Stock or Hull and very different from Larson and O'Hare. Instead of approaching the writing as a critic, an editor, a knowledgeable guide, a facilitator, a coach, or a mentor, Elbow assumes the role of an individual reader and spends much of his response simply playing back his way of reading and reacting to the writing. Over one-third of his comments are framed as interpretations and reader responses, dramatizing his way of experiencing the words on the page and providing his own personal views (*not* about the writing—that's the job of a critic or teacher or mentor) but about the subject (see the comments below in italic):

> What I noticed first are the places where you talk about your feelings while being in the gang: the oddly, interestingly, low-key "burden" as you put it. *I would feel flat out fear.* Also the feeling of comfort and support and family quality. Seems important.

> At the bottom of 1 you give the example of picking on people at the pool. You tell it in a kind of deadpan way, *but it's kind of horrifying for me. I think I was the kind of person who was picked on—or always felt I was about to be.* There's something intriguing or even moving about your low key tone here, [but I'm also curious to

know a bit more how you actually felt–and feel.] Something
mysterious here: perhaps it's more interesting this way, despite
my unsatisfied curiosity.

Elbow positions himself sitting across from the student, a reader talking
with the writer, not standing over or above him. He foregrounds his own
immediate reactions and highlights his subjectivity as a reader: "What I
noticed first," "Seems important," "it's kind of horrifying for me,"
"There's something intriguing or even moving about your low key tone
here."

He doesn't limit himself, however, to playing back the text. He presents several praise comments, makes a few criticisms, and offers several
pieces of advice. But he weaves these teacherly judgments in and around
his readerly responses and filters even these authoritative comments
through his experience as a reader:

Praise

This is interesting to read and sometimes has a strong impact on
me.

The symbols of the gang are nice and concrete.

I really like it [the point about growing up at the end].

The heart and strength is your investment and relation.

Advice and Criticism

I would enjoy getting a bit more exploration here: but not just
finding more words for it but more examples: [what does all that
look like in events or scenes?]

[Perhaps it's more interesting this way, despite my unsatisfied
curiosity.] But I do know I'd like you to flesh it out more as an
example: it's a specific scene or incident, *but you don't let us see
any particulars.*

[The symbols of the gang are nice and concrete.] I had the
thought of somehow starting with them–or at least finding some
way to start that has some zip to it; *it's a little bit of a soggy opening as you have it. And the ending sentence is very sudden*—though
now I see you were building to it. *I need some kind of help here;* not
sure what; don't want some abstract discussion of "growing
up"—but somehow this important point (I really like it) needs
something.

In his letter to Rusty, Elbow presents just as many evaluative comments
as reader responses, but they are shaded by the surrounding comments
and tempered by the way they are presented. Half of his praise comments

achieve? These are the questions that make teacher response, again like writing, a matter of perpetual adaptation and revision. A matter of style. A matter to work out over time, with each new class, with each batch of papers, with each student, on every response.

2

A Way to Analyze Comments

The best way of developing an effective response style is the most direct: intuiting, over time, the ways good responders comment and importing their strategies into your own responses. But such a process can take place only over time, with a lot of trial and error. Here I'd like to make the process more deliberate and present a fairly detailed method for analyzing comments. The idea is that the better you can identify different types of commentary and the more you understand the options available to you as a responder, the better you will be able to develop your own response style and make comments that are more responsive to the needs of your students.

There are any number of ways of analyzing comments: short comments versus long comments, comments about content versus comments about form and style, comments that criticize versus comments that praise, comments that make corrections versus comments that offer suggestions. Elaine Lees identifies seven modes of response: correcting, emoting, describing, suggesting, questioning, reminding, and assigning. Peter Elbow and Pat Belanoff distinguish between "reader-based" comments and "criteria-based" comments. Lil Brannon and C.H. Knoblauch, less confident of the usefulness of the ways comments are presented formally on the page, suggest that teachers look to distinguish between two general responding attitudes. In a "directive" style the teacher evaluates the writing and dictates what the student should do (or should have done) with the writing; in a "facilitative" style he indicates where the writing may or may not be realizing the writer's intentions and encourages the writer to make substantive revisions. Others like Elizabeth Hodges and Francine Danis call on teachers to listen for the voices and roles they create in their written comments: the critic, the judge, the coach, the questioning reader. Some methods of analysis are specific and formal; others are more general and impressionistic.

The following method zeroes in on specific comments. It looks at a teacher's comments, first individually and then holistically, from two key perspectives: the *focus* of the comment and the *mode* of the comment. The "focus" identifies *what* a teacher is calling attention to in the writing—for instance, whether the comment mainly addresses the writer's wording, organization, or ideas. The "mode" of a comment describes *how* the comment is framed. It looks to characterize the relationship the comment implicitly establishes between the teacher and the student and the implicit control the comment asserts over the student's writing. Analyzing a set of comments involves labeling each individual comment—each statement that the teacher presents to the student, whether it occurs between the lines of the student's text, in the margins, or in an end note of some kind—according to its "focus" and its "mode" and then looking for patterns and emphases that are suggestive of a given response style. Each comment is classified in one of five broad categories under "focus" and one of nine categories under "mode":

FOCUS	MODE
Correctness	Corrections
	Criticism
Style	Qualified Criticism
	Praise
Organization	Commands
	Advice
Content	Closed Questions
	Open Questions
Context	Reflective Statements

The Focuses of Commentary

The "focus" of a teacher's commentary describes what the teacher attends to in a comment. It identifies what the comment refers to in the writing—or, more accurately, what the teacher calls attention to, through the wording of the comment. Two comments can *refer* to the same word or sentence but *focus* on different concerns. Consider the following comments made next to the statement: "We all know drugs are dangerous to the body and society without any explanation, therefore, you shouldn't legalize something that is dangerous":

> Not all things that are dangerous are illegal. Think of cigarettes, alcohol, parachute jumping, and white-water rafting.
>
> [The teacher underlines "dangerous to the body and society" and next to the passage writes:] Vague.
>
> Comma splice.

The first comment calls attention to the idea the writer is asserting. It focuses on content. The second comment calls attention to the wording and focuses on style. The third focuses on correctness. The focus labels the teacher's *predominant* concern in a comment. The following classification establishes five general focuses of commentary.

1. Correctness

Comments about correctness deal with errors in grammar, mechanics, punctuation, and spelling—matters that are conventionally viewed in terms of right and wrong:

- Sentence fragment.
- "It's" is always "it is." You need "its" for the possessive.
- Place commas and periods inside the quotes.
- You want "lose," not "loose."

The category also includes comments that deal with formal conventions, such as paragraphing, citation, documentation, and manuscript format:

- Indent five spaces for a new paragraph.
- Place the title of the source and page number in parentheses at the end of the sentence.

2. Style

Comments about style deal with wording and with the structure within a sentence, between consecutive sentences, or within a paragraph:

- This language is pretty abstract.
- I'd look for a more appropriate word.
- Avoid putting a lot of words between your subject and verb.
- These sentences are hard to follow.

Included in this category are comments that ask the student to get more specific with the wording or phrasing *within a sentence*:

- What is the name of the lake?
- How many were in the gang?
- Which character are you talking about?

3. Organization

Comments about organization deal with the overall arrangement of the essay, the relation of materials within different paragraphs, and the order of paragraphs; the unity, coherence, and emphasis of the work as a whole; the thesis, focus, or organizing principle of the writing; and the effectiveness of introductions and conclusions:

- A good, engaging introduction.
- Does this idea go with the material above in paragraph 2?
- You might give too much space to this minor point.
- Is this your main point in the essay?

4. Content

Comments about content address the writer's ideas, assertions, arguments, examples, explanations, and support. They include comments that acknowledge the detail that is already achieved in the text and that call for development.

- Good explanation.
- A rich, insightful idea.
- This evidence is not convincing by itself.
- I'd like to see some examples.
- What happened? Tell us more.
- What would your opponents say in response to your argument?

5. Context

Comments about context focus on concerns beyond the formal text—for instance, the audience, the writer's intentions or purpose, the topic, the writing assignment, the work in class, the student's writing process, and the student's experience:

- Write as though you're talking with the members of this class.
- This is an interesting topic.
- The assignment asked you to express your views.
- This paper is a real improvement on your previous draft.
- I suggest doing some brainstorming before the next draft.
- I like the material you've added in this revision.
- How much do you know about the seat-belt law?

Most comments about voice—the tone, persona, point of view, authority, and credibility of the writing—are also considered matters of context, because they view the text in terms of writers, readers, and genres:

- You sound too casual for a formal academic essay.
- How does this sentence make you come across as a writer?
- This sounds like an advertisement.

Also placed in this category are comments that address the essay as a whole, the student's work on the writing, and the student's work in class:

- I think you have the makings of a very good paper here.
- You've made only a few minor revisions on this draft.
- This is your best paper of the semester.

Comments don't usually refer exclusively to these extra-textual features. Instead, they address some textual concern in light of these larger contexts. In such cases it's useful to note how frequently comments about content, organization, style, and correctness are seen in relation tothese contexts.

The Modes of Commentary

The "modes" of commentary describe the different ways that teachers speak to students and set up tasks for them to do. They attempt to catalog the typical ways teachers construct various images of themselves through their comments and in doing so implicitly assert varying degrees of control over student writing. This classification of modes is based on three complementary assumptions. First, the form of a comment strongly influences how the comment functions and what it comes to mean. Second, the form of a comment is not enough: any analysis of how a comment functions must consider, in addition, its voice and content—and the fact that the statement is made by a teacher to a student, with all the power relations that conventionally adhere in such a classroom situation. Third, the meaning and control implied by any given comment may be influenced by the surrounding comments.

The analysis of modes goes beyond a simple analysis of the outward, grammatical form of a teacher's comments—that is, whether they are presented as statements, commands, or questions. But the surface forms of teachers' comments are not unimportant. Consider, for instance, the following comments:

> Place this argument at the end.

> I wonder if this argument would be better to save for the end.

Both comments raise the issue of rearranging the order of the arguments. But that is not to say that the two are synonymous. There is a definite change in meaning—and in the constructed relationship between teacher and student—when the sentence changes from an imperative to a conditional declarative statement. The form of a comment makes a difference in the meaning and in the authoritativeness of the response..

At the same time, it is not enough to analyze the form of teacher comments. To capture the different ways teachers shape their comments and, through them, enact various relationships with their students, we must also take into consideration the voice and the content of their comments because changes in the substance of a comment may of course make a critical difference in its meaning and in its implicit control, as in the following case:

> Add detail.
>
> Add a sentence about your parents' views.
>
> Consider whether it'd help to add some detail.

Different forms of the "same" response amount to different comments. Thus, the following comments deal with the same issue and can be seen as having the same general goal—to lead the writer to consider refocusing his essay on his own experience with gangs— but they are all different comments:

> Focus on your own experience with gangs.
>
> You could just focus on your own experience with gangs.
>
> Can you deal exclusively with your own experience with gangs?
>
> This essay doesn't deal enough with your own experience with gangs.
>
> I found myself most interested in those places where you talk about your own experience with gangs.
>
> How would the essay change if you focused on your own experience with gangs?

Although all six versions of the comment—in a particular context, with particular teachers and students—may have the force of a request, each of the comments has a different immediate sense. Only the first example, "Focus on your own experience with gangs," immediately directs the student to make a change. The other versions offer advice, indirectly call on him to make a change, present criticism, provide a reader's response, and ask the student to consider refocusing the essay. Different modes implicitly create different images and roles for the teacher, establish different roles and tasks for the student, and enact different degrees of teacher control over student writing.

The way a comment is viewed may also be affected by the comments that immediately surround it. Notice how the meaning of the second comment in each of the following sequences is influenced by the first:

> I'm curious about the wildlife in the area. Are there bears in Syracuse?
>
> Much of your writing is marred by carelessness. Do squirrels hibernate? Are there bears in Syracuse?

And notice how the second half of the following comment *functions* as an explanation:

> This talk about Jack Frost nipping at your nose doesn't work. It's a cliché about winter.

The categorization that follows provides nine general modes of teacher commentary. While some modes tend to exert firm control over the student's writing (corrections, criticism, and commands), other modes tend to exert moderate control (qualified criticism, advice, praise, closed questions), and others only mild control (open questions, reflective statements).

It is important to note that all comments by their very nature employ some degree of control. Every time a teacher responds to a student's text, the comment identifies some issue the teacher finds significant and wants the student to attend to in some way. In a sense, then, all comments are evaluations of the writing and directives to the student. The question of control lies in the extent to which the teacher overtly evaluates the writing and directs changes that are to be made—or, alternately, the extent to which the teacher encourages the student to retain control over her writing choices.

1. Corrections

The teacher actually makes corrections in the student's text:

- [The teacher crosses out words and inserts others in their place:]

    This critic argues that Nick Carraway
    ~~Nick Carraway it is argued by this critic~~ is just as important as Gatsby.

2. Criticism

The teacher points unequivocally to problems in the writing, asserting distinct control over the writer's choices:

- Awkward sentence.
- Comma splice.
- The paper ends too abruptly.
- This argument needs more support.

3. Qualified Criticism

The teacher points to problems, but he tempers some of the control he exerts over the writing by using qualifiers or acknowledging his subjectivity:

- I'm not sure I'm following your point.
- This is a bit too technical for me.
- This paragraph seems out of place.
- I think you're missing some of the author's argument.
- This argument is not as strong as the one above.

4. Praise

The teacher presents positive judgments about the writing or the student's performance:

- Good point.
- This is a solid revision.
- I like this example.

5. Commands

The teacher directly requests changes in the writing, asserting distinct control over the student's course for revision:

- Add some specific details.
- Don't use "you."
- Use this paragraph as your conclusion.
- You need to support this argument with evidence.

6. Advice

The teacher suggests changes but, by casting his call in the conditional or highlighting his role as a single reader, tempers some of the control he exerts over the course for revision:

- You might present your own views here.
- I'd try to find a better title for this piece.
- Think about whether you need another example.
- I wonder if you'd lose anything if you started the essay here.

7. Closed Questions

The teacher asks a question but strongly implies a criticism or the need for a correction, makes an implicit request, or somehow insinuates that there's a certain answer to the question:

- Roommate?
- Right word?
- Change to present tense?
- Is this paragraph really necessary?
- Aren't there exceptions to this rule?

In another form of closed question, the teacher uses a question to guide the student to add specific information to the text—information that is usually readily available from her experience:

- Who was your favorite player on the team?
- How long were you in Italy?

8. Open Questions

The teacher asks the student to consider some issue and allows her the responsibility to think about it on her own:

- Is this your main point?
- Who do you envision as your primary audience?
- How is fall in Syracuse different from fall in other northern cities?
- In what ways has this experience changed you?

9. Reflective Statements

This category is a catch-all for declarative statements that are not evaluative, directive, or advisory. Comments in these modes usually present the responder's reflections about the writing, either as an instructor or as an individual reader. They include descriptive, interpretive, reader-response, explanatory, instructive, and hortatorical comments. Responses that cannot be labeled reliably in one of the other modes are placed here.

In *descriptive* or *interpretive* comments, the teacher describes what the text says or interprets its meaning or significance. The teacher points to a passage or "plays back" the writer's words and ideas but does not offer a judgment or reaction:

- Your first argument is that drugs are harmful to the individual. Your second is that they are a menace to society.
- You seem especially interested in talking about fishing this one time at Lake Ivanhoe.
- So you're saying you aren't really different from your brother.

In *reader-response* comments, the teacher assumes the role of a reader more than a teacher and says something about his way of reading the writing—the ways he experiences the text, his thoughts about the subject, and his reactions to the writer's ideas:

- I found myself getting bogged down on the third page.
- It took me a while to figure how this sentence follows from the previous one.
- This makes me think that Gatsby knows his dream is over.
- I love winter too.

In *explanatory* comments, the teacher explains or elaborates on an earlier comment:

- [Confusing sentence.] It's not clear who is doing the action.
- This is a comma splice. You're joining two main clauses with only a comma. You need a conjunction like "and" or "but."

In *instructional* comments, the teacher offers information or explains a concept:

- When you place lengthy quotations in an indent, you don't need to put quotes around the passage. The indent signifies material that's directly quoted.
- Writing is meant to <u>ex</u>press, not <u>im</u>press. Too often in this writing you opt for the impressive word instead of the right word.

In *hortatorical* comments, the teacher encourages or exhorts the student to adopt some attitude or take some action:

- You can do it—give it a try.
- I'm looking forward to reading your next draft.
- Now see what you can do to push yourself on the next draft.

In analyzing a set of comments, the goal is not to determine how the teacher actually intended a given comment or to predict how the student would likely understand it. The proposed analysis is concerned with the way the teacher creates himself in his comments, his persona as it may be construed from the words on the page. The teacher's comments—how they are presented and what they say—create their own image of the teacher, their own context, and play a significant role in determining how comments come to mean. Although it is true that comments written on a student essay are shaped by the larger classroom context, it is no less true that the context itself is shaped by the teacher's comments. Arguably, during the time the student looks over the response, they *are* the context of instruction and have an immediate impact on how the student reads and interprets the response. To the extent that the comments stay fixed in mind, they may even *become* that teacher for that student. The ways a teacher frames his comments, then, are crucial to the ways those comments come to mean. By analyzing his comments, a teacher can see if the image he is creating for himself—and the relationships he establishes with students—are working in line with his classroom persona and his course goals.

The complete rubric for analyzing the focuses and modes of a set of comments is presented in the appendix. It is designed to chart individual comments and detect key patterns in a teacher's responses.

Using the Rubric to Analyze Comments

In order to analyze a set of comments, you have to isolate individual comments, label them, and then look for patterns and emphases in the response as a whole. Basically, each statement (word, phrase, or sentence) that addresses the writing or the writer's work, whether it appears in marginal comments or an end note, is considered a comment. Marginal comments are easier to mark than end comments because they are placed next to the passage they refer to and are separated spatially from other comments. But in both cases comments are marked by their focus and function. Whenever the focus or mode in consecutive statements shifts— or whenever the responder takes on a new subject or tact—there's a new comment. All of the comments below—except for the last one—are single comments:

> A vivid description.
>
> This is a sharp and vivid description of spring.
>
> Pretentious language.
>
> This lofty language seems inappropriate for such a homey essay.
>
> These paragraphs need to be developed more fully and arranged in an orderly sequence.

Each comment is characterized by a particular focus and mode. The first comment deals with one of the writer's ideas and is labeled as focusing on "content." It offers a positive evaluation of the writing, and so it is labeled as "praise." The second comment, though it takes a different grammatical form, is marked the same way: a single comment focusing on "content" and presented as "praise." The third and fourth comments both deal with the wording of the writing and are labeled as focusing on "style," but the third comment is presented in the form of a direct negative evaluation and is labeled "criticism," and the fourth qualifies its criticism and is labeled "qualified criticism" or "qualified evaluation." The final example—"These paragraphs need to be developed more fully and arranged in an orderly sequence"—is different. Although it is a single statement, it contains more than one focus. The first half of the sentence calls for additional support, the second for changes in organization. There are two comments, then, the first labeled "content-command," the second labeled "organization-command."

Take a look now at the next list of comments, again placed in the margins next to the student's writing:

> Good description. You provide specific, concrete details that accompany spring.
>
> What kind of flowers? In Tallahassee, they would be azaleas. What would they be in Syracuse?
>
> What kind of flowers? What kind of trees?

> Your language gets very general: "the sun beats down," "the
> spirits are high," "long winter's nap," "Jack Frost nipping at
> your nose."

These are combination comments, in which two or more comments are
joined in a sequence and one comment is followed (and elaborated,
explained, or qualified) by another. In the first sequence, a praise comment about one of the writer's descriptions is followed by an explanation
of why it is successful. It is labeled as two comments, the first "content-
praise," the second "content-nondirective statement." The second
sequence opens with a question asking for information that should be
readily available to the student and may be easily inserted into the exist-
ing sentence; it focuses on "style" (because it deals with wording within
a sentence) and is presented in the form of a "closed question." This question is followed by two comments, marked by different modes. "In
Tallahassee, they would be azaleas" is an explanatory comment, providing information to the student. "What would they be in Syracuse?" is
another version of the opening question, but because it represents a
change in mode from the previous statement it is identified as a separate
comment. The third sequence contains two statements that deal with the
same focus ("style") and are presented in the same mode ("closed question"), but they are marked as two comments because they deal with different concerns: flowers and trees. The fourth sequence at first glance
might also appear to be a single comment. But the two halves are dealt
with separately in order to capture the detail of the response: labeling it
all as one comment would fail to account for the way the responder provides examples in the second half of the statement. The response is
marked as two comments, labeled, respectively, "style-criticism" and
"style-reflective statement." Again, the rule of thumb to remember when
marking comments: whenever the focus or mode changes, or the
teacher's subject, there's a new comment.

The same principles are used to distinguish comments that are presented in paragraph form in end notes. Consider the following end comment by Anne Gere, one of the compositionists whose comments are
highlighted earlier in the book:

> [1] This paper is filled with excellent descriptions. [2] You have
> done a very good job of conveying to your audience the "feel"
> of the seasons. [3] Phrases like "V formation," "heat waves rest-
> ing on the pavement," "auburn, garnet and gold," and "soft
> scrunching" make your descriptions particularly vivid. [4] I come
> away from this paper with a clear sense of place. [5] Your use of
> the second person (you) is also effective because it draws the
> reader into your account. [6] The significance of the four seasons
> for you remains somewhat vague. [7] Although I understand that

you take pleasure in each of the four seasons, I'm still not sure if they have any other meaning for you. [8] As noted in the margins, there are several usage problems in this paper. [9] Please check each one and see me if you have questions about any of them.

The statements are viewed one-by-one, with an eye to when the focus or mode changes. The first five sentences all offer praise. They comprise five separate comments because they deal with different focuses. The first clearly deals with the content of the writing. The second is a tough call. It deals with the content too, but it also addresses the audience. Here, audience seems to be the responder's main focus—and her concern for the descriptions themselves have already been acknowledged. So the comment is best seen as focusing on audience and labeled as "context." The third comment shifts from the broad perspective to the local. It focuses on the specific language choices that make these descriptions come alive and is labeled "style." The fourth comment returns to the content of the writing and seems to call attention simultaneously to the assignment and the effect the writing has had on the teacher as an individual reader. If you were looking for a full description of the comments, you would mark this comment as focusing on content and then note in addition that the comment is oriented to these larger contexts. The fifth comment compliments the writer's use of the second-person point of view and is labeled as focusing on "context." It is also oriented to the reader.

The next two comments in Gere's end note change tact, looking at where the writing does not yet succeed. The sixth comment points to the writer's failure to clearly indicate the significance the seasons have for him. It is presented in the form of a qualified evaluation ("somewhat vague"). The comment focuses on content and, like the fourth comment, may be marked in addition as being oriented to the writer's personal experience. The seventh comment, if it were presented in isolation, would be considered two comments: the first half, an interpretation of the writer's ideas, the second half, a qualified criticism of the content. But in the context of the response, the comment functions as an explanation of the previous comment. It is labeled "content-reflective." The last two comments shift to matters of correctness. The eighth comment is a direct negative evaluation and is labeled "criticism." The final comment directs the student to engage in a composing activity (in this case, proofreading) and is a process directive. It is labeled "correctness-command."

I'll use the rubric now to analyze two sets of comments on "What If Drugs Were Legal?" by two noted composition teachers, Jane Peterson and Tilly Warnock, and show how such an analysis can be used to describe responding styles.

What If Drugs Were Legal?
Jane Peterson's Comments

Nancy S.
First Rough Draft

What If Drugs Were Legal?

What if drugs were legal? Could you imagine what it would do to our society? Well according to John E. LeMoult, a lawyer with twenty years of experience on the subject, feels we should at least consider it. I would like to comment on his article "Legalize Drugs" in the June 15, 1984, issue of the *New York Times*. I disagree with LeMoult's idea of legalizing drugs to cut the cost of crime.

LeMoult's article was short and sweet. He gives the background of the legalization of drugs. For example, the first antidrug laws of the United States were passed in 1914. The laws were put in effect because of the threat of the Chinese imagrants. In addition, he explains how women were the first to use laudanun, an over the counter drug, as a substitute for drinking; it was unacceptable for women to drink. By explaining this he made the reader feel that society was the cause of women using the substitute, laudanun, for drinking. LeMoult proceeded from there to explain how the money to buy drugs comes from us as society. Since drug addicts turn to crime to get money we become a corrupt society. Due to this we spend unnecessary money protecting inocent citizens by means of law enforcment, jails, and ect. LeMoult says that if we legalize drugs that "Overnight the cost of law enforcement, courts, judges, jails and convict rehabilitation would be cut in half. The savings in tax would be more than $50 billion a year."

1
This is in his 4th prgh. What's he doing in the first 3 prghs?

2
I think you've fallen into the interesting detail trap here.

3
? crime-filled ?

4
Good use of quote

PETERSON

LeMoult might be correct by saying that our cost of living in society would be cut in half if drugs were legalized, however, he is justifying a wrong to save money. In my opinion legalizing drugs is the easy man's way out. Just because crime is high due to the fact that the cost of drugs is unbeleivable it doesn't make legalizing them right. We all know drugs are dangerous to the body and society without any explanation, therefore, you shouldn't legalize something that is dangerous.

5   6
Do we? All drugs?
7 Whose bodies?
8   9
How? Legal or illegal?

10 Cigarettes? alcohol? car racing?

My only and most important argument to LeMoult is the physical harm it would bring by legalizing drugs. People abuse their right to use alcoholic beverages because they are legal. For example, LeMoult himself says the amount of drug addicts is small compared to alcoholics. Why? –of course it is because of the legalization of alcohol. When you make something legal it can and will be done with little hassel. Why allow something to be done with ease when it is wrong? LeMoult's points are good and true but I believe he is approaching the subject in the wrong manner. Drugs are wrong, therefore, should not be legal!

11 To whom?

12 All people? This would mean everyone is an alcoholic because alcohol is legal.

13
Do you mean morally wrong or dangerous?

Nancy,

14 Your first draft is a good starting point— 15 you clearly understand the structure expected (opening with source info, summarizing the article, responding with your view). 16 Before beginning a second draft, I suggest you do a barebones outline on the article (16a you're missing a couple of LeMoult's points) and 17 then do one on your response (17a you seem to have at least two objections instead of one).

What If Drugs Were Legal?
Tilly Warnock's Comments

Nancy S.
First Rough Draft

What If Drugs Were Legal?

What if drugs were legal? Could you imagine what it would do to our society? Well according to John E. LeMoult, a lawyer with twenty years of experience on the subject, feels we should at least consider it. I would like to comment on his article "Legalize Drugs" in the June 15, 1984, issue of the *New York Times*. I disagree with LeMoult's idea of legalizing drugs to cut the cost of crime.

LeMoult's article was short and sweet. He gives the background of the legalization of drugs. For example, the first antidrug laws of the United States were passed in 1914. The laws were put in effect because of the threat of the Chinese imagrants. In addition, he explains how women were the first to use laudanun, an over the counter drug, as a substitute for drinking; it was unacceptable for women to drink. By explaining this he made the reader feel that society was the cause of women using the substitute, laudanun, for drinking. LeMoult proceeded from there to explain how the money to buy drugs comes from us as society. Since drug addicts turn to crime to get money we become a corrupt society. Due to this we spend unnecessary money protecting inocent citizens by means of law enforcment, jails, and ect. LeMoult says that if we legalize drugs that "Overnight the cost of law enforcement, courts, judges, jails and convict rehabilitation would be cut in half. The savings in tax would be more than $50 billion a year."

1
What's your main point here? If it's that you disagree, put that idea up front and explain.

2
Why do you disagree? Would letting your readers know here set up clearer reader expectations?

3
How do these ideas relate to your purpose as stated in the last sentence of prgh 1?

4
You summarize the article here, but how does what you say here relate to your view stated in the last sentence of prgh 1?

5
You've given us a summary of the article—why? You can give your view.

LeMoult might be correct by saying that our cost of living in society would be cut in half if drugs were legalized, however, he is justifying a wrong to save money. In my opinion legalizing drugs is the easy man's way out. Just because crime is high due to the fact that the cost of drugs is unbeleivable it doesn't make legalizing them right. We all know drugs are dangerous to the body and society without any explanation, therefore, you shouldn't legalize something that is dangerous.

6
Here you're giving your views.

7
Here you begin to give your views.

My only and most important argument to LeMoult is the physical harm it would bring by legalizing drugs. People abuse their right to use alcoholic beverages because they are legal. For example, LeMoult himself says the amount of drug addicts is small compared to alcoholics. Why? –of course it is because of the legalization of alcohol. When you make something legal it can and will be done with little hassel. Why allow something to be done with ease when it is wrong? LeMoult's points are good and true but I believe he is approaching the subject in the wrong manner. Drugs are wrong, therefore, should not be legal!

8
Is this your most original and most important argument?

Nancy–

9 *As you write, you seem to discover what you think.* 10 *How can you explain and support your views to make them convincing for readers of the publication?* 11 *What specific points does LeMoult make that you can argue for or against?* 11a *How?*

Peterson and Warnock write a similar number of comments, in a similar format, making extensive use of marginal comments and offering only a brief overview at the end. Both of them are concerned about the writer's arguments, the lack of development, and the organization of the essay, and they pay little, if any, attention to matters of editing and correctness. They also rely heavily on questions. The responses may at first glance seem very similar in style—and to an extent they are. But a closer comment-by-comment study reveals notable differences. One clear difference lies in the length and fullness of the comments. Peterson writes 22 comments, Warnock 17. But while Peterson averages six words per comment, Warnock averages nine. And while Peterson casts half of her comments in terse, elliptical phrases—Do we? All drugs? How? Legal or illegal? Cigarettes? alcohol? car racing?—Warnock writes out all of her comments in full sentences, half of them in the form of combination comments, for example:

> What's your main point here? If it's that you disagree, put that idea up front and explain.
>
> Why do you disagree? Would letting your readers know here set up clearer reader expectations?

There are other differences as well. Peterson is mainly interested in having Nancy sharpen and rethink specific phrases and statements. She casts eight of these comments in the form of closed questions:

> Crime-filled?
>
> Do we? [i.e., Do we all know that drugs are dangerous?]
>
> All drugs? [i.e., Are all drugs dangerous?]
>
> Whose bodies? [i.e., Dangerous to whose bodies?]
>
> How? [i.e., How are drugs dangerous to society?]
>
> Legal or illegal? [i.e., Legal or illegal drugs?]
>
> Cigarettes? alcohol? car racing?
>
> All people? [i.e., Do all people abuse their right to use alcohol?]

Two of the questions are designed to elicit specific information from the writer, but most of them imply a correction, criticism, or command and are designed to lead the student to recognize some problem in the writing. These comments, in principle, allow the student to make her own decisions, but the very form of the comment enables the teacher to insinuate her own judgments into the comments.

Warnock is interested, more broadly, in calling on Nancy, through questions, to define her main ideas and shape the essay more clearly around them. She goes one step further than Peterson, moreover, when she presents these comments in the light of the larger rhetorical context, namely, the writer's audience, purpose, and individual views:

> [1] What's your main point here? [1a] [If it's that you disagree, put that idea up front and explain.]

> [2] Why do you disagree? [2a] Would letting your readers know here set up clearer reader expectations?

> [3] How do these ideas relate to your purpose as stated in the last sentence of prgh 1?

> [4] *You summarize the article here,* [4a] but how does what you say here relate to your view stated in the last sentence of prgh 1?

> [5] *You've given us a summary of the article—* [5a] why? [[5b] You can give your view.]

> [6] *Here you're giving your views.*

> [7] *Here you begin to give your views.*

> [8] Is this your most original and most important argument?

> [9] *As you write, you seem to discover what you think.*

> [10] How can you explain and support your views to make them convincing for readers of the publication?

> [11] What specific points does LeMoult make that you can argue for or against? [11a] How?

Five of Warnock's comments are designed to indicate where Nancy is presenting either a summary of LeMoult's article or her own ideas (in italic). They simply play back the text, and each is labeled "content-interpretive." Ten of the comments are presented as open questions. One deals with the focus of the writing and is labeled "organization-open question" (comment 1). Three pose questions about the arrangement of ideas and are labeled "organization-open question" (comments 2a, 3, and 4a). Six of them ask Nancy to consider her ideas (comments 2, 5, 8, 10, 11, 11a). Two additional comments offer advice (in brackets). Warnock's focus, then, is more global than Peterson's and her modes are much less controlling. Such analyses of the number, length, focus, orientation, and modes of commentary help identify a teachers' typical strategies and picture the way she creates herself in relation to her students and their writing. (To see how these two sets of comments may be charted using the rubric for analyzing comments, see the appendix.)

Peterson's comments present her point-by-point questions as a critical reader and, at the same time, guide Nancy to make certain clarifications. They ride a fine line between assistance and directiveness.

Inasmuch as they are specific and clearly targeted, they offer guidance. Inasmuch as they imply that certain changes should be made, they are somewhat controlling. Warnock's comments are specific but open-ended. They don't indicate definitive changes in the text but raise issues for the writer to consider. Although both responders try to keep the writer in charge of the writing, Peterson's comments on this paper are more directive, more set on inducing certain changes in the text, and Warnock's are more interactive and, ultimately, nondirective.

Using the Rubric to Analyze Your Responding Style

Labeling your comments in terms of their focuses and modes is a key step in defining your style of response. But it's not the only step. To define your own responding style, gather a number of responses, optimally 5 to 10 sets of comments to students from the same course, on papers of varying quality. Count the number of comments you make and the number of words per comment. Note how many responses are presented in single-statement comments and how many are presented in combination comments. Do a comment-by-comment analysis of the focuses and modes you employ, and then look at your predominant focuses and modes in relation to the number of comments you make, the length and specificity of those comments, and the larger purposes you are bringing to bear in your response. What kind of roles do you enact through your comments? What kind of concerns do you take up? How much do you determine the nature and course of the student's revision? How much do you leave issues of revision in the hands of the student writer? A response style looks to characterize the strategies and concerns you typically take up in your comments, the voice and character you typically construct for yourself as a responder, and the control you typically exert over student writing.

You can use such an analysis to check whether what you intend to concentrate on is what you actually do in your written comments. You can check to see if the amount of attention you give to certain areas in your comments matches your stated priorities as a teacher. You can also examine the ways you create yourself on the page. If you see yourself as a facilitator and most of your comments are framed in directive modes, you might look to present more advice, explanations, and open questions. If you are intent on encouraging students and yet you find that you don't offer many praise comments, you can make an effort to work more positive evaluations into your responses.

Here is a heuristic for analyzing your comments, a set of questions that can help you reflect on your commenting strategies and define your style:

1. How many comments do you make?

2. How detailed are your comments? Do you rely on a lot of short, general comments, or do you tend to write out your responses in full statements?

3. How many areas of writing do you cover?

4. How much do you deal with global matters? With local matters?

5. How much do you deal with the larger contexts of writing?

6. How do you frame your comments? How many are directive, imposing your own views on the writing? How many are interactive, looking to engage the student in investigating an issue of the writing? How many are moderate, looking to suggest certain directions but not imposing them on the student writer?

7. How frequently do you establish some context for your remarks by playing back the student's text in an interpretation or a reader-response comment? How frequently do you elaborate on your key comments?

8. How would you describe the voice of your comments? How casual or authoritative do you sound?

9. What responder's comments in this book do you find your comments most similar to? Most unlike?

Discovering your typical strategies as a responder—the voices you construct, the concerns you take up, the modes you employ—will tell you a lot about your responding style: how you use your comments to talk with students about their writing, what you really value in student writing, and how much control you exert over students' work as writers. But the real task is to *use* this analysis to reflect on your comments and see if they are riding in tandem with your teaching style, your immediate and long-term goals, and the needs of your students. If you decide to modify your comments, take the changes up gradually. Concentrate on limiting the scope of your comments and dealing with areas of writing that are most important to your instruction. Look to make your comments more specific and explicit, or try to employ more comments that play back the student's text or that explain your responses. After a while, work on developing a favorite set of modes that complements your teaching style. Then you can start giving more and more consideration to shaping your commentary to the needs of individual students. To help you decide what might work best for you and your students, bring copies of your comments into class from time to time and talk with them about what you are trying to accomplish—and not trying to accomplish—when you respond. Ask your students to identify comments that they find most helpful, comments that they have trouble understanding, and comments that they find least helpful. See which kinds of comments they appreciate and are making use of and which kinds they are having trouble understanding or not taking up in their writing. Look for ways to help students learn to read and make use of your comments and for ways to adjust your responses to your style and goals.

Because response takes up so much of our time and energy as writing teachers and because our comments can be only as useful, finally, as they beget equal and complementary responses from students, it makes sense to study our response styles and make sure that the comments we make are doing the kinds of things we want them to do—and to make sure that the time we spend responding is well-spent.

Sources Cited

Brannon, Lil, and C.H. Knoblauch. "On Students' Rights to Their Own Texts: A Model of Teacher Response." *College Composition and Communication* 33 (May 1982): 157-66.

Danis, M. Francine. ""The Voice in the Margins: Paper-Marking as Conversation." *Freshman English News* 15 (Winter 1987): 18-20.

Elbow, Peter, and Pat Belanoff. *Sharing and Responding*. New York: Random House, 1989.

Hodges, Elizabeth. "The Unheard Voices of Our Responses to Students' Writing." *Journal of Teaching Writing* 11 (1992): 203-18.

Lees, Elaine. "Evaluating Student Writing." *College Composition and Communication* 30 (December 1979): 37-74.

3

Comments in Context: New Compositionists' Responses to Student Writing

In Chapter 1 we examined how a group of recognized writing teachers responded to a common sampling of student essays. We considered what these teachers comment on, how much they take up in their responses, and how they shape those comments. We saw how they present their evaluations, set up certain tasks for revision, and implicitly create various relationships with the student writer. All of the sample comments, however, are just that: *samples* of how these teachers would comment on student writing, reenactments, as it were, of strategies that they have found useful and that they would encourage others teachers to employ. The comments, after all, were written on hypothetical papers, to hypothetical students, in hypothetical situations.

In this chapter, I'd like to examine response more fully, in terms of real students and real classroom settings. How do well-informed teachers respond to their students in their own classes? How do they integrate their comments into the larger work of the course? To consider these questions I asked six composition specialists who have done research on response—one associate professor, three assistant professors, one instructor, and a doctoral student completing her dissertation—to submit a set of classroom materials that would somehow represent the kind of work they do with response in their own writing classes. I had three goals in mind: first, to test these new compositionists' "live" responses, made to actual students in actual classroom settings, against the clinical responses of the established teacher-theorists; second, to examine various ways that response is being integrated into the larger work of the class; and, third, to present a wider array of sample teacher comments.

I asked these six teachers to select a set of comments from one of their recent writing classes that would illustrate how they used response in the class and to describe the circumstances that informed the writing and motivated their responses. (Most of them, in fact, selected materials from a course they were teaching at the time, fall semester 1998.) "I'm not looking for an exemplary response or even an unusually good response," I told the contributors. "I'm looking for a response that is representative of

most of your actual classroom responses, one that shows what you typically do in your comments to students in a composition class." The paper
could be in any nonfiction genre, a rough draft or a final draft. In addition to the student paper, I asked them to submit a copy of the writing
assignment, a brief description of the course, an explanation of the work
they were doing at the time the paper was turned in, and a short profile
of the student. They were also encouraged to submit, if they chose, earlier drafts or later revisions of the student's writing, any responses they or
other students wrote on the writing, writer's memos about the writing,
scoring guides, and notes about what they were trying to accomplish in
their comments. All of these materials, I hoped, would offer a fuller picture of the way these teachers used written response in their writing
classes. Here is a listing of the teachers, the assignments, and the draft
stages for their responses:

> Ron DePeter
> Paper 2: an exploratory essay (final draft)
> "The Education of Richard Rodriguez"

> Tom Thompson
> Paper 2: thesis-and-support essay (rough draft)
> "One-Third of Europe Killed by Fleas"

> Margaret Lindgren
> Paper 2: argumentative essay (rough draft)
> "Learning Through Interaction"

> Summer Smith
> Paper 2: technical proposal (final draft)
> "Project Proposal"

> Simone Billings
> Paper 1 and Paper 3: expository essays (final drafts)
> "Collecting Interest" and "On Truth and Fiction"

> Peggy O'Neill
> Paper 3: expository essay (rough draft and revision)
> "On The Freshman 15"

In each case, I'll present the teacher's outline of the classroom context,
then the student essay with teacher comments, and then my own brief
analysis of the comments in light of the larger work of the class, along
with a list of questions raised by the scenario.

Ron DePeter's Classroom Context
Paper 2: Exploratory Essay
Final Draft

This is the second in a series of 10 exploratory writings that asked students to examine the theme of success. During the course we read Richard Rodriguez' *Hunger of Memory*, J. Paul Getty's *How to be Rich*, Adrienne Mendell's *How Men Think*, and watched the film *Citizen Kane*. Each text presents a version of success and also illustrates the more complex aspects of success, such as its costs or the sacrifices involved. The writing was done in English 102B, a required second-semester course in Reading and Composition at James Madison University. The "B" in the title indicates that the course is part of a core of courses in Package B, which includes two other courses that most students take simultaneously, Speech Communication and Business Decision Making in a Modern Society.

The writing assignments, especially the early ones, encouraged students to explore, speculate, wonder about, and complicate their own thinking, without concern for writing formal essays. They were challenged to delve deeper into their thoughts, interact more closely with the texts, and push themselves to arrive at new, or more fully realized, insights about success. Students also wrote 10-12 freewrites about their own experiences with success, ambition, failure, and sacrifice. The final essay, taken through drafts and revisions, required students to consider the texts we studied within a longer, reflective essay.

We opened the semester by studying Rodriguez' *Hunger of Memory*, and the sample writing is the first of two that students wrote in response to the text. The first assignment asked students to work through their reading of the first three chapters, while the second pushed students to tackle a particular concept in the text, such as Rodriguez' ambition or the costs of his successful assimilation into American society. There were no rough drafts for these early writings; in later essays, students worked on drafting, revising, and shaping their essays.

In my assignments and early responses, I was more concerned with encouraging an exploratory mindset in the writing than I was with such elements as organization or mechanics. As my assignment sheet illustrates, I spent more time urging students to use writing to think and speculate rather than worry over composing a formal, polished essay. (Concurrently, I was teaching students a peer-response method that emphasized a similar focus on global rather than local matters.)

It was too early in the semester to have developed an image of this student either through her writing or her class presence. However, I thought Molly's piece showed a worthwhile investment in the assignment, and a willingness to engage closely with the text. My comments on the writing were not intended to improve this particular piece, but to help her consider the potential of her ideas and claims.

Assignment

Write a reflective response to the first 70 pages of *Hunger of Memory*. However you get into the piece, make sure that you approach it with an exploratory mindset. I am not looking for you to make official-sounding pronouncements and tell me things that you already know or have read about the author, and I certainly don't want extensive plot summaries. Instead, I want to see you pursue lines of thought and speculation, generate possible understandings, and work toward some kind of insight that emerges from the act of writing. Rather than proving, defending, or arguing, I want you to use the writings as occasions for thinking, questioning, searching, and, ultimately, learning.

Some questions to consider: What is it you like or dislike about the text? What draws you in or keeps you from becoming more engaged? What struggles are you having as a reader? What parts do you have to work at to comprehend? Try to explain such reactions fully, and use *specific details* from the text to help you give substance to those reactions and to develop lines of thought.

To explore the text and your reactions to it you might try to ask yourself questions. Why are you reacting as you are? What have you read so far that you don't understand? What have you read that makes you think, wonder, or feel confused? Don't feel you have to produce an organized, polished essay from start to finish. Allow yourself to pursue hunches ("I think," "maybe," etc.) and follow digressions that occur to you. Don't worry about coming up with correct or final answers to all your questions. Go into this essay with an open mind willing to learn more about your initial impressions, and about *possible* ways you might read and think about Rodriguez' writing.

The writing should be at least 500 words, and is due Thursday, September 17. *Bring three copies.*

DePETER

Student Paper with Teacher Comments

Molly Ping
GENG 102B
Writing 2B

The Education of Richard Rodriguez

Try to work on more original titles.

The first seventy pages of *Hunger of Memory: The Education of Richard Rodriguez* gave me a weird mixture of feelings on Richard and his book. There were several points that I found really provocative because they showed me a part of America's society that I never have put much thought into before. Living on the East Coast of the United States has a lot to do with this fact. I'm sure that people who live close to the border of Mexico have a much clearer understanding of the social status of these immigrants and their roles in the community because they are around it constantly. The one major problem that I kept having getting into the book dealt with Rodriguez's style. He would describe these wonderful stories about his family and then all of a sudden he would break it off and go into a philosophical reason for why he had such a hard time balancing Spanish and English. This bouncing around became repetitive and also through my train of thought. I found myself struggling to comprehend Richard's point way too often. Personally, I find it more intriguing and more impressive when an author can get their whole message out through stories rather than bluntly telling the reader what they want them to get from the book. It was a lot like hearing someone complain over and over again.

I'd have liked an example here. Which one would best show his narrative tendency? And how did it throw you?

There were a few pieces of the book where I became confused or didn't understand the message Richard Rodriguez was trying to get across. The first bit of trouble

Do you talk enough about the messages you grapple with?

that I ran into was the chapter titles, but after looking up the words "Aria" and "pastoral," I realized their relevance in the text. A pastoral is a portrayal of country life; usually these people are shepherds and are looked at in an envious way. Richard relates this to his roots by stating, "I still am a shepherd (p. 4)." <u>It also seems like he is implying that he would have rather never known about education in the U.S. because ignorance can be bliss.</u> The word "Aria" really <u>through</u> me and I thought that I would never find it in the dictionary, but I did. It means a melody that is usually accompanied by a lone singer <u>with musical backdrop</u>. This symbolizes Richard's life going through a white, English speaking society as a Mexican American. I thought it was very impressive that Rodriguez picked a title that was so appropriate, yet so abstract at the same time. There were also many authors and people sprinkled throughout the prologue that I have never heard mentioned before. I hope it isn't hurting my understanding of the book by not knowing people like Sammy Glick, Garcia Lorca, and Garcia Marquez.

I really thought Richard Rodriguez did a great job with imagery when he was telling stories about his youth. The way he described his father's garbled English at the gas station as confusing "as the threads of blue and green oil in the puddle" created such a vivid picture (p. 15). <u>I loved it</u>. The description of Richard's grandmother in the casket was also moving. I thought that it was strange that this little boy associated the look of dressed up death with the look of confusion and ignorance. <u>I liked the symbolism that this image created</u>. The clear cut personification, like the "clicking tongue of the lock" was also a good way to keep my attention focused on the separation of Rodriguez's family and community life (p.17).

Nice to see you pursue these two definitions.

I like how you work through this.

A thoughtful statement.

"threw"

Any thoughts on what his musical backdrop might be in the book?

But more than that— what sense does it help evoke of the father? See any similarity betw. how the father + grandmother are evoked? What might he be trying to say about their lives in English-speaking America?

I like how you give specific details. To go further, what did you make of his choice to describe it that way? What is he suggesting about the private and public worlds his g'mother had to live in?

The book really showed me the amount of pain and loneliness that Richard went through as a boy. I'm not really sure why he couldn't find a medium between his home and academic life as he grew out of adolescence at least, but his struggle seemed genuine. The picture of this little boy waiting for the screen door to shut out the world outside his house so he could be happy sounds horrible. Education gave Richard a way out of being a social outcast, but it also took away his childhood. I have a hard time reconciling whether it was better for him to stay a part of the Spanish community or become highly educated. I also think it is wonderful that he feels foreigners should not be taught in their native language and that voter ballots should be in English only. If you choose to be an American, then you have the responsibility of assimilating yourself into the language and culture. For me, *Hunger of Memory* has opened up a lot of new ideas, like the idea of the U.S. as a melting pot, and made me fascinated in Mexican-American culture. I can't wait to learn what else Rodriguez has to say on the topic, even though sometimes it is hard for me to follow and stick with his thoughts.

I would have liked to see more of your struggle, more of the thoughts, doubts, concerns . . . on that issue.

And why is he so strongly in favor of this, you think? Esp. given the losses he experienced assimilating?

You were kind of vague here as to what you want to say about the melting pot.

Analysis of Ron DePeter's Commentary

In this response to "The Education of Richard Rodriguez," Ron DePeter sets out with a clear and tightly focused aim. He is looking, through his comments on this writing and the other early writings in the course, to lead students to concentrate on pushing their thinking and developing the content of their essays. The assignments and classwork are structured in a way that allows a stretch of time in which everyone can give their undivided attention to what they have to say. Because they will have a shot at so many assignments across the course, students have the advantage of focusing their early work on discovering and developing their ideas; as a teacher, DePeter has the luxury of dealing, both in his work in class and in his comments, almost exclusively with these areas.

Not surprisingly, then, he devotes all but two of his 19 comments on Molly's paper to the ideas she already has down on the page and ways she might develop them more fully. A number of comments praise an assertion she makes or her use of detail:

> S: It also seems like he is implying that he would have rather never known about education in the U.S. because ignorance can be bliss.
>
> T: A thoughtful statement.
>
> S: The first bit of trouble that I ran into was the chapter titles, but after looking up the words "Aria" and "pastoral," I realized their relevance in the text.
>
> T: Nice to see you pursue these two definitions.
>
> S: A pastoral is a portrayal of country life; usually these people are shepherds and are looked at in an envious way. Richard relates to his roots by stating, "I still am a shepherd."
>
> T: I like how you work through this.

But most of his comments, the real work of his response, call on Molly to look back on an assertion she has made and consider what else is wrapped up in it, what else she might say about the idea:

> I'd have liked an example here. Which one would best show his narrative tendency? And how did it throw you?
>
> Do you talk enough about the messages you grapple with?
>
> Any thoughts on what his musical backdrop might be in the book?
>
> [I like how you give specific details.] To go further, what did you make of his choice to describe it that way? What is he suggesting

about the private and public worlds his grandmother had to live in?

And why is he so strongly in favor of this, you think? Especially given the losses he experienced assimilating?

Notably, he does not get distracted by matters of organization, sentence structure, or correctness, although (if they *were* his concern) there'd be plenty to discuss along these lines.

DePeter's modes of commentary—the ways he frames his comments—also seem appropriate to his purpose. Four comments are presented as praise. They acknowledge ideas that are particularly promising and look to strengthen Molly's confidence as an author whose task is to find something to say. Ten of them are in the form of open questions that are meant to challenge her to think further about what she has said.

All of the comments are placed in the margins and written out in full statements. On several occasions, a cluster of comments is presented on a single passage, to dramatize for the student the richness of an idea, it seems, and to prompt her thinking on the subject. He writes no separate end note that summarizes his line-by-line comments or highlights his main concerns. The reason seems clear enough. The comments are not designed to guide revision; they are meant to use the statements Molly has already come up with to lead her to reflect on her ideas and consider how they may be captured in text. The series of short comments on isolated ideas seems a useful strategy for leading her to re-envision what she has said so that she might come up with even more to say and, more importantly perhaps, get a better understanding of the kind of thinking she can reach for in her subsequent writing.

Questions

1. How well do DePeter's comments get at the key ideas of the essay? Is it okay if they don't?

2. What other options are available for responding to such student writing in order to achieve the aims that DePeter sets forth for his class? In what ways might they be more or less adequate to his purposes?

3. What are the benefits and the drawbacks of not commenting to any appreciable extent on organization at this time? On sentence structure? On Molly's many problems with mechanics and punctuation?

Tom Thompson's Classroom Context
Paper 2: Thesis-and-Support Essay
Second Draft

This paper was written in ENGL 101: Composition and Literature at The Citadel, a school of approximately 1700 undergraduate students that combines a liberal arts education with a military lifestyle: students live on campus (in rather Spartan barracks, not dorms), and students and professors alike wear uniforms and observe military customs and courtesies. Most professors have traditional academic backgrounds—military experience is neither required nor expected—and although the student culture is largely southern white male, the academic culture is similar to that at any small, southern liberal arts college. The college catalog says the course is to focus on the "development of the basic skills of writing, reading and analysis," and departmental guidelines identify "writing clear, correct prose" sustained in a "750-word essay" as the skills students should demonstrate at the conclusion of the course.

This particular section of ENGL 101 was linked with a section of HIST 103 (Western Civilization); all students in ENGL 101 were also in a single section of HIST 103. Readings came from the history textbook, and the professors drew up the writing assignments together. The sequence of assignments moved from straight summary to thesis-and-support-style papers answering a specific question and using an assigned source. The paper shown here came from the second thesis-and-support essay: a direct answer to an assigned question, using evidence drawn from a single assigned article. This is the second of three drafts: the first received feedback only about the appropriateness and depth of the thesis and support; the second received feedback and a grade based on a scoring guide; the third draft would go to the history professor for a grade in that class. (All course materials—the syllabus, assignments, scoring guides, links to on-line help, and samples of previous assignments—were posted on a class web site.)

The student who wrote this draft had turned in only two assignments all semester. Several sources indicated that he should be capable of succeeding, but he was clearly on course to fail the class. Though I doubted that he would attend to many of my specific comments, I nevertheless addressed a variety of problems in the paper so other students might learn from his mistakes. I typically have students read each other's papers—with my comments—as a way to increase the potential value of each set of comments: students who do poorly get to see some successful responses to the assignment, and everyone learns from the successes and miscues of others in the class. It is also worth noting that, because the Honors program drains off the best students and most students with strong writing skills place out of ENGL 101, many of the students who do take the course have weak reading and writing skills. That emphasis on "clear, correct prose" influences my responses to ENGL 101 papers; my responding style is quite different for upper-level and graduate papers.

My running commentary—what I wrote while I read the paper—focused almost exclusively on grammar and mechanics, in part because the paper was so far below acceptable standards that it would fail for errors alone, and in part so other students could learn from these fairly typical punctuation and diction problems. The other main problem was that this student (like several others) summarized the article rather than using material from the article as evidence. In the final comment I explained the problem with the paper as a whole—that, in effect, it missed the point of the assignment—and suggested that he start over before turning in the next draft.

Assignment

The goal of this second assignment is to have you read and understand an article, then use the key information from that article as support for a claim of your own. To that end, write a paper of 650-900 words in response to one of the prompts below. Be sure to state your claim clearly, and show how information from the article supports that claim. Note: Each prompt includes a directive (i.e., "explain," "describe," or "comment on"), but I have also rephrased each prompt in question form. I recommend that you read the article to find an answer to the question, then use that answer as the thesis of your paper and use information from the article as support for your thesis.

1. Drawing on David Robert's "In France, an Ordeal by Fire and a Monster Weapon Called Bad Neighbor," explain why the Cathars attracted so many followers in southern France in the 13th century and why a crusade was launched against them. ("Why did the Cathars attract so many followers, and why was a crusade launched against them?")

2. Drawing on Charles Mee's "How a Mysterious Disease Laid Low Europe's Masses," describe medieval European society in the 14th century and explain how it was changed as a result of the plague. ("How did 14th century Europe change as a result of the plague?")

3. The Knights Templar combined two great institutions of medieval Europe: monasticism and the Crusades. Drawing on Helen Nicholson's "Saints or Sinners? The Knights Templar in Medieval Europe," comment on the Knights Templar as monks and Crusaders. ("How well did the Knights Templar combine monasticism and the Crusades?")

Scoring Guide (10 possible points)

For a grade of C or higher, the paper must:

· answer the question (This statement will be your thesis.)
· use information from the article to support your claims
· use standard class header (name, course, Paper 2, second draft)
· use MLA style for all citations
· be relatively free of errors in grammar and mechanics
· use an appropriate title
· include a word count and be 650-900 words long
· be typed or word-processed, double-spaced
· use 1"-1.25" margins
· use 12- or 14-point type

For a B or higher, the paper must meet C criteria and some of the following criteria:

· use tight, dense prose
· be virtually error-free
· show an awareness of audience
· incorporate sources smoothly
· use a variety of ways to incorporate sources
· use a variety of sentence structures
· use precise diction
· use grammar and mechanics to contribute to meaning

If you're having trouble writing Paper 2, try these steps:

Invention
· Read the assigned question
· Read the article, looking for an answer
· Write/highlight facts and quotes
· Write summaries and related thoughts
· Draw a conclusion that answers the question

Arrangement
· Write your thesis (i.e., the answer to the question)
· Select facts/quotes that support that thesis
· Arrange material in an order that will make sense to the reader

Style
· Create an outline to let you see the whole paper at a glance
· Add transitions between key points
· Add lines to tie each piece of evidence to whatever claim it supports
· Add examples or summaries as needed
· Add metaphors, similes, or analogies to clarify points
· Add definitions of key or unfamiliar terms
· Work in quotes gracefully
· Check sentence types; add variety as needed
· Check grammar, mechanics, and conventions
· Have someone else read it and give you feedback

THOMPSON

Student Paper with Teacher Comments

Eddy Bohlander
English 101
Paper 2

One-Third of Europe Killed by Fleas

In Mee's article "How a Mysterious Disease Laid Low

Europe's Masses," it depicts how the Bubonic Plague took

the lives of one-third of Europe's people. Today's scientists

believe that the bubonic plague was started when rats

interacted with humans in trading ports. These rats which

were infested with fleas, had a bacteria called (not at the

time) *Yersinia pestis*. When word spread that a disease had

started to take the lives of many people, the townsmen and

women started to lock up their towns and communities

from people coming in and out. During this time period,

there was an incline in economical standards for town-

ships. To this day there has not been a more single disease

to top the Black Plague.

To this day no one actually knows where the Bubonic

came from, but it was believed that it came from a trading

ship in Messina. Aboard this ship were a couple of

Teacher comments in margin:

At least 6 errors in the first paragraph—having so many errors makes you look either lazy or uneducated, both of which are bad options.

Use both commas

This info isn't really necessary.

"increase" maybe? you don't need the "-al"

I think you mean "a single more devastating disease" or something to that effect. What you've written makes no sense to me.

black rats; these black rats were very common on trading

ships in that day. There was something different about

This could be the end of the sentence; a semicolon signals the possible end

these rats, though, little did they know that they were

caring fleas with a certain bacteria called *Yersina pestis*, a

bacteria that would shut down the nervous system in a

couple of days. These fleas would change their hosts to

humans, after the rat, the flea had been eating on had

These commas made it hard for me to figure out your meaning. See me to explain your thinking when you added them.

died. Once on a human, the flea would start to suck his or

her blood like normally and spread the disease. After the

bacteria had entered the body of its victim, it would spread

throughout the lower section of the body for the first day.

Once the second day had come about the victim should

This is wordy. You could simply say, "On the second day."

become weak with aches and chills. After this has

w

occurred the lymph nodes should begin to swell on the

Now you've switched into present tense. Why?

third day. By this time the nervous system already has

begin to shut down, and during the fifth or sixth day the

victim should die from the disease. This is not that accu-

rate, though; it could have been a longer or shorter

same construction as earlier

time span depending on the person. It was a long and

painful death for the victim, and there was no cure for any-

body (Mee 186).

THOMPSON

To try to prevent the spread of the Bubonic plague (also known as black death), towns would not let people in or out of the town. If a person had to leave the town, he or she would not be *"allowed"* <u>aloud</u> back in. There would be no linen or cloth imported from other cities. If someone from the immediate family had died, the family would not be able to bring the corpse into the town, and only would [the family] be able to go to the funeral. These would be the guide lines for most cities or towns, but no matter how hard they tried the people still could not keep the black plague out. Some men and women had the right idea and moved away from the big cities into the mountains, were there was little flea action going on ~~these areas~~ (Mee 187).

"Where" = "these areas" (You don't need to say it twice.)

Since there were so many bad things going for the Europeans at the time, there had to be something good going for them. Since there *singular* <u>was</u> so many *plural* <u>people</u> dying at the time, there was room to better one's self through employment. People could get jobs, only because there were spots opening up() from the people dying. This caused <u>better</u> luxuries for the common man or women.

same as on page 2

There is a flip side to this() though() since most of the

I think you mean "more," not "better." They didn't have poor quality luxuries, then get <u>better</u> quality ones; they didn't have many (or any), then finally got some.

people lived or worked on farms, and there were so many

people dying, there was nobody to work the farms. This

caused agriculture to go way down, and some towns found

themselves with food shortages (Mee 188).

The Black Plague ~~caused great reform~~ in Europe.

Many people died because of this tragic fate. ~~Many

people turned to religion for answers~~, and never found

them, but there was nothing God could do for them.

Maybe God wanted to punish the people of Europe or

maybe it was just fate that it should have happened. No

one knows for sure, but we do know this, that the Black

plague was one of the most horrible things ever to hit this

earth, and we pray that nothing like that should ever

happen again.

You've said very little about "reform." Define it, explain it, give me some examples of it.

This is a major way the plague changed Europe—worth at least a paragraph or two.

Eddy—

Most of my comments focus on mechanical errors because (1) you must meet a certain baseline of correctness or you won't pass anyway, and (2) you basically missed the point of the question. You told me about the plague as a disease (i.e., what caused it and how people tried to "treat" it), but you were supposed to tell how it changed Europe. I recommend that you keep the first three sentences of your closing paragraph as part of your introduction, but cut everything else. Focus on the reforms—what they were and why they happened. (See me if you need help getting started on your revision.)

Analysis of Tom Thompson's Comments

"One-Third of Europe Killed by Fleas" won't inspire many teachers. The paper does not address the question it sets out to discuss. Its detail is spent describing the circumstances of the disease instead of providing support for any arguments about its effect on fourteenth-century Europe. It has a slew of problems with sentence structure. And, sure enough, it is plagued by errors. The paper has so little going for it that most teachers would have a hard time coming up with something productive to say to Eddy—especially given that this is the second draft of a paper that has already received comments and the student hasn't been keeping up with the work in class.

Tom Thompson hedges his bets, interestingly, by assuming that Eddy is not the only—and maybe not even the principal—target of his comments. This double audience may explain a number of Thompson's choices, including the focus of his comments and his aggressive tone. Because he is commenting as much for other students (who will get to review the comments on this paper) as for Eddy, he does more work on local matters than he otherwise might and he is less concerned about how he comes across to the writer.

Thompson foregoes any involved attempt at leading Eddy to revise the content of his essay for the final draft. There's no sense in commenting on the material that's here, he reasons at the start of his end comment, because almost all of it is off topic, and the paper is not going to pass anyway because of his rash of errors. Instead of looking to lead the writer to refocus his essay and find evidence for his argument, he chooses to concentrate on mechanical errors. Twenty-five of his 30 marginal comments are focused on sentence structure, wording, and correctness. He makes only a few comments about content and focus in the margins and a few summary remarks in his end note. Most of the comments are critical, and several of them are sharp and aggressive:

> At least 6 errors in the first paragraph—having so many errors makes you look either lazy or uneducated, both of which are bad options.

> I think you mean "a single more devastating disease" or something to that effect. What you've written makes no sense to me.

> You've said very little about "reform." Define it, explain it, give me some examples of it.

Yet Thompson also seems to go out of his way to make his comments clear and instructive. He writes out all of his comments in full statements. He doesn't simply say "unnecessary," for example, in his comment at the end of the first paragraph; he says, "This info isn't really necessary." He doesn't just correct the punctuation or a write "comma splice" next to a sentence in the second paragraph; he circles it and explains: "This <u>could</u> be the end of the sentence; a semicolon signals the <u>possible</u> end." He doesn't say, "misused commas"; he says, "These comments made it hard for me to figure out your meaning." And he goes back over the ground of his earlier comments to explain or develop them in a dozen cases, among them the following:

> This is wordy. You could simply say, "On the second day."
>
> "Where" = "these areas." (You don't need to say it twice.)
>
> I think you mean "more," not "better." They didn't have poor quality luxuries, then get better quality ones: they didn't have many (or any), then finally got some.
>
> This is a major way the plague changed Europe—worth at least a paragraph or two.
>
> You told me about the plague as a disease (i.e., what caused it and how people tried to "treat" it).
>
> Focus on the reforms—what they were and why they happened.

The comments might help Eddy and the other students learn something about what to do—or not to do—in their writing. The question is, how much will they help Eddy with this writing and his work as a writer? Thompson seems resigned not to have the comments do anything more for the student writer than explain to him why he has failed.

Questions

1. There are many ways to respond to error in student writing, of course. Thompson shows a more direct way than we have seen to this point. What do you think about Thompson's choice to give so much attention to local matters at this time, given how much there is left to do with the substance and organization of the revision and given that the due date for the final paper is fast approaching? What do you think about the way he addresses them?

2. What do you think about the number of comments Thompson makes on errors? Is it an effective way of dealing with these problems? What other strategies might be employed to deal with so many errors?

3. Thompson obviously sees his aggressive style of response as an appropriate strategy in this academic environment. Do you see it as an effective strategy, given the circumstances of the class and the larger academic setting, a military school where there is an unyielding emphasis on "basic

skills of writing" and "clear, correct prose"? Would it be an effective strategy for use at your own institution?

4. What other methods might be employed to address a paper, now in the second of three required drafts, that misses the point of the assignment as much as this paper? What other methods might be used to deal with the deep problems that such a paper has in sentence structure, usage, and punctuation? What other methods might be used to respond to a student writer with these problems and Eddy's history in the class?

5. A teacher's comments are usually kept private, to be seen only by the student writer. Thompson chooses to flout this convention and make his responses on a student's paper public, for use by other students in the class. What do you think of this strategy? Would responses to another students' writing, namely, about problems with usage, mechanics, punctuation, and sentence structure, be helpful for other students? Are there other ways to achieve the end that Thompson seeks—having other students learn from the mistakes and successes of others?

6. In his statement about the backdrop of the course, Thompson says that the emphasis in the first-year writing program on "clear, correct prose" influences his way of commenting on ENGL 101 papers; "my responding style is quite different for upper-level and graduate papers." What do you think about a teacher assuming different emphases and styles of response for different courses and different levels of instruction? To what extent do you think a teacher's response style should be geared—or can usefully be geared—to the emphases and goals of the larger writing program?

Margaret Lindgren's Classroom Context
Paper 2: Argumentative Essay
Rough Draft

Janet was enrolled in English 102, the second course in the three-quarter sequence in the English Composition Program at the University of Cincinnati. This course emphasized research, critical reading, and constructing arguments in response to academic texts. This paper was the second draft of the second essay in the course. Students would take the writing through at least one more draft before handing it in for final evaluation. In essay one, students were asked to construct an argument in response to the ideas proposed by an author whose work they had read and discussed in class. In this essay they were asked to construct an argument in response to the ideas proposed by several authors. In addition to addressing the formalities of citation, the goal was to help students learn to identify the important claims in an academic essay and focus on and develop an idea of their own, taking at least some of the author's words or ideas into consideration. In her paper Janet considers the ideas presented in Shirley Brice Heath's "The Fourth Vision: Literate Language at Work" and Paulo Freire's "The Banking Concept of Education," as anthologized in *Writing Lives: Exploring Literacy and Community*, 1996.

Janet had been a student in my 101 class the previous quarter, so I had an established relationship with her even at the time of this essay. She was highly motivated and a good writer, but she had little experience complicating her ideas. She consulted me frequently during my office hours, and I generally spent the time asking her questions to help her think more complexly about her topic.

My comments have various functions. With my marginal comments I do a little of everything: identifying grammatical concerns (not necessarily all of them), highlighting areas that might be developed further, and trying for a bit of humor. The letter I attach, however, is where I do my most coherent responding. Because I want students to have the first word in the conversation about the essay, I ask them to write a memo to me about their writing, indicating their thoughts about the paper and raising questions they would like to see me address. These memos are crucial; I simply refuse to respond unless a memo is attached. Though I don't confine my responses to elements the students identify, I am careful to address any problems or concerns they raise. A student may revise an essay as often as she likes, and I will respond. I "grade" the essay only when the student tells me it is finished.

Assignment

Write an essay in which you express and support an argument about literacy and community using *at least two* of the readings we've read and discussed in this unit. You may use the other authors' words and/or ideas to introduce your argument, to support your argument, or to explain the relevance of your argument. The goals of the assignment:

- to practice summarizing and analyzing academic essays
- to practice making connections among several authors' ideas
- to practice developing an argument in the context of other arguments
- to practice supporting assertions with evidence
- to practice using quotations in expository prose
- to practice editing and proofreading

Guidelines:

1. As you read the essays be sure to take careful notes. Concentrate on outlining the main points of each writer's argument and recording your own reactions. Also, be alert to connections and contradictions between arguments: these points of intersection might provide you with a starting point for an argument of your own.

2. Narrow your topic by posing a specific question about one issue. In a short essay, you can't address every aspect of literacy and community, so just focus on one issue.

3. You don't need to provide a complete summary of the essays to which you refer; just quote or paraphrase passages relevant to your argument. Just be careful not to misrepresent the author's overall position by taking her/his statements out of context.

4. Again, make sure your work is carefully proofread and presented in MLA format with a "Works Cited" page attached. Your completed paper should be at least 1000 words long.

Student Writer's Memo

1. How have you changed this essay since the last draft? *I have changed this essay by taking out unclear sentences. I made my counterarguments more specific. I also made my examples more specific to help my focus.*

2. What is your argument at this point? *I feel my argument is everyone learns best through interaction.*

3. Are you finished? If not, about what aspect would you like me to respond? *This essay is far from being finished. There is a lot of revisions that need to be made still. I am unsure if my focus is becoming more clear and less confusing. The main thing right now is my introduction. Basically, it stinks! I am aware of this but nothing has come to my mind yet on how I want to change this!*

Student Paper with Teacher Comments

Janet
English 102
Paper 2

Learning Through Interaction

Literacy is not just things that are learned in class-rooms and ^ textbooks, but rather by everyone sharing   ^ *from*
their knowledge through interaction. This argument is
similarily posed in Heath's essay, "The Fourth Vision" and
~~of~~ Freire's essay, "The Banking Concept of Education."

Freire voices his opinion that the problem-posing
method is better for education. This problem-posing
method makes no authoritarian out of anyone. Rather it is   / *p*
a process in which everyone shares their knowledge,
learns, and therefore grows. Learning from everyone in a
classroom is beneficial not only to the student, but [it is]
also [beneficial] to the teacher. For example, students usually fill out evaluations of the class at the end of the year,
and their feedback helps the teacher to possibly figure out
a different way to teach things so the ^ students are able   ^ *next*
to understand. This is ^ how the teacher-student relation-   ^ *one way (I could give*
ships are developed.   *you others too—from my*
                                                                perspective.)

Similarly, Heath states that people learn by talking
and considering together. From this vision, three conclusions seem to point to past achievements that we must use
to challenge both the future organization of institutions
and simplistic definitions of literacy. "These include all of
us–children and adults, students and teachers, shop work-   *See Hacker for the proper*
ers and supervisors, clerical workers and managers—learn   *format for including a*
most successfully with and from each other when we have   *long quote.*
full access to looking, listening, talking and taking part in

authentic tasks we understand. Secondly, we can complement each other in particular areas of expertise if we learn
to communicate our experiences; sharing what we know

It would be better if you didn't quote this whole thing at once.

helps bring the group higher performance than private
reflections of individuals do. Finally, humans must move
beyond information skills to meaning and interpretation
for learning to take place and to extend itself" (Heath,
157). Both of these authors argue that we all can learn
from each other to benefit everyone, whether it be at
school, work, or home.

However, ~~because~~ the argument ~~by~~^ both ~~of~~ these

^ *of*

writers ~~helps support the fact~~ ^ that the teacher is not the

^ *is*

only "knowledge giver" [does not mean that textbooks
should be taken out of classrooms nor should lectures.

You state this but don't develop it at all. Even though it's not your position, your readers will take you seriously only if you give counter-arguments a fair hearing.

Textbooks are a very important part of learning], but there
is more to learning than just reading the text. [I agree with
this.]* To me, a good teacher is one who will respect the

* *Needed?*

students equally and listen to them. I learn more if a

/ *p*

teacher teaches the text, by relating it to our lives, rather
then a teacher who gets up in the front of the classroom
and rambles on about the text. For example, my English
teacher ng my senior year, would sit in a students desk and

/ *sp*   / *p*

be part of the discussion when we would talk about
Shakespeare. At times, some of Shakespeare's plays
seemed to be too confusing, but with her interaction, I was
able to understand <u>on my level</u>. This type of learning does

Maybe give an actual example?

not occur just in the classrooms, but also in the workplace.
It makes the inferior person (student or employee) have a
chance to be heard and from their knowledge, their over-
seer can learn more.

Some may disagree with this argument that everyone
can and should learn from each other through interaction
and cooperation. They may feel that Heath and Freire do

not believe in teaching the text and instead they believe in just sitting around and talking. However, this is not true. I think, they still believe in the text, but they just feel everyone should have an equal chance to say what they feel instead of the teacher lecturing ^ the whole class. Maybe this is what Heath meant when she said, "Learning can be dangerous." ¶ Others may add, that this would give children a bigger role than what they should have. If we have the teacher-student relationships at school, the children may start to voice their opinion too much and take advantage of this when they are at home also. But I do not think this is so because the students would be in better learning environments if they were to ask questions to understand the material. Others may also add that people learn better by themselves through practicing. Of course, <u>this is true</u>, but is not the interaction of the teachers that first helps the students to understand what they are doing. Such as in Math class, <u>if the teacher throws up</u> a couple of problems on the board, chances are the students will be clueless. But, if the teacher explains how to do them and then wlks around the room and checks to see if everyone is doing them right, <u>they</u> will understand better and then will be able to go home and be able to practice them on their own.

Just like Heath stated in her three conclusions, everyone learns best from each other—young or old. Teachers can really make a difference in the way they teach so can any authoritive figure for that matter. For example, I would much rather be in a classroom setting where you would sit around and discuss what you read, just like in English class, instead of sitting in my Chemistry class where my professor lectures for an hour that, to me, sounds like he is speaking some foreign language because I do not understand. I ~~would be~~ ^ more inclined to not

Margin notes:

^ *to*

Maybe expand on the danger?

✓ *p*

Example?

Always?

I don't think this is what you really mean, is it? :)
See if you can fix this sentence on your own.

/ *sp*

Sounds like you mean the teacher.

Maybe be even <u>more</u> specific?

RS

^ *am*

show up for the class that ^ lectures because [it would not]   ^ *are*

keep my interest. In order to get more out out of learning,   ^ *[they don't] The tense*
you've used here sounds
one's interest level has to be high. Keeping one's level of   *unnecessarily vague to*
me.
interest is usually easier for the teacher when they interact

with the students as they teach. Literacy is gained by   *Although this is true,*
most of your essay has
everone sharing their knowedge.   *aimed to establish how*
students learn more by
interacting. So why end
with this?

Janet,

    I wonder if you (or we, together in a conference) could figure out how Heath and Freire suggest slightly different, though still complementary, forms of interaction? Or perhaps there's a way to look at the opposite side of learning from that you've focused on here . . . how the teacher is a learner. Or perhaps you could differentiate the type of learning Heath and Freire are talking about from some other type of learning. I think all of these thoughts, Janet, because my biggest concern is that your argument here is thin; the fact that people learn better through interaction isn't particularly new or astounding—and few folks would be likely to disagree with you. I wonder if you could focus your argument further so that what you say has more power.

    In part of your essay as it is you seem to be putting problem-posing education in opposition to textbooks—but I don't think that's quite accurate. In fact, many textbooks now try to teach students how to pose problems for themselves. If what you want to do is to show the benefits of problem-posing education, then I'd say your best bet is to bust your head open thinking up examples. And I don't mean vague allusions, I mean like when my English class was discussing Cassius' speech about Brutus in Julius Caesar. See the difference between something that specific and the kinds of examples you're working with so far?

    I bet if you focused your argument further you'd also solve the problem of your opening. You say in your memo that you think it needs work, but I'd say that it's better to wait on that until you have something to say that is really exciting and stimulating.

    I'm afraid this still isn't passing, but I think you have the beginnings of a good idea. Why don't we meet to see how to help you work profitably on your next draft? Let me know.

Maggy

Analysis of Margaret Lindgren's Commentary

Margaret Lindgren says that Janet has a hard time developing and complicating her ideas, and both problems are evident in this draft. Her line of argument frequently meanders and strays, and she seems to have trouble getting beneath the surface of her assertions to give them substance. But her problems run deeper. Janet has trouble shaping her ideas plainly and directly in her sentences and building a series of assertions into a line of thought. It seems appropriate, then, that Lindgren gives a good deal of attention both to sentence-level concerns and large conceptual matters in this essay. She sprinkles comments liberally, like seeds, across the margins of the essay, looking to see which ones might take root and grow. She makes 29 comments on the pages of the student's text. Ten address the ideas and areas for development in the draft; 19 address local matters of sentence structure, wording, and correctness. Lindgren doesn't mind making these comments about local matters on an immature rough draft, in ways that are directive. She's also not afraid to use abbreviations to signal mechanical problems and even occasionally to edit the writing. Notably, however, all but one of her comments on global concerns are presented in moderate modes, as advice, questions, explanations, and interpretations:

> Maybe give an actual example?
>
> Maybe expand on the danger?
>
> Maybe be even more specific?
>
> Example?
>
> Always?
>
> [You state this but don't develop it at all.] Even though it's not your position, your readers will take you seriously only if you give counter-arguments a fair hearing.
>
> Although this is true, most of your essay has aimed to establish how <u>students</u> learn more by interacting. So why end with this?

With these content-based comments, she seems more interested in giving way to Janet's authority as a writer.

In her end note, Lindgren's attention is locked on the content and purpose of the essay. Seventeen of her 19 comments are focused on ideas, development, and the overall focus of the writing; the other two are concerned with the essay as a whole. No comments are given to local matters. Here, Lindgren's comments seem to hit their stride. The voice is casual and searching, a blend of openness, support, and direction. It is the voice of an ally, a helper. Almost half of the comments suggest ways of looking at the task of revision: "I wonder if you could figure out . . . ," "Or perhaps there's a way to look at the opposite side," "Or perhaps you could differentiate the type of learning Heath and Freire are talking about from some other type of learning." Another four are explanatory comments that go back over and clarify earlier comments:

> I think all of these thoughts, Janet, because my biggest concern is that your argument here is thin; the fact that people learn better through interaction isn't particularly new or astounding—and few folks would be likely to disagree with you.

> In part of your essay as it is you seem to be putting problem-posing education in opposition to textbooks—but I don't think that's quite accurate. In fact, many textbooks now try to teach students how to pose problems for themselves.

> If what you want to do is to show the benefits of problem-posing education, then I'd say your best bet is to bust your head open thinking up examples. And I don't mean vague allusions, I mean like when my English class was discussing Cassius' speech about Brutus in Julius Caesar.

She uses only a few critical evaluations, only after she has set the tone of the response and established a positive, forward-looking approach to Janet's work. And all of the criticisms are couched in terms that are meant to soften their edge:

> I think all these thoughts, Janet, because my biggest concern is that your argument here is thin.

> In part of your essay as it is you seem to be putting problem-posing education in opposition to textbooks—but I don't think that's quite accurate.

> I'm afraid this still isn't passing.

Nevertheless, each one of these criticisms carries its weight, points unwaveringly to a real problem in the essay, and lays a solid foundation for her other comments. Overall, her response achieves a genuine give-and-take relationship with the writer. Lindgren *talks* with Janet in her comments: "I'd say your best bet is to bust your head open thinking up examples," "I bet if you focused your argument further you'd also solve the problem of your opening," "Why don't we meet." Yet even as she talks with Janet she engages her in the problems with the draft and engages her in revision. And even as she offers her assessments and advice, she refrains from making crucial decisions for her: she tells Janet that she needs to focus her argument further, not what to focus it on; she suggests that she look for more examples about the benefits of problem-posing education *if* that is the direction she wants to take the essay. Finally, both symbolically and practically she involves Janet directly in the work of response by having her write her own assessments and questions about the writing and making them a viable part of her commentary. Her response, in a very real sense, is a collaboration with the writer.

Questions

1. There are obvious benefits to addressing the problems with correctness, wording, and sentence structure in this paper. Is Lindgren's way of addressing these problems effective? Are there other ways to address them that would be as effective, or perhaps even more effective?

2. The dominant feature of this letter to Janet is its casual, engaging voice. Look back at the commenting styles and voices of other responders. Consider: How important is the voice we employ in our comments to students? Are some voices more engaging than others? Is there a certain voice or style that appeals to you when you read the comments? Is there a voice that you are most comfortable with using as a teacher?

3. What are the advantages to Lindgren offering a number of options to the writer? Would there be any advantage to giving Janet more direction in her work toward the next draft?

Summer Smith's Classroom Context
Paper 2: Technical Proposal
Final Draft

The proposal is the second assignment in my English 418 course, Advanced Technical Writing and Editing, at Penn State. The course is designed to give seniors and graduate students practice with the types of writing they will do as professional scientists or technical writers. First-year composition and an introductory technical writing course are prerequisites. English 418 continues the emphasis in these courses on rhetorical principles; however, students learn more sophisticated rhetorical approaches and genres, and are expected to demonstrate writing skills characteristic of novice members of technical communities.

The proposal fits into a series of assignments that culminate in a substantial semester project designed to solve through writing a significant problem facing a technical community. At the beginning of the semester, students arrange meetings with technical experts in an area of their choosing and interview them about their writing practices. Then, based on the results of the interviews and on their own interests, they develop the individual semester projects they will propose. For example, a student might propose to write a journal article reporting the results of lab research she is conducting as part of a senior thesis or graduate work. Another student might propose to write an instruction manual that will be used to train new hires in her workplace. Another might propose to write a handbook explaining the applications of research to practitioners in the field. The genres and purposes of the proposed projects are as individual as the students, because the projects are based on the students' expertise and on problems they consider important. The proposal, addressed to me, requests permission to proceed with the semester project.

In teaching and evaluating the proposal, I emphasize the importance of describing the semester project as the solution to a pressing problem faced by the project's audience. This strategy creates purpose and exigence for the project. Class sessions focus on strategies for establishing the significance of projects within their disciplinary contexts, analyzing rhetorical situations, and persuasively covering the details called for in the outline portion of the assignment sheet. After I approve their proposals, the students spend most of the rest of the semester (about seven weeks) working on their projects. (Some students must revise their proposals before I can approve them, but this delay is relatively rare. I ask students to revise their proposals only if they have failed to provide enough persuasive detail to convince me that they can complete a good project.) Because the projects represent a variety of genres and subjects, my instruction focuses on generalizable rhetorical principles and on strategies for discovering, applying, and modifying discourse conventions.

The proposal presented here is a final draft. The author, Lauren Beste, was an honors undergraduate who had co-authored a journal article with her advisor. She had spent the previous summer studying the health services of five Lakota Indian reservations in South Dakota, and she had recently asked me to advise her on an application for a major national fellowship for graduate school. She often stayed after class to ask focused questions about her proposal, but she never showed her draft to me. Her proposal was reviewed by a fellow student during a draft workshop.

Assignment

Write a formal proposal in which you convince me that a certain person or group of people has a significant problem and that you should be permitted to solve the problem through a writing project. While I am willing to consider a wide range of projects, you must persuade me that you have chosen a worthwhile, carefully thought-out project that you are capable of handling well. Your project should result in a document that is similar to the types of writing you will do as a professional scientist or technical writer. It should have a real audience and fulfill a pressing need for that audience. Use the following basic structure for your proposal, adapting the content and structure as needed for your situation. You may rename the sections listed in this outline:

Problem statement: Use one of the three forms we discuss in class to create a tight problem/solution connection.

Problem and context: Describe the problem and its significance for some group of people. Convince me that the audience is facing a pressing problem.

Proposed solution: Explain how your document will solve the problem for the audience. Describe your plans for the document. Convince me that you know what the audience needs.

Work plan: Describe the work that must be done in order to complete the project. Establish a schedule that shows specifically when certain activities must be completed. Convince me that you have thought through the project and can complete it on time.

Qualifications: Describe your qualifications for the project, your access to necessary resources (including people to contact for information), your position relative to your audience, and factors that affect your credibility with the audience. Convince me that you are prepared to work on this project and that you understand how you fit into the rhetorical situation.

SMITH

Student Paper with Teacher Comments

Lauren A. Beste
English 418
Paper 2

Project Proposal

Problem Statement:

Penn State's Biobehavioral Health department <u>is interested in</u> the outcome of a cultural awareness assessment project conducted at Pine Ridge Public Health Hospital. <u>The researcher</u> will give a presentation to the Biobehavioral Health faculty detailing the methodology and results of the assessment, and the rationale for the cultural orientation packet based on the results. The researcher will benefit from the review and critique by the faculty, and the faculty will be exposed to the results of the project.

Here's an idea to expand on. Why are they interested? How does your work contribute to the field (fill a gap in knowledge)?

Go ahead and use "I" here, as you did in the rest of the proposal.

Problem and Context:

Researchers share their findings both to educate their colleagues and to strengthen their research techniques with peer feedback. Undergraduate researchers, in particular, need the advice of their technical community to help develop their skills. <u>The Biobehavioral Health department at Penn State has requested that I present findings</u> from a cultural awareness assessment project I conducted on five Lakota reservations in South Dakota during the summer of 1998.

From our talks, I understand that this is not actually your situation, right? You face a more common situation that would be useful to explore because it is the same situation faced by expert researchers who must request that their articles be published or that they be given a chance to speak at a conference.

Two measures of cultural awareness were used to assess the physicians: physician questionnaires and patient interviews. The questionnaires were carefully structured to evaluate three facets of physician cultural ▼

Great details, concisely stated. Now, argue for their significance. Why do the faculty need to hear your presentation?

awareness: sensitivity to economic and environmental conditions on reservations; knowledge of traditional Lakota beliefs and etiquette; and receptiveness to cultural education. The patient interviews assessed patients' opinions of the physicians' levels of cultural awareness, and will serve as a yardstick with which to measure the accuracy of the questionnaires.

The presentation should last approximately fifteen minutes. As a junior researcher, I must be careful to firmly establish my credibility. My primary concern is proving that my study has a sound design and has yielded valid results. I also desire to receive constructive criticism from the faculty that can be incorporated into future presentations and journal articles. A well-organized and informative presentation will educate the faculty and produce useful feedback that may improve the study.

Solution:

I must structure my presentation to the Biobehavioral Health faculty in a way that reveals the sound design and valid findings of my study. When discussing the theory, methodology, and results of the project, I must reinforce its strong technical foundation. I must also be careful to support my credibility as a researcher, despite my status as an undergraduate.

These are good points that show your awareness of your position within the community. But you are focusing mainly on solving your problems (credibility, etc.) not the faculty's problem (gap in knowledge).

The presentation will follow a standard format of introduction; discussion of theory and methodology; results; and audience comment period. I will introduce my project with a brief description of the cultural miscommunication issues facing reservation health care workers. I will establish my credibility on the subject of reservation health care by drawing attention to the fact that I lived and worked on a reservation while conducting the study.

Furthermore, I will cite the work of other researchers and demonstrate similarities between our projects.

Good strategies for establishing credibility in a scientific community!

Next, I will address the design of my study, with particular attention to the technical concerns of validity and accuracy. I will emphasize my use of multiple measures of physician cultural awareness, and describe my careful rationale for inclusion of each survey and interview question.

Finally, I will describe the conclusions that I drew from the data. I will present correlations that I found and make comparisons between the interview and questionnaire data. I will also describe the cultural orientation packet that was based upon the project results. I will outline my rationale in selecting the contents of the packet. I plan to conclude the presentation with a discussion of the potential for physician education to improve the quality of reservation health care.

The knowledge that fills the gap?

When I finish my presentation, I will give the faculty audience an opportunity to ask questions and make comments. They will gain insight into the issues facing reservation hospitals and American Indian patients. I will benefit by their comments and criticism, and by the opportunity to disseminate my results to a technical audience.

The details in this solution section give me confidence that you have already begun to plan some lines of argument for your presentation, and that you have studied the presentation genre.

Work Plan:

Date	Item due
10/21	Complete data analysis
11/1	Establish rough outline
11/14	Refine the outline
11/21	Complete a rough draft of presentation
12/1	Final draft of presentation
12/10	Project due

What are the smaller steps that make up these big steps?

Qualifications:

A combination of research and practical experience qualifies me to present the results of the cultural awareness assessment to the Biobehavioral Health faculty. First, three years as a student in the Biobehavioral Health department has made me intimately familiar with the needs of the faculty audience. Second, I am the Principal Investigator in charge of the cultural awareness assessment project at Pine Ridge Indian Reservation. Since I have spent nearly eighteen months designing, executing, and analyzing the cultural awareness of IHS medical staff, I have a thorough appreciation for the nuances of the project. Having lived and worked as part of the Caucasian minority of Pine Ridge Indian Reservation, I have a practical, as well as academic, appreciation of the need for cross-cultural communication in reservations hospitals.

Excellent combination of main point and forecasting!

You are certainly qualified!

Lauren—

Your proposal is approved. You clearly demonstrate an understanding of your position within your disciplinary community, and you have identified several widely accepted methods of boosting credibility within that community. Your proposal gives me confidence that you will be able to use conventions to create a presentation that demonstrates membership in your community. You can also use disciplinary conventions to develop a strong purpose for your presentation. The "knowledge gap" problem-statement form might serve you well. My marginal comments offer some suggestions for ways to present your work as filling a gap. Remember that purpose derives from your audience's problems, not your own. See yourself as contributing knowledge to your field, for you do in fact have a strong contribution to make!

Analysis of Summer Smith's Commentary

Summer Smith's response is, as she indicates, not intended to prompt revision on this project proposal. The proposal, a request to prepare an academic presentation on the cross-cultural awareness of physicians at five Lakota reservations, has met the requirements of the assignment and is approved. But Smith has other purposes, and revision of another sort, in mind when she makes 27 comments where otherwise essentially one comment—"This proposal is approved"—might do. Her first purpose is to stroke the writer's confidence and exhort her to push ahead with her work on the actual presentation. Her second, more substantive, purpose is to indirectly lead Lauren to recalibrate the focus of her presentation.

Smith is lavish in her praise of this writing. She is keen on the project and well-satisfied with Lauren's ability to work within the conventions of the genre and the discipline. She writes a dozen positive evaluations and, at the close of her end note, an applauding hortatorical comment—all of them presented in precise detail. Four comments praise the content of the writing and underscore the importance of following the conventions of such academic discourse:

> Great details, concisely stated.
>
> The details in this solution section give me confidence that you have already begun to plan some lines of argument for your presentation and that you have studied the presentation genre.
>
> Excellent combination of main point and forecasting!
>
> Your proposal gives me confidence that you will be able to use conventions to create a presentation that demonstrates membership in your community.

Six comments praise the writer's ethos and her appeal to the prospective audience:

> These are good points that show your awareness of your position within the community.
>
> Good strategies for establishing credibility in a scientific community.
>
> You are certainly qualified!
>
> You clearly demonstrate an understanding of your position within your disciplinary community, and you have identified several widely accepted methods of boosting credibility within that community.
>
> See yourself as contributing knowledge to your field, for you do in fact have a strong contribution to make!

Beyond looking to reinforce these rhetorical principles through praise, Smith subtly but insistently draws Lauren to recognize (and reaffirm) her purpose as responding to a need in the community—what she calls filling a gap in the disciplinary knowledge. She directs no fewer than six comments to this aim:

> How does your work contribute to the field (fill a gap in knowledge)?

> But you are focusing mainly on solving your problems (credibility, etc.) not the faculty's problem (gap in knowledge).

> The knowledge that fills the gap?

> You can also use disciplinary conventions to develop a strong purpose for your presentation. The "knowledge gap" problem-statement form might serve you well. My marginal comments offer some suggestions for ways to present your work as filling a gap.

These comments are framed in various modes—open and closed questions, advice, explanations, and even one criticism—but they all share the aim of directing Lauren to sharpen the focus of the presentation to come.

The very number of comments across the response and their length and detail—on a prospectus that will not itself be revised—reflect just how intent Smith is in using her comments to teach. The comments don't simply look to make improvements on a piece of writing; they serve to tie the student's work in the text to the ongoing work of the class—in this case, the importance of writing according to the demands of a particular situation, employing the conventions of the community—and quietly exhort her to push herself as a writer. Even as her comments look to enhance the prospective conversation between the writer and her audience, they seek to advance the larger conversation of the class. In doing so, they illustrate how much teacher response may do beyond simply correcting, critiquing, directing, and advising.

Questions

1. Would it have been helpful for Smith to present these comments more explicitly as advice meant to guide Lauren's work on the writing of her actual presentation?

2. Would it have been helpful to offer more critical comments, with the aim of emphasizing the importance of defining the project as filling a gap in the discipline's knowledge of physicians' cultural awareness?

3. Would it have been helpful to have Lauren sharpen her understanding of her purpose in a revised proposal before pursuing her work on the actual presentation?

Simone Billing's Classroom Context
Paper 1 and Paper 3: Expository Essays
Final Drafts

This is the final draft of an expository essay, the third paper out of five in the quarter. It was submitted in the middle of the term. The student wrote the paper for an English I Honors class (Composition and Rhetoric 1) at Santa Clara University in Fall 1998. This draft is the result of feedback from both peers and me on earlier drafts: students provided written feedback, using guidelines for response I had handed out; I provided feedback during a half-hour conference. At the beginning of the term, students had written on topics related to non-fictive readings from the *Ways of Reading* anthology edited by Bartholomae and Petrosky; this assignment was the bridge between those readings and the fictive readings they would write about during the second half of the course. The anthology categorizes readings by topics such as The Aims of Education and Experts and Expertise.

The group of readings for this assignment was labeled Writing and Real Life. The readings featured an excerpt from John Edgar Wideman's nonfictive text *Brothers and Keepers,* an excerpt from Joyce Carol Oates's novel *Marya,* and a Lewis Nordan short story, "Music of the Swamp." The course would move from an examination of the aims of education to an examination of the criteria we use to determine expertise (such as educational degrees) to an examination of our own expertise as writers and readers. As subsequent assignments would be based on readings of short stories, I wanted students to see that they could have valid opinions about the readings, whether the text was fictive or non-fictive, without having to research what critics had to say about them; they could rely on their critical thinking and reading abilities and on their use of specific detail from the text or from their experiences.

In class discussions across the term I suggested specific topics for their essays, but I generally asked students to select subjects that addressed the umbrella heading *and* that were meaningful to them because I believe students write bloodless prose if they feel no emotional and/or intellectual connection to the topic. From start to finish I also reminded students that they needed to consider the elements of the rhetorical situation—writer, audience, subject, and purpose. At the point of the term when this piece was written, the class as a whole was still working on making their topics significant and incorporating concrete evidence from either the text(s) or real life to support the general contention of their thesis. Just before this assignment, however, we had spent a few days working, in addition, on introductions and conclusions and on ways of weeding out wordiness. Through the readings and the writing assignments, I sought to help students hone their critical thinking, reading, and writing abilities.

Like most of the other students in first-year honors courses I have taught, Christina was bright and eager to please. She readily contributed to class discussions and believed herself to be a strong writer: at the beginning of the course, she had written on her student fact sheet, "I do a pretty good job of presenting an issue and analyzing it. My weakness is not possessing 'eloquent' writing. . . . My favorite thing to do is rereading an essay when I get a good grade from a teacher. I usually marvel in surprise at the success of my paper." However, her first paper for the course had been the weakest one in class, filled with broad generalizations and generally lacking a cogent argument and any patent organization (oh, heck, it was a failing essay, to be utterly blunt about it). Then, in our first conference, when I mentioned some glitches in the draft of her second assignment, she rapidly replied, "Of course!" or "Yes, definitely, I see!", usually running over the last word I had uttered, trying to assure me that she had understood but only leading me to believe that she wasn't so much listening as she was trying desperately to please. She wanted that first conference to continue well into the next student's time so that we could review every word and sentence. Christina was clearly worried about her writing—and her grade for the class. Fortunately, although her final, submitted draft for the second assignment was also weak, still the weakest in the class, she had revised it substantially so that it contained at least a modicum of specific detail in one or two paragraphs; I could therefore justify a barely passing grade. During our conference on the second draft of the third assignment, I still felt as if Christina were trying to please, but I knew that we had to deal with the fact that somewhere a break in communication still existed, for that second draft seemed underdeveloped despite her peers' encouragement for her to add specific detail; they too had encouraged clearer organization when they'd commented on the first draft. Because she seemed clearly to be trying to improve but also seemed wan and confused at this point in the term, I wanted genuinely to praise whatever improvement and strength I perceived and gently move her toward more organized and better developed expository prose.

Assignment

Now that we're working with short stories as well as non-fictive prose, we will modify the guidelines we used in our last assignments. You need still to narrow to a topic meaningful to you, using at least one of the pre-writing strategies discussed in class; you need still to consider the writing rhombus (Writer-Audience-Subject-Purpose) as you move from writer-based prose to reader-based prose; you need still to revise both globally

BILLINGS

and locally as you work toward producing a product that does your ideas justice and that reflects serious inquiry on the topic. But the topic—ah, that shifts somewhat. You can use the umbrella heading of Writing and Real Life to discuss the role of writing in life, but in writing about short stories, among other possibilities, you can also choose:

- to document the unfolding of the theme in one of the short stories through analyzing various literary devices;

- to document how one particular literary device contributes primarily to the reader's discernment of the theme;

- to compare two of the pieces on the basis of craft, of theme, of characterization;

- to discuss solely characterization or tone or style (e.g., using the traditional five-part structure of short stories).

However, you must ensure that you address the "who-the-heck-cares" criterion in your piece: you must do more than demonstrate that you know, say, how to trace a symbol through a literary work. You must have a thesis, a point, that holds larger significance, greater implication, than the mere act of dissection of the story or part of the story/ies. And if you choose to relate any personal anecdotes, attend particularly to the who-the-heck-cares criterion because you'll need to consider the significance of some personal comparison to anyone outside your family and friends.

Editor's note: The following section presents the essay that Christina composed in response to this third assignment, but first it presents Christina's opening paper in the course, to provide a sense of her earlier writing. Billings makes two dozen interlinear comments on this first paper, almost all of them, as in her comments on Paper 3 to come, on sentence-level problems. Only her end comments on Paper 1 are reproduced here.

Paper 1 with Teacher Comments

Christina Wai
English 001H
Paper 1

Collecting Interest

Humans are defined by their never-ending desire to attain a state of divinity. By divinity a condition of being perfect and omniscient is implied. Of course knowledge is inevitably linked to perfection. It is the route by which humans believe they can reach divinity. Becoming divine is a difficult process and must be attained through a process of learning and development. Therefore the proper way of forming genius is through an educational process that deposits ideas into the minds of people to the extent that it enables one to use what they have been given and develop it into something further.

What separates humans from other known beings is the self-centered nature by which they try to view themselves. People believe that since they have the intellectual capabilities of understanding and reasoning, they are above all other creatures. But the realization that all things can't yet be explained by human minds has caused people to feel insecure about their significance. In an attempt to reassure their superiority, humans have continually tried to discover the truth behind the world. To know everything would allow one to attain perfection and thus have complete control over one's life.

History has demonstrated itself as proof of people's attempt to become divine. The development of verbal and written language has been one major step in that direction. Communication was done before through body movement, gestures, and other forms of physical language; so communication was not a motivating factor. What inspired the need for written and spoken language can be attributed to the desire to chart and control things. Naming is a means of domination. By being able to label something, one exercises authority over it, since one has defined it. The process of naming things, creating rules, and developing structure are all means to simplify the complexity of the world and allow one to possess an understanding of it.

Education plays an essential role to the pursuit of knowledge. It has been used by those who have uncovered some secrets of the world as a means to preserving their discoveries as well as investing in others to continue their work. Since not all things in the world have been accounted for, the search for knowledge has yet to cease. Rather, it is a continuing process accomplished through generations and generations of people. In each age these scholars are agents of this continuing quest. Therefore the process by which education is administered to them is vital to the survival of the past discoveries and wisdom collected by those predecessors, as well as the future of scholarship.

One way education has been presented by Paulo Freire is through the banking concept. It is where "education thus becomes an act of depositing, in which the students are the depositories and the teacher is the depositor . . . the scope of action allowed to the students extends only as far as receiving, filing, and storing the deposits" (213). In his view, this type of teaching fosters an environment of conformity where intellectual growth is stunted and a group of dehumanized victims are oppressed by a select few that are in power. Students aren't set free to question the world as taught and are not inspired to seek out more truths hidden in the world. Susan Griffin aptly defines how people develop:

> At a certain age we begin to define ourselves, to choose an image of who we are. I am this and not that, we say, attempting thus to erase whatever is within us that does not fit our idea of who we should be. In time we forget our earliest selves and replace that memory with the image we have constructed at the bidding of others. (325)

With education spoon-fed to students, the students are more likely to grow into beings that are shaped by the feeders who are in power. Hence education is only limited to what is given them, and so creativity and imagination are not allowed to blossom inside the students.

Freire proposes a way of teaching, which he believes can liberate students. It is described as the problem-posing method. It is one that fosters and stimulates students to question and to develop their intellectual capabilities to the fullest, which will free them from the control of oppressors. "Liberating education consists in acts of cognition, not transferals of information. It is a learning situation in which the cognizable object (far from being the end of the cognitive act) intermediates the cognitive actors" (Freire 218). In order for this method to work it must be administered to students from the beginning of their educational paths.

What Freire has propounded is a little extreme. His supposition is that all people have the passion and drive to pursue a stimulating path of discovery. Also, without any basics ingrained into students, it is difficult for them to embark on a education based on problem-posing, for one wouldn't know where to start or how to go about doing it. Therefore the best type of education for fostering intellectual pursuit would be a practice that merges the problem-posing method with the banking theory to create the "collecting interest" technique.

The collecting interest technique is based on the idea of depositing to expand. The banking method allows for only deposits to be made to students, permitting no potential for growth. Continuing along the lines of the banking parallel, the problem-posing theory allows for only growth but there is no initial deposit. The best way would be to deposit and then let that develop through various paths. The collecting interest theory of education would begin with lower level education leaning towards the educator providing the students with information. Of course problem-posing methods wouldn't be completely obliterated. They would be kept to a minimum. As a student develops intellectually, problem-posing education will gradually take over. In this way, students initially are given the basics and then stimulated to develop further and explore their curiosities later on. "Knowledge emerges only through the invention and reinventions through the restless, impatient, continuing, hopeful inquiry men pursue in the world, with the world, and with each other" (Freire 213). Through this method scholarship can be fostered in a well-rounded atmosphere.

In seeking to encounter answers to all the questions that plague humans about the world, they are merely trying to become perfect. By reaching perfection, people can satisfy their human need for the reaffirmation of their high significance in this vast universe. Finding the best type of education is necessary to maintaining scholars who can satisfy the human condition of wanting to explain the universe, so as to fulfill their ultimate desire of wanting to be reunited with the "creator."

Christina—

First, do not despair: you have several strengths working for you. You control sentences' structures adequately, and you control surface features a bit more than sufficiently. Sometimes students have problems in these areas, but you do not—good!

However, to improve your writing, you'll need to narrow your paper's topic more quickly right from the start, permitting yourself generally only a single paragraph of introduction for a paper under six pages, so that you're stating your thesis right at the end of the first paragraph. Narrowing the topic will enable you to contextualize your paper's topic more immediately, more precisely, so that you aren't trying to cover an overly broad topic. Narrowing the topic will also enable you to provide concrete, sensory detail for your generalizations. That's the second area you need to work on, Christina: supplying specific, often visual support for your generalizations so that readers truly can see your points as you see them. When you write, consider yourself the instructor, in a way: you're teaching your audience your ideas.

For the next assignment, then, work especially on those two areas: narrowing your topic and supporting your generalizations, whether the thesis or topic sentences or generalizations within the paragraphs, with concrete detail. You can do it. Now onwards!

Paper 3 with Teacher Comments

Christina Wai
English 001H
Paper 3

On Truth and Fiction

Last month on the radio, KGO news broadcasted an interesting segment reporting that more and more individuals <u>have a need</u> to see psychologists. What is the root of their problem? Often it is difficulties in communicating—between husband and wife, parents and children, or even friends and friends. People find it tough verbalizing their thoughts and emotions clearly. In recent studies, medical professionals have declared writing as an effective means of therapy for individuals. It reveals to others the complex thoughts shifting through one's mind. For a piece of writing to be successful in conveying a message, it must elicit emotions from the audience. An effective way of writing to achieve desired responses is through nonfiction writing as opposed to fiction writing.

No -ed for the past tense of this verb

Wordy verb phrase

<u>The fact that nonfiction works mirror reality</u>, more credibility is established. In seeing a truthful example, audiences are more likely to believe authors readily. That is, in Homer's *The Iliad*, the Greek poet paints a vivid picture of the Trojan War revealing both the brutal reality and romanticism of war. Glorifying and graphic details of Achilles, Agamemnon, and Hector in battle fill the poem. However, since Greek historians know it to be a fictive poem, they hesitate to use the work as an accurate representation of the Trojan War times. Rather they look to factual writers, who recorded actual data, for historical comprehension of the Greek times. Historians accept

Sentence organization—no grammatical function for this noun phrase in this sentence (not a subject, an object, or an appositive).

Thucydides's nonfiction account of the Peloponnesian War as valid evidence of such times. By using personal anecdotes, proven facts, gathered data, or real problems and consequences, authors substantiate a claim. The authors show, not just tell the audience their ideas. In seeing tangible proof, readers can accept what authors say as genuine.

Authenticity, in the sense of a complete grounding in reality, is what many fictional works lack. Fiction writers produce some or all the details of a piece. The possibilities are endless, for truth is not required. Vampires can lurk through the dark night while werewolves cautiously hunt prey under the bright moonlit sky. Fiction conjures up hypothetical situations and offers speculative solutions that do not require validity. In [Michael Crichton]'s *Jurassic Park*, the author writes a story based upon an imaginary scenario. He writes of a world where dinosaurs are capable of exisiting. Crichton describes how scientists discover dinosaur DNA and through a complicated process reproduce actual dinaosaurs. In real life, scientists have yet to discover how to reconstruct dinosaurs. Since the book is a fictional work, the authors established his own predicaments and explanations. Critchton does not possess scientifically accurate information nor does he incoporate genuine scientific theories into his work. In their writings, authors can create characters that possess only good attributes and live perfect lives. Fiction allows writers to fill in blanks unanswered by facts and delete imperfections at their own discretion. Therefore, fiction works do not convince readers of an author's message or idea as ^ well as nonfiction works. Readers feel that the authors may not have actually experienced what they have written about and therefore are not as capable of accurately depicting it.

Weak to be verb—as the main verb in a topic sentence, to be leaves little for a prgh to argue or support.

Wordy, unnecessary

That world did exist in the past; it's not imaginary.

p

Didn't he? Most good writers base their fictions on fact in some way.

^ "so"

Overgeneralizations—if one reader feels differently, your assertion is proven false.

In order to convince readers, writers <u>must</u>^ stick to portraying all the facts precisely. Authors should not cover up events or omit details since these truths will exist no matter what the authors feel towards them. Writers should present information <u>at surface level</u> ^ , making sure not to exaggerate or undermine it. For instance, in describing routine, spring rain showers ʌ writers must not characterize it as sprinkling or pouring. <u>It is critical for</u> writers to strike a balance between interpreting information and distorting it. John Edgar Wideman in his piece "Our Time" discusses his difficulties in taking his brother's stories for face value: "I had to root my fiction-writing self out of our exchanges. I had to teach myself to listen. Start fresh, clear the pipes, resist too facile an identification, tame the urge to take off with Robby's story and make it my own" (667). Wideman demonstrates that accepting details without contorting them is not a simple task. People often prefer to accept what they like instead of what is the truth. When writing accurate experiences, writers must not add details that <u>suit their fancy</u> and stray from the truth.

Truth must stand valid on its own merits, something fiction writing does not allow for. In creating fiction, writers often lose sight of reality since they are so enveloped in their own fantasy world. Fact and fiction become blurred. In her work "Theft" Joyce Carol Oates states," "A writer's authentic self, she thought, lay in his writing and not in his life; it was the landscape of the imagination that endured, that was really real. Mere life was the husk, the actor's performance, negligible in the long run . . ." (474). With fiction, authors can distort truth because their imagination is the basis of all reality. They see their truths as the only reality through which to live. Wideman writes: "And even if I did learn to listen, wouldn't there be a point at which I'd have to take over the telling . . . Do I write to

Overgeneralization—not all writers convince this way.

^ *"non-fictive writers prefer to OR choose to"*

Only for accuracy— satirists and humor writers routinely exaggerate.

^ *Odd modification— implies superficiality, shallowness.*

Wordy <u>it is</u> construction. Focus.

Eschew clichés.

escape, to make a fiction of my life?" (667). He struggles to face reality since his common <u>method</u> of escape <u>is</u> through fiction. Writers must see that in choosing to retreat into their own fictional world, they distance themselves from the reality their audience lives in.

Focus: abstract subject + <u>to be</u> verb.

Authors can convey a story with a powerful message and validate the message's significance by writing in a real context. Nonfiction develops familiarity between the reader and the situation, because the situation is authentic. The audience can relate to the genuineness of the episode; therefore, they exhibit emotions for the writer and towards the situation. Effective writing comes down to knowing the audience and being capable of convincing them. Wideman, in his piece, captivates his audience by sharing his personal story of dealing with his brother. He shows them a human side to a criminal. After reading the story, one is ready to embrace Robby and forgive him for what he has done. Had it been a fictional work, readers may have doubted the possibility of seeing a criminal as human.

In all cases? What of <u>Crime & Punishment</u>? <u>Great Expectations</u>? <u>Macbeth</u>? <u>The Scarlet Letter</u>?

Christina—

Work as a peer critiquer: You did well in reminding Chris of the WTHC criterion and to note the redundancies on the paper, just as you did well to note the lack of connection between details and topic sentences for Parnell; however, in both cases you need to curb your desire to edit the writer's work—editing is the writer's job.

Work as a writer: You can commend yourself for having a stronger thesis and a more organized piece here than you have had in the previous two assignments. Your paragraphs also work better with their topic sentences here than the paragraphs in previous papers. Perhaps because you were writing from a stance of greater knowledge, using information from both our class and your Honors 11, you had greater confidence in your material. Whatever the reason, you can commend yourself for those improvements. Further, you are reducing the wordiness in your sentences' structures and controlling the surface features a bit better.

To continue improving your writing, you'll need to scrutinize your development still, asking yourself whether the statements you make in the words you choose to make them truly are accurate or whether they're overly general. Learning to support generalizations both specifically and accurately is a skill you'll find useful regardless of discipline, but you'll find that skill particularly useful in communication, your major. Keep going in this direction—onwards!

BILLINGS

Essay Evaluation Sheet

Thesis and unity (everything—every sentence and each paragraph—works together to support a clear, precise, and concise thesis).   12/15

Organization (both within each paragraph and over the essay as a whole: a reader can follow the whole essay easily because each paragraph has a topic sentence holding it together, connections between the details within paragraphs are clear, there are smooth transitions between paragraphs, and the points—all of them germane to the thesis—are in the most effective order.   12/15

Development (both within individual paragraphs and over the essay as a whole: the essay responds to the topic fully, the topic selected sufficiently challenges the writer and is appropriate for the course, paragraphs contain several sentences of specific, sensory, visual details to support the topic sentences, and the essay goes into sufficient detail to substantiate the thesis. *odd insertion* [2] / *overgen* [3]   10/15

Sentence structures (sentences are not only grammatically correct but rhetorically clear, well-organized, varied, and sophisticated).
wv ph / *s.o.* / *w* [2] / *odd mod* / *focus*   11/15

Surface features of written English (essay is virtually free of errors in spelling, grammar, punctuation, idiom, reference, and usage).
no -ed / *p* [4] / *wv*   13/15

Clarity of style (double-whammy: all of the above categories contribute to a collegiate, individual style; prose is not gray). *Cliché*   6/10

Quality of ideas (triple-whammy: none of the above categories detracts from logical, reasonable, and worthwhile reading; subject is worth writing on; paper looks professional and shows that the writer has taken time and care to prepare the manuscript).   6/10

Introductory and concluding paragraphs.   2/05
- - - - - - - - - -
TOTAL   72

GRADE   C -

Analysis of Simone Billings' Commentary

"On Truth and Fiction" is not an easy essay to comment on. How do you respond to a student who says, within the space of a few pages of writing:

> Authenticity, in the sense of a complete grounding in reality, is what many fictional works lack.

> Fiction conjures up hypothetical situations and offers speculative solutions that do not require validity.

> Writers should present information at surface level, making sure not to exaggerate or undermine it.

> Truth must stand valid on its own merits, something fiction writing does not allow for.

With such statements staring you in the face, you might be inclined to settle for talking about the writer's half-hearted choice of topic, her unsupported claims, or her confusing sentences. That is, you might avoid her ideas themselves altogether. Or, taking an aggressive tact, you might call her on these outlandish claims: tell her that her ideas are not thought out, that her writing is careless. Billings takes a more prudent course. She'll wrestle with Christina about her ideas in her marginal comments, but in her end note she'll play up the strengths of the paper and encourage her to work to improve these areas. Weighing the problems of the writing against the needs of the writer, she decides that it would be best to work with the writer.

Billings relies on her marginal comments and evaluation sheet to point out the various problems in the paper and impress on Christina the need to be more vigilant about her assertions. Half of the marginal comments address matters of word choice and sentence structure they have been talking about in class. But half of them challenge her claims:

> S: [Michael Crichton] writes of a world where dinosaurs are capable of existing.
> T: That world did exist in the past, it's not imaginary.

> S: Crichton does not . . . incorporate genuine scientific theories into his work.
> T: Didn't he? Most good writers base their fictions on fact in some way.

> S: Fiction works do not convince readers of an author's message or idea as well as nonfiction works. Readers feel that the authors may not have actually experienced what they have written about and therefore are not as capable of accurately depicting it.

T: Overgeneralizations—if one reader feels differently, your assertion is proven false.

S: In order to convince readers, writers must stick to portraying all the facts precisely.

T: Overgeneralization—not all writers convince this way.

S: Writers should present information at surface level, making sure not to exaggerate or undermine it.

T: Only for accuracy—satirists and humor writers routinely exaggerate.

S: Had [*Brothers and Keepers*] been a fictional work, readers may have doubted the possibility of seeing a criminal as human.

T: In all cases? What of <u>Crime and Punishment</u>? <u>Great Expectations</u>? <u>Macbeth</u>? <u>The Scarlet Letter</u>?

Billings reinforces these criticisms on her evaluation sheet. She takes off 9 of 15 points for problems of style and another 9 points together for problems of development, overgeneralizations, and the overall quality of ideas.

In her end note, Billings concentrates on improvements Christina has made over earlier papers. She praises Christina—or, rather, tells her she can commend herself—on three counts: a stronger thesis and a better organized essay than in her past two assignments, tighter paragraphs, and less wordiness in her sentences. In fact, Christina's writing *has* improved. Although she still has problems focusing her discussion and saying precisely what she means, she has gotten better at keeping on track, her paragraphs are more coherent, and her sentences are more simple and direct. She has even managed to get more concrete detail into her writing, though many of these examples and details are lacking in strength. She still has a long way to go, but Billings decides not to ask her to take on more than she has already taken on over the past weeks in her writing. As she puts it in her prefatory note, Christina "seemed clearly to be trying to improve but also seemed wan and confused at this point in the term. I wanted genuinely to praise whatever improvement and strength I perceived and gently move her towards more organized and better developed expository prose."

With this plan in mind, Billings avoids any direct criticism in her end note and does not make any call for revision on the paper. She questions Christina's claims, but only in the context of a call for continued improvement and even then only in general terms: "To continue improving your writing, Christina, you'll need to scrutinize your development still, asking yourself whether the statements you make in the words you choose to make them truly are accurate or whether they're overly general." She holds back and does not go into the issue. Instead she aims her sights on the next paper, hoping that Christina will continue working to improve her writing on the two assignments left in the class. This course of action may be best, for Christina has shown herself to be motivated and able to improve when she is asked to.

The case illustrates how much the writer behind the text (or at least the writer we construe on the basis of the text) can affect the way we look at and respond to student writing. If this were Christina's first paper of the semester or if her earlier writings were stronger in focus, coherence, and sentence structure, our evaluation of the work (maybe not the paper, but the work) might be very different. Billings' way of dealing with Christina reminds us: We don't so much comment on student writing as we respond to students and help them develop as writers. Not better writing, as process teachers have suggested, but better writers. Billings' response illustrates how comments, to be effective, must be shaped to the contours of the individual student—to her abilities, her earlier work in the course, and her particular needs as a learning writer.

Questions

1. Should Billings have done more to address the problems in this draft, especially the problems with overgeneralizations and half-truths?

2. Should we expect this student to take on anything in addition to the issues she has already taken on in her work as a writer so far this semester?

3. Is there a point at which emphasizing the positive over the negative is ungenuine and counterproductive?

4. How much should a teacher direct her comments toward improving the writer's content and her ways of thinking? How much should the teacher emphasize the craft of writing and the shaping of prose?

5. When we look to the student writer when we respond, to what extent are we looking at the student behind the text, the real flesh-and-blood writer? To what extent are we looking at a construct of the student, an implied author that we create based on the text and our prior experience with the student's writing?

6. To what extent can an evaluation sheet like the one Billings employs communicate to students the strengths and problems in a piece of writing? More broadly, how are we to negotiate the act of responding to students about their writing with the institutional business of grading and informing students about their progress in a course?

7. What role do assignments play in reading and responding to student writing?

Peggy O'Neill's Classroom Context
Paper 3: Expository Essay
Rough Draft and Revised Draft

This writing was produced as part of a Composition I course at Georgia Southern University during the fall 1998. Although Pertrina was starting her second year of college, she was taking first-year composition for the first time. She explained that she didn't want to take it as a first-year student. She attended class regularly, was always prepared, and actively participated in class. The course was set up as a workshop that required students to submit writing for review weekly, write weekly responses to published essays, and participate in response workshops, discussions, and other in-class writing activities. Students wrote on topics of their choice, with the aid of regular invention exercises.

The first six draft workshops were devoted to responding to rough drafts of 1 to 3 typed pages. The next six workshops were focused on responding to revised drafts. At the end of the semester students were to produce a 10 to 15 page portfolio of polished writing (culled from their drafts) and a formal, introductory letter to the portfolio reader. The portfolio's purpose was to demonstrate that students had achieved the course goals, which included the understanding of composing processes as well as a sense of their own composing process, an understanding of rhetorical concepts such as purpose and audience, and an ability to adapt their writing for a variety of rhetorical situations. Students received written feedback from me on their weekly drafts and reading responses. One midterm conference was required, but there were opportunities in the two-hour computer workshops for informal conferencing.

The first of these drafts was produced after an in-class invention exercise that focused on using journalists' questions (Who, What, Where, When, and Why) to generate material about the student's topic of choice. It was the third rough draft Pertrina had submitted up to this point in the course. She brought the draft to class for peer review and submitted a copy of it to me for response. Accompanying the draft was a Letter to the Reader in which Pertrina specified some of the problems and questions she wanted her readers (both her peers and me) to respond to. After receiving the feedback, Pertrina submitted a revised version of the draft with a new Letter to the Reader. Again, she received feedback from her peers and me. With this draft she also included some of the research material she had used for the paper. After receiving my feedback on this revised draft, Pertrina took advantage of the opportunity to respond to my comments and ask any questions she had about the comments or the paper. I then responded to her concerns both orally and in writing. She decided to continue working on the paper to include in her end-of-the-semester portfolio.

My response really starts with the writer's own response to her writing as articulated in the Letter to the Reader. I try to think of the response as part of the ongoing conversation that I have with the student throughout the semester. This conversation, which I see as central to teaching and learning, takes place in writing as well as through face-to-face interactions with the student during class or during conferences. Consequently, what is represented here is just a snippet of the dialogue that Pertrina and I—along with her peers—carried on over the semester about her writing.

Rough Draft with Teacher and Peer Comments

Pertrina Cross
Composition 1
Midterm Portfolio Writing (3rd RD)

On The Freshman 15

When entering college everyone has their own fears. "Will I fit in, will anyone like me, am I going to like it ...?" No one ever thinks about me. That is why I hit everyone so hard, sometimes they do not even see me coming. Before I tell you what my name is, let me tell you a little about myself. A can be a response to fatty foods, or stress. I love when you late night snack, and when you eat Lakeside's great hamburgers, french fries, and chicken fingers. I can't wait to see those weekends when you go home and eat mom's great home cooked meals. Some of you even goes to grandparent's house and eat more and more. I really love when you tell your friends that they can go on to the RAC without you. You never want to exercise, and my self-esteem rise when yours get lower. My main goal is to watch how your perfect figure turns to not so perfect. My name is The Freshman Fifteen.

[These are the teacher's marginal comments.]

The Freshman 15 is a nickname given by college students. It is where you gain weight, commonly 15 lbs., from the change in atmosphere and food. Many other factors can cause this weight gain of new college students. For one, if you do not exercise regularly or do not watch what you eat. Another major factor is stress. College students sometimes do not realize how stressful college can be. If you are not mentally prepared for it, it can hit you harder than you think. This is why this situation apply to males, females, and even new teachers. Because everyone

How does this affect F-15?

is different, we all respond to changes differently. While some are gaining weight, others may be losing weight. No matter what, we all respond to stress and new environment.

The response of the Freshman 15 can be very damaging. If you are not prepared for it, you can more than 20 lbs. It can be very stressful if you are already a little overweight. This can be another stressful situation that can cause your mind to wander off of school work. This can lead to many different eating disorders. ~~They may include~~ *, including* beliuma and/or anorexia. ^ There are many different solutions that can help prevent a college student from being affected. First, you must decide if your weight gain is a problem. If it is, you must then decide if it is a response to stress of the change in eating habits. If it is a response to bad eating habits, set up a plan that decides what you should and should not eat. Avoid fatty foods and late night snacking. Get some motivating friends and set up an exercising program and stick to it. Also learn to say no! If you are gaining weight because of stress find out what is stressful in your life. This can lead to very serious problems, that may result to suicide or dropping out. Is being away from home for the first time, the schoolwork, the transition from high school to college, or being away from your boy or girlfriend, or even your family that you left back at home. There may be other problems that you might not recognize. That is why there are counselors on campus to help you with problems that you may be having. Stop, think, do not let the Freshman 15 control your life.

^ Combine sentences such as these

How do you do this?

O'NEILL

Letter to the Reader and Three Responses

My goal of this paper was to inform you about different things in college life. I choose The Freshman 15, because it is commonly known. In this draft, I talk about what it really is and how it can affect you. Not to many students look at the problem the way I did in this paper. I tried to be informative, to let you, the reader, know that it can be more than just 15 pounds. In the opening paragraph, I let the "Freshman 15" talk. I did it this way to make the reader think. I felt that if I started it off by saying "The Freshman 15 is . . ." it would not give the same impact.

1. Do you think my strategy worked to get my point across?

2. I think that paragraph 2 was short, should more information be added, or was it enough?

3. If more revisions are to be made, what are your suggestions? For one, should I give some examples of people who have been affected by it?

Student Response 1

I thought the first paragraph was really neat. There were a couple of unclear parts that I underlined. In the second paragraph you should name more factors that can cause the F-15—like some guys get it from drinking beer a lot. Maybe you should go more in depth about how you can lose the F-15. Overall it is a very interesting and well worded paper.

Student Response 2

This is a really good paper I can definately relate to. In the first paragraph I think you could be a little clearer that you are talking in the Freshman 15's point of view. There are a couple of sentences in the first paragraph that are a little confusing. Overall this is a really good paper.

Peggy O'Neill's Response

I liked your opening and the personification of F-15. It caught my attention. You have a lot of good info but try beefing it up with some student experiences and some info from the Health Center. A couple of quotes from people will add weight (no pun intended) to your argument. For example, I wonder how common the problem really is?

Revised Draft with Teacher and Peer Comments

Pertrina Cross
Composition 1
Midterm Portfolio Writing (Rev)

On The Freshman 15

When entering college everyone has their own fears.
"Will I fit in, will anyone like me, am I going to like it ...?"
No one ever thinks about me. Sometimes they do not even
see me coming. Before I tell you what my name is, let me
tell you a little about myself. I can be a response to fatty
foods, or stress. I love when you late night snack, and
when you eat Lakeside's great hamburgers, french fries,
and chicken fingers. I can't wait to see those weekends
when you go home and eat mom's great home cooked
meals. Some of you even go to grandparent's house and
eat more and more. I really love when you tell your friends
that they can go on to the RAC without you. You never
want to exercise, and my self-esteem rises when yours get
lower. My main goal is to watch how your perfect figure
turns not so perfect. If you haven't guessed by now, my
name is The Freshman <u>Fifteen</u>.

[These are the teacher's marginal comments.]

Be consistent

The Freshman <u>15</u> is a nickname given by college students ~~to~~ a result of weight gain. This weight gain is commonly 15 pounds, that is a response to a change in atmosphere and a change in eating habits. This situation can
apply to males and females. Because every body is different, we all respond to changes differently. While some are
gaining weight, others may be losing weight. In college,
many think "thin is in", and students become afraid to gain
weight. This may lead to eating disorders such as, bulimia and anorexia. Bulimia is where a person bing, purge,

^ *as*

vomit, and fast to lose weight. Other characteristics may include, abusing laxatives and overexercising. Anorexia is an condition where one is afraid to gain weight. They starve themselves, and are thin to the point of emaciation. Both of these disorders are severe and life threatening.

No matter what, we all respond to new environments. This is why The Freshman 15 is an very important topic. If you are not prepared for it, it can be very damaging. Stress is an form of a response to psychological changes. Being away from home for the first time, the transition from high school to college, or being away from a boy or girlfriend are all changes that my disrupt someone life. Whether it is minor or severe, it all should be taken seriously.

^ "going": Structures should be parallel

** Will do add on later **

Take control of your life. Figure out how you are responding to The Freshman 15. There are many different solutions that can help prevent a college student from being affected. First, you must decide if your weight gain is a problem. If it is, you must then decide if it is a response to stress, or the change in eating habits. If it is a response to bad eating habits, set up a plan and stick to it. Establish a regular eating pattern, this will help to avoid fatty foods and late night snacking. Set realistic goals, and maintain them. Set up an exercising schedule that is convenient, and stick to it. Get a support group of friends and people who are being effected by a weight gain. If you make eating healthy and exercising fun, it will become apart of your daily routine. It will become a goal to reach for. When you reach it, the results will be rewarding. For those who are gaining weight because of stress, find out what it is that is stressful in your life. This can lead to very

Response to the F-15 or rather to the change in going to college?

serious problems, that may result to suicide or dropping ^ *Too much stress*
out. There may be other other problems that you may not
recognize. That is why there are counselors on campus to
help you with problems that you may be having. Join
clubs and organizations that will help your out look on life
be more positive. Stop and think, do not let the Freshman
15 control your life.

Letter to the Reader

My goal of this paper was to inform you about how college students are affected by the Freshman 15. I talk about what it is and how it can affect us all. I tried to be informative, and started off funny so the reader will want to continue to read. In paragraph one, I open up telling you what the Freshman 15 is. I give characteristic of it. In the second paragraph I tell about how it affects people by leading to eating disorders. I tried to be informative, but is it boring? My biggest problem came with the third paragraph. I ran out of things to say. What can I add to this paragraph to give it more length, and make it better. My conclusion contained methods that may help you to deal with the Freshman 15.

Overall what did you think of my revision. My main problem with this paper is that I am too informative. I think it makes it boring, and I feel that it takes away from the real purpose of why I was writing about the Freshman 15. Do you feel that I stuck to the topic at hand? As a reader, what do you think I can do to make this paper informative, but fun to read? Also is there things that I need to take out? Is my transition from paragraph to paragraph easy to follow?

Two Peer Responses and Teacher Response

Student Response 1

The intro to the essay was good. A little confusing at first, but I thought it fit togeth-er well. The second prgh is not boring and it is informative. Only question I have is if it is called the "Freshman 15" that means you gain weight. Most people won't come to college, gain 15 pounds, and become anorexic. Freshman 15 usually comes from drinking alcohol. In 3rd prgh write on how to avoid gaining 15 lbs. The transition of essay is good. Another area to add on in the essay can be describe someone you knew in high school and write on how much they have changed if they got the Freshman 15. [*Teacher note: Some good suggestions.*]

Student Response 2

I really liked your essay—I thought it was very helpful and informative and inter-esting to read (not boring). I really liked the unique way that you started the paper! Some of my suggestions are:

1. Prgh 2, 4th sentence: Don't use "we" because you didn't use it anywhere else in the paragraph.

2. After "... others may be losing weight" in prgh 2: Continue with prgh 3. Then, when you write "minor or severe ..." (about the stress, transitions, etc.) you can lead into anorexia / bulemia.

3. The sentence in 3rd prgh, "Stress is a form ... changes" doesn't seem to fit too well.

The last paragraph was very good. It's helpful to have suggestions in your paper for those that may be struggling with Freshman 15. Good job.

Peggy O'Neill's Response

Your letter is very helpful in reading your essay and responding to it. I like the open-ing because it did pique my interest, making me want to read. I don't think your information is boring. For paragraph three, you note that you ran out of things to say. Consider these questions: Does the Freshman Fifteen affect male or female stu-dents more? How can the F-15 be "dangerous"? Can you get any info specific to our campus from the Health Center or Counseling Center?

As you continue to work on this, consider how to cite your sources. It looks like you got great information but you don't give credit to them. Also, I noticed some prob-lems with tense and sentence structure that you need to be aware of as you polish this. Finally, I didn't think this was "too" informative. I think you do a good job of making it readable and informative.

Student Reactions to Teacher Comments

In response to the suggestions that you gave to me for paragraph 3, someone else told me to add how men are affected by it. Their suggestion was that men gain weight because they start to drink more when they go to college. To cite my sources, will it be okay if I just say something like "The Health Center has lots of info on . . . of where I got info on and used in this essay"? I did not understand what you meant by my structures should be parral-lel. Does that mean they should agree? When you don't write too many comments, does that mean the paper is good? Maybe you could write on our paper what you think it may be worth. For example, you could say that with the mistakes you have, and all the grammer mistakes, this is about a "C" paper. Then you could say "to make this an A paper you need to do . . . .", or "to make this an B paper you need to rewrite the whole thing." Maybe you can even tell us if this is a good paper to revise, should we choose another one.

[These are O'Neill's responses to the student's reactions.]

Yes—you want to use a variety of ways.

Do you understand now?

Usually

Trina—

Good suggestion but I don't want to indicate grades for individual papers because that may mislead students. The Pass / Fail grade will encompass more than just a paper. If you want more indication of a "grade" come by my office. I do think you are doing well-above just meeting the require-ments.

Peggy

Analysis of Peggy O'Neill's Commentary

This case demonstrates just how tightly effective response is tied to the day-to-day work of the course. The talk that goes on about a student paper, at its best, is part of the ongoing classroom conversation: what gets said in a set of comments reiterates and gives substance to what is said in class, in conference, and in the hallways after class is over. Response at its best is also a dialogue—a two-way communication between student and teacher, one student and another student, reader and writer. The writer writes. The reader reads the text and replies. The writer, seeing how the reader responds, decides what changes are required to make the text more fully achieve what he wants it to achieve. He revises the writing and gives it back to the reader, looking again for how well the text prompts the effects he intends. Discourse engenders discourse, response begets response.

All too often this give-and-take quality of an exchange goes slack. The teacher reads the paper solely in terms of her agenda, often as a critic or judge, in isolation from the larger work of the class or cut off from the history of the individual student. Students are left to take on subjects, genres, and purposes set down by the teacher and revise according to her wishes. Peggy O'Neill looks to restore the naturally dialogic quality of writing and response. Her class is saturated with response and two-way discussion between writers and readers about their writing. The very design of the course is built on writing, response, and revision, and looks to give students the authority they need to see themselves, and develop, as writers.

In O'Neill's class there are no formal assignments doled out according to a course schedule. Students take up their own writing tasks and subjects, and they set their own schedule, deciding how many papers they will draft and which ones they will revise and submit in their final portfolio. Writers don't just hand their papers to the teacher for commentary, they also hand them to other students at various points in their drafting. Moreover, they don't give them to readers to have them respond as they will, according to their own agendas; they take an active role in deciding what readers will attend to in their reading. Students include a memo (what O'Neill calls a Letter to the Reader) with each paper telling the reader what they are trying to accomplish and what they want feedback on. As a result, responders are encouraged to see their work as in the service of helping the writer accomplish what he wants to accomplish in the writing. The writer retains greater control over the response and greater authority over his writing. The class is truly a workshop. Students bring in writing, other students and the teacher respond, and then they revise or work on another piece of writing, according to their own schedule and purposes. Students comment on the writing of the course as much, if not actually far more, than the teacher. Response is woven into the very fabric of the course and is integral to whatever is accomplished. Any analysis of response in the class, then, must include the full circle of response: the writer's memo, peer comments, and teacher comments.

The rough draft of "The Freshman 15" has real promise. The writer engages readers through the use of an unconventional point of view. She defines the "Freshman 15," notes who is susceptible to it, and identifies its causes and looks to offer some way of dealing with it once it strikes. She does a particularly good job with the solutions section of the paper, which is fairly detailed and, for the most part, well-organized. By the end of the essay, she comes to a keen insight: that the stress that leads to the Freshman 15 may be caused by some more serious problems "that you might not recognize." Still, there is much yet to do. The writing lacks substantive detail. Pertrina notes that the Freshman 15 "can be very dangerous," but she doesn't define the dangers. She says that it can lead to "many different eating disorders" but doesn't go into the likelihood that they might happen. She says that it "can be very stressful if you are already a little overweight" but gives no example or sense of how stressful it is or how this stress can be manifested. The solutions she offers begin to be helpful, but they are over-simplified. She points to some sources that may cause stress, but she offers no real advice about what to do once the causes have been identified. She mentions nothing of the impact added weight may have on self-confidence or social life. The language and detail remain at a fairly general level, and the essay is marred by problems in usage and sentence structure. Pertrina sees the paper as trying to inform readers about this phenomenon and its dangers. She wants to be informative but in an interesting way. She has a pretty good sense of some of the limitations of the draft: she sees that she probably needs more information in the second paragraph and perhaps some examples of people who have been affected by it. She asks her readers to advise her on these points.

The peer responders restrict their comments to the questions asked by the writer, offering, for the most part, straight yes or no answers, praise or criticism, in response. Her peers like the strategy she uses to introduce the paper, but both of them indicate that the writing in parts of this first paragraph is unclear. The first response is somewhat fuller than the second; it directs the writer to identify more causes for the Freshman 15 and suggests that she give more detail about how to lose the added weight. O'Neill herself jots down two marginal comments about the sentence structure and a single comment asking Pertrina to develop one of her statements. In her end note, she focuses on the writer's ideas, praising them, and points to the need for greater development. In response to the first question in Pertrina's memo, she praises the introduction. She doesn't address the second question directly, but she does offer a couple of suggestions, one in the form of straight advice ("try beefing it up with some student experiences and some info from the Health Center"), the other in the form of a reader's question ("I wonder how common the problem really is?"). It is a modest response and not very detailed. You get the sense that O'Neill is holding back, perhaps relying on the student responders to take up a lion's share of the response, and waiting for Pertrina herself to come up with changes on her own.

In spite of this minimal response (or perhaps because of it?), Pertrina comes up with a quietly impressive revision. The improvement, however, does not come (at least not yet) as a result of adding the kinds of detail and information suggested by her responders. She adds nothing about the causes of the Freshman 15 and nothing in the way of sample student experiences or information from the Health Center. Following the advice of one of her peer responders, she does add some helpful material on how to lose weight through exercise. But the vast majority of the improvement comes from her work with reordering, recasting, and tightening the material of the draft—work instigated perhaps by the shared view of the peer responders that the writing in a few places could be clearer. Pertrina restructures no fewer than a dozen sentences. She deletes two chunks of material, about seven lines from the middle of the second paragraph and another four lines from the start of the third paragraph. She moves and recasts several chunks of sentences in the second half of the paper and makes them flow with the sequence of her argument.

> Draft: College students sometimes do not realize how stressful college can be. If you are not mentally prepared for it, it can hit you harder than you think. This is why this situation apply to males, females, and even new teachers. Because everyone is different, we all respond to changes differently. While some are gaining weight, others may be losing weight. No matter what, we all respond to stress and new environment.

> Revision: This situation can apply to males and females. Because every body is different, we all respond to changes differently. While some are gaining weight, others may be losing weight. In college, many think "thin is in", and students become afraid to gain weight. This may lead to eating disorders such as bulimia and anorexia.

> Draft: The response of the Freshman 15 can be very damaging. If you are not prepared for it, you can more than 20 lbs. It can be very stressful if you are already a little overweight. This can be another stressful situation that can cause your mind to wander off of school work. This can lead to many different eating disorders. The may include beliuma and/or anorexia.

> Revision: No matter what, we all respond to new environments. This is why The Freshman 15 is an very important topic. If you are not prepared for it, it can be very damaging. Stress is a form of a response to psychological changes. Being away from home for the first time, the transition from high school to college, or being away from a boy or girlfriend are all changes that may disrupt someone life. Whether it is minor or severe, it all should be taken seriously.

Pertrina adds a half-dozen new sentences outright in the second half of the essay, adds five sentences about bulimia and anorexia, and revises and expands another five or six sentences, including most of the following section:

> Establish a regular eating pattern, this will help to avoid fatty food and late night snacking. Set realistic goals, and maintain them. Set up an exercising schedule that is convenient, and stick to it. Get a support group of friends and people who are being effected by a weight gain. If you make eating healthy and exercising fun, it will become apart of your daily routine. It will become a goal to reach for. When you reach it, the results will be rewarding.

The revised paper is far from smooth or complete, but Pertrina is getting a better and better sense of what she is aiming for and what she still has to do. In her second Letter to the Reader, she wonders if the paper is boring. She still feels the paper has too much information and not enough material to stir interest. She wonders if she has stuck to the topic and if her transitions from paragraph to paragrah are easy to follow. She admits that she has run out of things to say about how stress can lead to the Freshman 15 and asks readers if there is anything she can add. She also asks if there are things to take out of the paper.

The peer responders, generally supportive in their overall reaction to the paper, offer a mixed bag of advice for revision. The second response praises the overall content and shape of the essay; it offers only three suggestions for sentence-level revision. The first response is more substantive. The reader addresses each of the issues Pertrina raises in her memo. He offers praise on four points and presents three suggestions. He wonders about how extensive the Freshman 15 problem is on campus. In response to her question about paragraph 3, he tells her to "write on how to avoid gaining 15 lbs."—a dubious bit of advice here because the paragraph focuses on the stress that can cause the problem, not on the weight issue itself. And he advises her, more promisingly, to add somewhere in the essay an example of someone she knows who has "got the Freshman 15."

Here, as in her response to the rough draft, O'Neill takes her lead from Pertrina's memo. She writes 18 comments—four in the margins, all but one of them editorial, 14 in the end note, dealing twice as much with global concerns as local concerns. She uses nearly the full range of modes: criticism, praise, corrections, imperatives, advice, open and closed questions, and explanations. Over half of her end comments respond in direct, matter-of-fact answers to Pertrina's questions: Is it boring? Does the information overwhelm the reader's interest in the paper? What might be added to the third paragraph? (She does not address Pertrina's questions about unity, transitions, or places to cut.) Most of these responses reassure Pertrina about her choices. O'Neill's most substantive response deals with the issue of developing the third paragraph, which she does through three questions:

Does the Freshman Fifteen affect male or female students more?

How can the F-15 be "dangerous"?

Can you get any info specific to our campus from the Health Center or Counseling Center?

Her other comments raise concerns of her own, namely about the citation of sources, mechanics, and sentence structure. Although these comments point to problems that Pertrina will be expected to address in her revision, O'Neill couches them in unassuming ways. She tells Pertrina to "consider how to cite your sources," praises her information, and only then, in a response that functions as an explanatory comment, notes that she hasn't given credit to the source of this information. What she does—and what she doesn't do—is telling. She doesn't tell the student that she's made errors in mechanics or that she's written awkward sentences; she says, "I noticed some problems with tense and sentence structure," problems, she then adds by way of explanation, "that you need to be aware of as you polish this." She closes the response, appropriately, on a note of praise, perhaps purposely holding this comment (which conventionally would have been better placed at the start of her response with her other positive replies to Pertrina's questions) as a way to close her response.

O'Neill's comments do not look to provide much in the way of direction or detailed advice for revision. They don't have to because the writer gets so much response from other students and, presumably, direct, spoken feedback in class from O'Neill. The written comments she makes look to get into an exchange with the writer and leave it up to her to decide on the best course for revision. Pertrina is left in charge of her work as a writer. O'Neill, like the peer responders, is cast in a supporting role, usually offering comments only on questions the writer herself raises and only sometimes, late in the composing process, raising her own concerns about the writing. It has become a tiresome commonplace: writing

162 COMMENTS IN CONTEXT

instruction should be student-centered. But here is a truly student-centered class. The students' writing, self-evaluation, and peer response beat at the heart of the course. At its best, response to student writing, as this course aptly shows, is not an isolated activity; it is woven into the very fabric of the course. In many ways, it is the course, the principal mode of instruction.

Questions

1. How well does Pertrina see her own purposes as a writer and evaluate the strengths and weaknesses of her writing? How successful are her Letters to the Reader?

2. How successfully do the peer responders take on the responsibility of reading and responding to this student writing?

3. As a teacher, what do you think would have to be done, if anything, to prepare students to do the kind of responding that they are called on to do here? How might they be prepared to do it (even) better?

4. What do you think of O'Neill's responses? Are they full enough? Demanding enough? Or do the moderate number of comments fit well in the framework of the course?

5. How would students react to this course structure? Would they appreciate and make good use of this kind of set up where their peers are given such substantial responsibility for responding to their papers and where the teacher looks to become just one more voice of response? What would have to be done during the early weeks of the semester in order to orient students to such a self-directed course?

6. How much does the structure of response in this course depend on a portfolio system of grading? Could this system of response work (or work as well) if the teacher graded individual papers across the course?

7. Just how important is response—informal spoken responses or formal written responses—to writing and writing instruction?

A Comparison of the Two Groups of Responders

The responses of these new compositionists, together with those of the experienced scholars examined in Chapter 1—the one group responding to students in their own classes, the other responding to student writing outside the immediate context of a class—offer a profile of effective responding strategies. They show what well-informed composition teachers advocate in theory and what they practice in responding to student writing. Across these 20 sets of responses, these 18 teachers write 491 comments—an average of 25 comments per paper. The comments are for the most part written out in full statements and deal specifically with the particulars of the student texts. They average a generous 10 words per comment. Tellingly, 57 percent of the comments focus on global matters of content and organization. Another 18 percent deal with the essay as a whole and such extratextual concerns as the writer's composing process, persona, audience, and purpose. Only 25 percent of their comments are given to local matters: mechanics, punctuation, wording, and sentence structure—this, in spite of the fact that 6 of the 11 papers responded to are final drafts. These responders are intent on deferring any substantive work with editing and proofreading until the overall content, focus, and shape of the writing are far enough along to justify such local commentary. Even on final drafts they are careful not to try to get a quick fix on all the local problems they encounter. Though their individual styles range from directive to advisory to moderately facilitative to receptive, their comments as a whole are only moderately directive. Thirty-nine percent of their comments are framed as corrections, criticisms, and calls for revision. Another 13 percent are presented as praise. The rest—almost half of their comments—are framed in nondirective modes: as questions, explanations, interpretations, and reader responses. As a group these teachers refrain from adopting a minimalist, hands-off posture, on the one hand, and taking over the text, on the other. In their various ways, they adopt the middle course. They are intent on pointing to problems and offering direction for revision, but they look to make comments that engage students in a discussion and leave them to work out their writing on their own. If learning to write is learning to make effective choices, these teachers want to place students, through their comments, in the position of making more and more informed choices for themselves and, in doing so, developing a richer understanding of how writing works.

The two groups' responses differ in interesting ways. The classroom teachers, responding to their own students' writing, make 15 percent fewer comments on content and organization and 20 percent more comments about local matters than the teachers who model their response styles on the sampling of essays. These classroom teachers also make 12 percent more corrections and criticism than the clinical responders. It would seem, as a group, they are more willing to point directly to the changes they want students to make. This is true, but only to a certain extent. Remove local comments from consideration, comments that are typically framed as corrections or criticism, and the two groups' modes of commentary are remarkably similar. With local comments out of the picture, there are only a few differences in the groups' modes of commentary: the clinical responders write more questions, and they write more comments that play back the teacher's reading of the text, and the classroom teachers write more praise and twice as many explanatory comments. The clinical responders who are modeling their optimal response styles may provide more playback because they present a substantial number of their comments in end notes and letters to the student, forms that (because they are removed from the lines of the student's text) put more demands on the teacher to supply a context for their comments. Their greater use of questions may grow out of their interest in modeling a form of commentary that aims to keep responsibility for revision squarely on the student writer. The classroom teachers may provide more in the way of praise and explanations simply because they have the real flesh-and-blood student more firmly in mind as they respond and feel a need to be more responsive to the practical realities of instruction. It is debatable whether the two groups of teacher comments are equally rigorous and intellectually demanding. But it seems clear that, because of their greater emphasis on local matters and their greater number of authoritative comments, the classroom teachers' responses, as a group, are somewhat more directive and controlling than those of the 12 clinical responders. Nevertheless, both groups of teacher comments are noteworthy for the way they engage the issues raised by the text, look to the needs of the individual student, modulate the control they exert over the writing, and look to engage the student in a give-and-take exchange about the writing. It is this tension between pushing and holding back, criticizing and encouraging, directing and helping, speaking and waiting, that seems to animate these teachers' responses and enable them to motivate revision.

Conclusion

These responses from actual classroom situations illustrate the astounding complexity in responding to student writing. They show the range of concerns and the rich layers of context that are involved in talking with students about their writing, with the aim of improving their texts, improving their writing over time, and, in the long run, helping them develop as writers. Good response requires good, close reading: knowing how to approach a piece of writing as a reader, sensitive to the writer's purposes and receptive to its content and effects. Good response requires consistent, incisive evaluation: not just knowing whether a paper is good or bad or mediocre, but knowing how your values as a teacher-reader fit into your aims for the course. Good response, moreover, cannot deal with just the words on the page; it must deal with a whole circle of contexts. If it is to be effective, it must take into account the assignment, the stage of drafting, the audience, the rhetorical situation, the work of the class, and the individual student: his attitudes, his earlier work, his particular needs as a writer. Good response also requires an emphasis on the positive and a belief in the student's ability to learn: What strengths can I find? What is the student doing here that he hasn't done, or hasn't done as much or as well, before? What does he most need to work on right now? Finally, response, if it is to be effective, has to view the writing in relation to the student and his ongoing work as a writer. The most keen, incisive evaluation is only as useful as it leads the student to work on his writing. Comments are made *on* student writing but, at their best, they are directed *to* the student writer. When we respond to a text we should be talking with the student behind that text.

Nevertheless, for all this complexity, for all the ways it depends on particular teachers, particular students, and particular classroom contexts, effective response comes down to a simple set of questions. What do I most want to achieve through this writing and this response? What is most important to work on in this paper, with this student, at this time? What is this writer doing well that we can build on? How can I use my comments to help this student learn? It takes time to learn to write well, and it takes time to learn to read student writing closely, according to your priorities, and to respond clearly and engagingly with student writers. But, in time, it can be done well by anyone who gives herself to the task. The responses of these writing teachers show how much can be accomplished.

4

Classroom Instruction, Response, and the Student's Evolving Text: Three Case Studies

In Chapter 1 we looked to identify the strategies that accomplished writing teachers use when they respond to student writing, based on their reading of papers written by students from a variety of settings and gathered into a test group for study. In Chapter 3 we considered how representatives of a new wave of composition teachers, informed about contemporary response, comment on their own students' writing in actual classroom situations. We examined how these teachers responded to one of their students on one of their papers, amid the circumstances of their own courses. Now, in this chapter, I'd like to get an even fuller, more holistic view of teacher response in context, amid the particular circumstances, activities, and goals that animate a writing class and help shape a teacher's responses—in this case, my own writing class and my own written responses. I'll analyze how I responded to three students' writing, on several papers, across a six-week segment of a first-year college writing course, a class I taught over a half-dozen years ago. My aim is to show how response—and a comprehensive study of teacher response—must be tied to the larger work of the class and shaped to the needs of the individual student writer.

The course I'll be examining here, English Composition 1101, is the general freshman writing course at Florida State University, the first of a two-semester composition requirement. The course, as I envisioned it, was a course in writing as a way of thinking, a way of making and sharing meaning through texts. For writing to be writing, it has to have something to say and communicate with readers. It is the *content* of writing—what the writer has to say—that makes writing writing and makes a text worth reading. Paradoxically, it is only through *form* that a writer can discover what he has to say and find ways to shape it for readers to understand. Traditional writing courses emphasize cleanness and clarity: it doesn't matter so much what you say so long as you say it clearly and effectively, without committing errors. Contemporary writing courses are distinguished from such traditional courses insofar as they go beyond a concern for the formal written product, especially the conventional five-paragraph theme, and give students hands-on practice with practicing writing as a social action, a way of saying something to someone else for some purpose, according to the conventions and aims of various communities. Contemporary courses may focus on helping students adapt their writing for various audiences and purposes. They may focus on helping students develop their composing processes or enhance their understanding of writing and reading. They may focus on writing as expression and self-definition. They may focus on the ways that writers must learn to assume various social roles in their writing and negotiate various conventions of discourse, depending on the community for which they are writing. Or they may focus on writing as a way of thinking and learning and a way of sharing one's (newly framed) understandings with others.

In my ENC 1101 course, I took up this last approach and looked to help students develop the content of their writing and share their views with readers. As I told students in the course description:

> Writing is first of all a way of thinking, a way of coming to terms with our experience, ideas, and views. It is also a way of sharing our thoughts with someone else. It is what writers say, their content, that gives writing its value—not correctness, not variety in sentence style, not clearly laid out thesis statements, not good organization. These may all contribute to good writing, but they do not constitute good writing by themselves.

I also emphasized students' improvement over time. The course was designed to immerse students in composition and encourage them to experiment with their writing. I was more concerned with their using writing to say something to someone else, with the possibilities they were opening up, with the signs of their development, than I was with simply correct, competent prose. If what they said mattered to them as writers, it would more likely be worth reading.

Students prepared 16 writings across the semester—seven informal exploratory writings and nine full-fledged essays, most of them in reply to a sequence of assignments on the subject of achievement. We wrote about the same topics at the same time so that we would have a common ground to work from, a set of shared experiences we could talk and think about. The exploratory writings, all of them written during the first half of the course, were informal exercises where students could give their full attention to getting their ideas about achievement down on paper and seeing where they might lead. The formal papers were to be more fully developed and more carefully shaped around a central focus, with an eye toward readers. Seven of them were essays dealing with the subject of achievement, addressed to the other members of the class; two of them (the last two papers in the course) were articles written for a general audi-

ence of newspaper readers, one a feature article on something they knew
a lot about, the other a response to an article they had read. Half of the
writings, especially the informal exploratory writings, were based on
readings, many of them on two novels, *The Great Gatsby* and *The Catcher
in the Rye*; half of them were based on the students' own first-hand experience. Here is an outline of the writing assignments across the semester:

Week 1	Informal Writing 1
Week 2	Informal Writing 2
Week 2	Informal Writing 3
Week 3	Informal Writing 4
Week 3	Essay 1
Week 4	Informal Writing 5
Week 5	Essay 2
Week 5	Informal Writing 6
Week 5	Informal Writing 7
Week 6	Essay 3
Week 8	Essay 4
Week 9	Essay 5
Week 11	Essay 6
Week 12	Essay 7
Week 15	Essay 8
Week 16	Essay 9

Through and through, the course looked to highlight the students' own
ideas and views, the kind of statements that would make them authors in
their own right.

Students were asked to develop casual voices even as they looked to
find ways of talking that would establish their authority. They were
asked to define their own positions, assert their own views, and pursue
ideas that went beyond the obvious and commonplace. They were to
explore their ideas and make a case for their views, not simply argue in
defense of a pre-established thesis. Students were required on occasion to
submit drafts of writing in progress for review and response, and they
were required to write substantive revisions of three papers. But they
could revise as many times as they wanted any paper they wanted; I
would read and respond to as many revisions as they submitted. Each
new writing could be seen in a very real sense as an opportunity for revision, a chance to clarify, extend, and refine their texts and their ideas, a
chance to learn to write better.

"Achievement" was the nominal topic of the course. The real subject, however, was writing, reading, and making and sharing meaning through texts. By looking at different ways writers in the class had taken up the same subject, I hoped to highlight the various strategies writers use to form their ideas in a text and share those ideas with others. By focusing on the same subject again and again, I hoped to prompt more substantive thought and give students practice not just in revising texts but with revisiting, re-envisioning, and deepening their thoughts on a subject, over time—the way practicing writers usually work with a topic: slowly, carefully, repetitively, using their writing to think through, clarify, and develop what they have to say.

In class, we spent the majority of our time talking about samples of the students' own writing. I'd hand out copies of sample papers, ask students to read and mark them up, and then engage them in a discussion about the writing. What do you learn from the essay? What does the paper have to offer to our inquiry into achievement? What passages stand out? What do you like most about the writing? Where do you find yourself not so interested in what the writer has to say? Are there any places where you find yourself unsure or confused? Where you need some explanation? Where you would like to know more? When it went best, our talk would focus on the words on the page and the techniques the writer used to form thoughts into text. From time to time, we would also discuss outside readings on achievement, discuss strategies for developing ideas, examine ways of shaping texts, and engage in peer-responding workshops. But more than anything else, our time in class was spent talking about—and trying to learn from—sample student papers.

We took our talk about developing the content slowly. We moved incrementally from concentrating on getting something more (more thoughtful, more distinctive, more substantive) to say; to developing a casual, talkative voice; to giving substance to key claims through the use of examples, details, and explanations; to extending, qualifying, and complicating ideas already down on the page. We dealt only later in the course, usually only after the fourth or fifth formal paper, with arrangement and matters of wording, sentence structure, and correctness. Even as we worked through this general progression of concerns, my work with students was shaped according to their individual needs. If a student, according to his writing, was not ready to work on new strategies, he was encouraged to continue work on old ones. If someone needed intensive work with their voice, say, or making use of examples, I would make an effort to direct their work back to these concerns.

The course was response-intensive. Students were given comments, however brief, from me or their peers, on almost everything they wrote. The comments were designed to create a dialogue with the writer and connect our moment-by-moment work on a paper with the overall work of the course. The number of writings—and the number of opportunities for response and further writing—allowed me to concentrate on certain concerns at certain times and yet still fit my comments and instruction to the needs of the individual student. I read students' writing with a double focus: one eye on their *writing*, looking at the text before me, in terms of its shape and meanings; one eye on their development as *writers*, as students learning to write, looking at the writing in relation to the student behind the text. I was less interested in the quality of students' texts as discrete written products than I was in the evolving text of their ongoing work in the course and their development, along certain lines, over time, as writers. I looked for places where they were putting (or trying to put) into practice some strategy or feature of writing we'd been working on. I looked for indications that they were experimenting with their writing and trying to push themselves as writers. I looked for occasions when students might be led to try something they had not yet tried or that they had tried but did not (yet) pull off: a sharper way of naming an experience here, a willingness to reach beyond an easily come by thought there, an experiment with a new voice in one paper, an attempt in another paper to develop a key statement that in earlier writing was left standing on its own. My comments on student writing would be only as successful as they enabled me to put these principles into practice and work toward these goals.

In the rest of the chapter, I will examine, as case studies, my responses to three students, on three assignments across the early-to-middle part of the semester: Writing 1, Writing 4, and Writing 5. These three assignments seem optimum for such a study because they came at the heart of the course, from week 3 to week 9, after we had gotten into our inquiry on achievement and as students were bringing the concepts I was looking to value in the course to bear on their own writing. These three students were at different stages in their development as writers and seemed to involve themselves in the work of the course to varying degrees. Their writings and my responses are as representative as any three cases could be of the class as a whole.

I did no lengthy introduction in the course. We dove right in, reading sample essays, talking about our views about what makes writing good, and getting into what would become a semester-long discussion about pursuing goals. In the first two and a-half weeks we read *The Great Gatsby* and did four informal exploratory writings—in effect, discovery drafts— about Gatsby's dreams and their own ambitions. What did they want to achieve through the class? What did they hope to achieve after college? Why does Gatsby pursue Daisy? How does his past, especially his life as a young boy, influence or even instigate his dreams? What did they think about Gatsby's pursuit of money, material goods, and status? I collected these writings one period, read them, and brought copies of selected samples of one or two to the next class for discussion.

I made no responses on the first two exploratory writings, relying instead on our in-class discussion of sample papers to speak for the group as a whole. Students read one another's third exploratory writings, but they made no written comments on the papers. The idea was simply to share their writing with readers, to give them a sense of what others were doing in their papers. I simply marked passages I found interesting with a vertical line in the margin. I wrote comments for the first time on their fourth exploratory writing, addressing a few passages that stood out, usually about the writer's ideas, many of them framed as open questions. I wrote no summary notes at the end of these writings nor made any attempt to grade the work. The comments were meant to lead students to think more fully about the subject and raise issues about their writing. They were also meant to orient students to the kinds of comments I would (and would not) be making throughout the course. I wanted them to get used to comments that were not corrections, criticisms, or missives, but that looked to get into real exchanges with them as writers.

In class during these first couple of weeks I tried to develop a sense of what it means to say something—really say something—to readers in a piece of writing. I looked to lead students to get beyond easily come by thoughts and empty generalizations. I set our sights on searching for richer assertions: ideas that were distinctive, engaging, or thought-provoking, statements that were adequate to the complexity of the subject and that they could substantiate. *Gatsby is obsessed with Daisy because she represents all the material wealth he lacked and the excitement he longed for in his own life.* How do you know? How can you make a case for your claim? Is there anything else wrapped up in his pursuit of this rich girl? Is there anything else you can say—about Gatsby's ambitions, the goals we set for ourselves, your own hopes and dreams? The assignments and discussions—and my responses—were meant to encourage students to pay more attention to the content of their writing and raise the standard of expectations for the writing to come in the class. They were meant to advance our discussion about achievement and prime student's thinking for their subsequent writing. They were meant to help students reconceptualize their views about what makes writing good and convince them that substantive content was within their reach.

Essay 1

The first formal assignment came midway through the third week of the course, after we had read *The Great Gatsby*, completed three exploratory writings on achievement (two of them on Gatsby's dreams), and discussed several of these writings in class. This was the assignment:

> How do you view what Gatsby strives for or how he strives for it? What does his case tell you about a life devoted to achievement? About a life focused on achieving what he hoped to achieve? Do you see yourself having any of the views or anything of the drive that Gatsby has? Are they something you think we should strive for?
>
> Up to this point in the course, we have been practicing writing to discover. You've been looking at your writing as a way of getting your thoughts down on paper and thinking through your ideas and experiences, looking to see where your writing and thinking take you. For this assignment (and all other formal writing assignments) I'd like you to still use your writing as a way of exploring the subject and finding out what you think, but I'd like you, in addition, to shape the writing carefully for yourself and your readers—the members of this class. Instead of allowing yourself to shift, where you would, from idea to idea, or instead of being content to stop after you've done such open-ended exploring, go back over your writing and shape your text in ways that will help you get at your key points and share them with us. In other words, get more selective with what you have to say and what to present to us as readers. What can you tell us that might get us thinking further about achievement and the drive to achieve?

As I told students, I was not intent on them addressing each of these questions. For that matter, I wasn't interested in having them "answer" any of the questions at all. I wanted them, instead, to use the assignment as a point of departure, a prompt for their thinking about achievement. It was fine if they found themselves pursuing only one of these issues or something only tangential to them, just so long as they found a way into the subject that they could make work for them. At this point, I was looking almost exclusively at the content of their writing. I was especially hoping to see students make statements that went beyond what we had been talking about in class, that were somehow distinctive, and that might add to our discussion of Gatsby's dreams. In my responses, I would restrict myself to marginal comments. Because the comments would be tightly focused on ideas and development, I felt no need to provide any larger perspective in an end note.

Rob's Essay 1

Sacrifice for Achievement

Someone who dedicates a portion of their life for achievement has numerous reasons for sacrificing certain aspects of their life. Whether the reason is for money, fame, or for a family the outcome can turn good or bad. In Gatsby's case, the reason was for acceptence into a society he never had a chance of being in and also for a love he wish to fulfill.

How do you sound here? How do you come across? I wonder if this kind of language will help you think about things, as you really see them.

I have the upmost respect for Gatsby. I respect him for his determination to achieve his goals. I also respect him for what he strives for. I can relate to one of his goals that he wishes to accomplish, <u>the goal for acceptence</u>. Speaking from experience, it is a hard task to accomplish. Trying to fit in with the "<u>in-crowd</u>" isn't easy and is often discouraging. I was accepted because of the friends I had made at the beginning of the school year and also I had the advantage of being the "new kid" in school. But for Gatsby, he had no friends in the high class society nor did he have an advantage of wealthy ancestors like the families who live in the East Egg.

I like this idea. Where do you see Gatsby striving for acceptance? What can you do to show that this is the case?

What in-crowd is Gatsby trying to join?

Gatsby never turned his back on a dream and that is what I admire most about him. The one thing that he did achieve was wealth and it was the one thing that he was hoping to capture his dream with. This leads us to his second goal and that was his dream to obtain Daisy. The woman he reaches out for in the night. The woman who brought him to his death. Strange as it may seem, Gatsby was attached to <u>pursuing the goal</u> rather than <u>actually accomplishing the goal</u>. I believe this is reason that Gatsby

Yes—that is admirable, isn't it?

Are the two goals separate and distinct?

Hmm. A nice distinction. I'd like to hear more.

could never have an established relationship with Daisy.

Ever since the age of seventeen, Gatsby had changed his future. Not only did he change his name but also his outlook on life. His motivation for success proved to be one of his best characteristics. Along with this motivation he brought immaturity of the seventeen year old boy he used to be. Gatsby was easily led into the realm of love, which made him very susceptible to the young woman who came across his path and this is what made him long for Daisy so much. I believe that there is no reason to actually sever yourself from your past in order to accomplish any goal or dream. If this was to happen certain problems may occur such as faulty relationships and inevitable occurences of terrible past experiences and nostalgia. These reasons may also be the drawbacks of being self-centered.

Yes, good point. But I don't see how it helps advance the discussion that you started above.

I should hope that neither I nor others should go as far as completely shutting ourselves off from our past in order to achieve a goal or dream, but if I need to make that sacrifice, so be it.

Chris's Essay 1

Who Am I?

Who am I? This statement is often used in trivia, but it should be a question that Jay Gatsby asks himself. In the book *The Great Gatsby* Jay Gatsby is the main character of the story. A puzzling life-style makes it difficult for the people who know Gatsby to understand him. I'm not even sure Gatsby knows himself. Some of the questions that give Gatsby such a confusing life-style are: Is Gatsby really a materialistic man? Why does he strive for Daisy so much?, and What makes him tick?

These are fair questions to ask. I just wonder if you'll be able to go into them all adequately here. Let's see.

Jay Gatsby, an extremely wealthy man, appears to be a materialistic person. By the way he treats people at his parties Gatsby has the image of a cold nonchalant man. If this is true how could he yearn for Daisy so much <u>without even caring for her</u>. A man with his affluence could have just about any woman he wanted in New Jersey. Somewhere behind his materialistic mask has to lie some feelings of kindness in his heart. I believe that Gatsby himself knows that he cares, but he is afraid that if he shows these feelings that his image would be shattered.

Yes.

Doesn't he care for Daisy? It seems she's the one person (at the very least) he cares about.

What in the novel makes you think so?

[It has been determined that] Gatsby does care for Daisy, but why does he strive for her so much? Daisy is married but that still does not deter Gatsby from her. I don't believe that Gatsby wants her just to make her a possession, or to boost his ego by stealing her away from her husband Tom Buchanon. <u>I think it has something to do with Gatsby's past relationship with Daisy</u>. Gatsby and Daisy were together a long time ago and then Daisy went off to marry Tom. <u>I think Gatsby still has feelings for</u>

O.K. Now you're onto something. What is it that captivates Gatsby about Daisy?

Daisy and that he will not give up on her until she commits to him or tells him no for good.

What is that makes Gatsby the way he is? Is it is because of his childhood experiences? Like most I believe it was because of the way he grew up. He grew up with nothing and wanted everything as an adult. Once he achieved wealth and fortune he realized it wasn't what it was cracked up to be. Gatsby is still the farm boy trapped in the body of an affluent person. I think the reason Gatsby acts the way he does is because he has to show the people around him that he is rich and live up to that expectation, when he would actually rather lead a simple lifestyle.

What people is he trying to impress? Where do we see them?

We all lead many different lifestyles and only one is suitable for every individual around. Gatsby tried to lead a lifestyle that was not suitable for him and he ended up to be confusing for him and the people around him. Some of us have masks that we wear for different groups of people.

Interesting.

If the masks are worn to often then we start to lose our individuality. Gatsby had this problem. He tried to lead a life that was not his own. Once a person cannot answer the

What was his life, then?

question Who am I? regarding themselves then their identity is lost. Once a person loses their identity then they will not be happy with what they are doing.

Cherri's Essay 1

Achievement

Achievement is a wonderful thing. Devoting your life to the achievement of your goal is good, but there should be other aspects of your life that are important too. To Gatsby the only thing that mattered was becoming the person he had always dreamed about for so long. Some people might say he was successful because he acquired a great amount of wealth from nothing, but I disagree with that thought. <u>I do not believe that Gatsby was really happy despite all that he had</u>. One must admire him for his hard work, determination, and faithfullness, but he was so focused on achieving his goal that he ceased to notice the world around him. He was too absorbed in himself to even make friends.

What makes you think so? What kept him from being happy? Was it Daisy? Would he be happy with Daisy?

Of course, there are always people at the other end of the spectrum. They have no pride in them selves and no goals. They wonder through life aimlessly never really accomplishing anything. They blame the world for their troubles by saying things like, "No one will hire me cause I'm from the wrong side of town", or "Why should I bother getting a job as long as I can collect unemployment." They believe people should feel sorry for them because they were born the wrong race, sex, or with a lack of money and status. I can relate more to Gatsby's way of thinking than to theirs because he did try to do something with his life instead of just giving up. Gatsby just let his goal become so important that he lost touch with reality. In the beginning I believe Gatsby thought he would be happy once he achieved his goal, but he just set his sights

I like this turn of thought to the other side of things. Where can you take it?

higher and higher <u>until the only thing left that he did not have was the past</u>, which was something even he could not acquire. He never allowed himself time to savor the victory of reaching a goal or enjoy the things that he had acquired, instead he just kept on striving, and for what? In the end there were only two sincere mourners at his funeral.

I'm not sure what you're getting at here. He also didn't have Daisy.

Do you think Gatsby ever comes to any recognition of this?

We should all have high ambitions and we should all strive hard to achieve them, but there are other goals in our lives, such as family, love, and happiness that should be equally important to us. Gatsby had none of these things, only an overwhelming desire to achieve. I think we can all learn from Gatsby's mistakes and set goals that can be balanced by the other things in our lives.

On Rob's Essay 1

This is not a strong paper. Rob leaves his ideas at a high level of generality. He's not sure where he wants to go. He closes off lines of thought as soon as he's about to open them up. His voice often gets in the way of what he has to say. And he writes a number of sentences in the second half of the essay that are flat out confusing. Nevertheless, though they may be easy to overlook, the paper has a number of things going for it. Rob brings a conviction to this essay that every now and then can be heard:

> I have the upmost respect for Gatsby.

> Gatsby never turned his back on a dream and that is what I admire most about him.

He plays with the form of his sentences to give added emotional weight to his ideas:

> I have the upmost respect for Gatsby. I respect him for his determination to achieve his goals. I also respect him for what he strives for.

> This leads us to his second goal and that was his dream to obtain Daisy. The woman he reaches out for in the night. The woman who brought him to his death.

And he opens up several ideas that, while none of them is earth-shattering, have promise. He doesn't settle for the commonplace idea that Gatsby is looking simply to get Daisy herself. He makes a more interesting assertion: Gatsby's goal is acceptance—acceptance, presumably, into the world of the rich and elite. It's an idea that goes against the grain, resists the obvious. He suggests that Gatsby isn't taken so much with Daisy as with the *idea* of Daisy: it's not the prize he seeks, but the seeking itself. And he asserts that we shouldn't separate ourselves from our past in order to accomplish some goal. Our goals, he implies, must be made consistent with who we are and where we have been. Although none of these ideas is developed, all of them, it seems to me, would be well worth exploring.

If the writing looks good or bad in its own right, it looks better in terms of Rob's earlier work in the course. When I read and comment on the text, I am also, no doubt, responding to Rob: the Rob I've seen in class and the Rob I've constructed from his earlier writing. I'm disposed to view the writing more positively than I might not just because of the potential I see in these ideas but because he gets so many more words down on the page than he has in his earlier writings. This first formal essay, in fact, is longer than his first three exploratory writings combined. And yet it seems I come not simply to praise Robert but to challenge him, again, perhaps because of his persona in the class and his earlier work as a writer.

Rob was a former all-state wrestler in high school, and he had brought a clear confidence into the course. He was outspoken—at times argumentative—in our class discussions and quite willing to counter ideas raised by others. He said what he had to say and he said it assertively. In his first four exploratory writings, however, he did not consistently have as much to say as he did in class. He showed some early promise in his first informal writing. His voice was strong at times, and he had something to say:

> I would like to achieve what every person wants to achieve in life: a financial foundation, a home, and most important, happiness. But nothing is handed to you on a silver platter. Hard work and dedication are the answers to achievement.

> Achievement fills the empty space in you. It makes you feel like you're on top of the world and no one can take you down.

But more often he took on the voice of the theme writer and spouted out platitudes:

> The road may be long and discouraging, but if the urge for success is strong enough you will come out on top.

> No matter which circumstance an athlete will come across, achievement is the ultimate reward.

He had served up a smorgasbord of general ideas in his second informal writing but ended up only pushing them around on his plate. He struggled especially when he spoke in a lofty voice: "Gatsby's need for Daisy is one of many strange reasons why he has made it a goal to possess her. His persistent dream of being with her combined with what he is doing to attain her has set the plan for achieving his goal askew." His third informal writing was no better, and his fourth was a brush off. Whereas other students by this point had been writing two or three pages, pushing themselves to find something more to say, Rob settled for four sentences. He was coasting. This won't cut it, I told him in a brief *tête-à-tête* after the class in which I handed back his fourth exploratory writing. You need to do a lot more with these writings or you're not going to make it in this course. Don't wait until it's too late. Now's the time to get going.

So while I come to this first formal essay with a certain overall agenda, looking for what the writer has to say and where I might lead him to say more, I also bring to Rob's paper a certain edge. I ignore the many muddled thoughts in the paper. I focus all of my comments on the content and voice of the essay. I respond positively to a couple of his assertions and follow them up with comments that are meant to lead him to think further about the subject:

S: I can relate to one of his goals . . ., the goal for acceptence.

T: This is an interesting idea—different. Where do you see Gatsby striving for acceptance? What can you do to show that this is the case? What in-crowd is Gatsby trying to join?

S: Strange as it may seem, Gatsby was attached to pursuing the goal rather than actually accomplishing the goal.

T: Hmm. A nice distinction. I'd like to hear more.

Yet I find myself—because I'm in a hurry? because I want to make only a few comments on this assignment? because I'm intent on seeing what he can do on his own? because I'm still put off by his start in the class?—missing some things that are worth praising and instead challenging Rob in my comments. I call into question his stilted voice in the opening paragraph—and yet fail to express my preference for the more straight-forward voice he adopts at the start of paragraph 3. I question his separating Gatsby's quest for wealth from his quest for Daisy, even though it seems he sees the two connected in the previous sentence. I don't spend much time explaining what I like about his ideas or what makes them work. Instead, I quickly note my praise and move on to what remains to be done. At the end of the paper I offer praise with one hand and with the other call him on not pursuing his earlier line of thought: "Yes, good point. But I don't see how it helps advance the discussion that you started above." My comments seem to be prompted just as much by Rob's earlier work in the course as they are by the writing before me. It seems I'm reluctant to really give myself wholly to a constructive response. Perhaps feeling that Rob has been issuing a challenge, I get down on the mat.

On Chris's Essay 1

Chris gives it the old college try in his first formal essay. He offers a lot of statements. He makes use of material from his earlier papers, in line with an invitation I had been making with all the assignments, and he even revises his take on some of these ideas. He makes a couple of statements that would be worth pursuing:

> Gatsby is still the farm boy trapped in the body of an affluent person.

> I think the reason Gatsby acts the way he does is because he has to show the people around him that he is rich and live up to that expectation . . . .

But he takes on too much in this essay—too many ideas that are too general to pursue in one paper. Like Rob, he doesn't pursue ideas, he accumulates them. He is versed in the five-paragraph theme and burdened by his over-reliance on it. I want to impress on him the need to focus his investigation and, more than this, to give substance to his statements. Yet I also want to praise him for the fullness of the content in this paper—especially in light of his earlier work, which (again like Rob's) was not what I had been hoping for.

Chris kept a low profile in class. So much so that I have a hard time conjuring up anything substantial about his classroom persona. As a writer in the first few weeks of the course, he showed a basic fluency— he could write a sentence without making errors and string statements together meaningfully—but little beyond it. His early exploratory writings had followed the worn path and never got out on the open road. His first informal writing was a list of tried-and-true generalizations:

> Goals have to be set in order to have achievements.
>
> By setting goals we are always striving to be better.
>
> Achievements are rewarding to all.

His second exploratory writing featured the same kind of statements and was shorter. His third exploratory writing, however, had more to offer: more words, more substantial assertions, more follow-up statements. He calls Gatsby a curiously uncaring person, wonders why Gatsby longs for Daisy, and sees her as yet another possession he would like to own. He wonders out loud what feelings Gatsby still has for her after all these years: "What these feelings are I'm not sure. Is it love? Is it lust? Or is it something else? Something personal?" I'm encouraged. But then he ends up backsliding on his next exploratory writing, presenting a series of truisms and summarizing Gatsby's childhood but never really investigating how it might have contributed to his later dreams. The paper was only 18 lines long and read like an answer to a test question, not like any investigation into the subject. In my comments I called him on the lackluster quality of his claims and raised questions that might lead him to look at Gatsby's past more closely and come up with more interesting assertions. I also talked with him after class about his work. I was concerned, I told him, about what seemed like a half-hearted effort on this last assignment, especially after the potential I saw in his third exploratory writing. Let's see what you can do, I urged him, to get back on track.

I make 13 comments on Chris's first formal essay. All of them deal with the content of the writing. Four of them praise his ideas, to acknowledge what he's accomplished and build a constructive framework for the rest of my response. One comment questions his claim that Gatsby doesn't care for Daisy, and another expresses my concern about whether he'll be able to deal with all these ideas adequately. Five comments raise questions that are meant to lead Chris to think further about his statements and get at what is underneath them:

> S: I believe that Gatsby himself knows that he cares, but he is afraid that if he shows these feelings that his image would be shattered.

> T: What in the novel makes you think so?

> S: I don't believe that Gatsby wants her just to make her a possession, or to boost his ego by stealing her away from her husband Tom. I think it has something to do with Gatsby's past relationship with Daisy.

> T: OK. Now you're onto something. What is it that captivates Gatsby about Daisy?

> S: I think the reason Gatsby acts the way he does is because he has to show the people around him that he is rich and live up to that expectation.

> T: What people is he trying to impress? Where do we see them?

> S: He tried to lead a life that was not his own.

> T: What was the life he led, then?

More than anything else, the comments look to build on the strengths of the paper and direct his attention to the importance of developing his key statements. Perhaps because his work is looking up, or at least he seems to be working on his writing, I am not nearly as sharp or challenging as I am with Rob on his first formal essay.

On Cherri's Essay 1

Cherri's paper is full of sharp, three-dimensional ideas. She has something to say, and she throws the full weight of her conviction behind it:

> Some people might say he was successful because he aquired a great amont of wealth from nothing, but I disagree . . . .

> He was so focused on achieving his goal that he ceased to notice the world around him. He was too absorbed in himself to even make friends.

> Gatsby just let his goal become so important that he lost touch with reality.

The ideas assert a position and advance beyond the familiar territory of commonplace ideas and our classroom discussion.

Cherri also shows a knack here for bringing ideas together and playing one off another, making her ideas elastic, more venturesome. She starts by presenting an idea that was aired in class—that Gatsby is successful because he becomes wealthy—and then works against it. She acknowledges that Gatsby should be admired for his hard work and determination, and then she blames him for losing a sense of perspective: "One must admire him for his hard work, determination, and faithfulness, but he was so focused on achieving his goal that he ceased to notice the world around him." She suggests that he's too determined to achieve his goals, and then she looks to the other side, at those who look for any easy excuse to relieve them of striving. Such repeated shifting may take a toll on readability, but in these early writings I'm much more concerned with encouraging students to use their writing as a way to learn and get richer thoughts down on the page. I'm especially inclined to be encouraging to Cherri because she has been using her writing to discover something more to say.

From the start Cherri had given herself to the work of the course. A long-time dancer who also taught dance and a student who envisioned a career as a writer, she had the discipline and the motivation to work at her writing. She was involved in our classwork and made regular contributions to our class discussions. She also tried to put into practice the principles and strategies I was advocating, though sometimes less successfully than at others. Her second exploratory writing was given to (and left at) such uninspired claims as "being successful is simply reaching all the goals you set for yourself" and "what is successful to one person may not mean anything to another." Her third exploratory writing made assertions that were sharper and more distinctive. *The Great Gatsby*, she says, is a tragic story of people whose lives were empty despite their countless millions. Gatsby is enamored of Daisy because she represents all the wealth and station he lacked as a young man. Gatsby strives for material wealth in order to impress Daisy and have her as his own. She also took her thinking further in this writing, going back over and explaining some of her key statements, as in the following instance:

> Gatsby seems to be trying to achieve the type of success Daisy would be impressed with. He bought the castle-like mansion just so he could be right across the bay from her, and he decorated it with the dream that someday she would see it and approve of it. All the partys he threw were just so that he might see her or find someone who knew her.

Her writing was more carefully developed in her fourth exploratory writing, but it was also less venturesome. In my comments I encourage her to squeeze more out of her statements. Gatsby went to Oxford, she says, so he could have more time to become wealthy, and I reply, "Why would going to Oxford get him more money? Did he go there just to get more money? What about status?" His search for material wealth, she says, became an obsession "to show the world who he was, or who he thought he was," and I reply, "Okay. But who would you say he was trying to be?" Cherri was looking to make some distinctions in her writing, reaching for something to say, and I want to nudge her to say something more insightful, more revealing. Now, as I'm reading and responding to her first formal essay, I want to continue to encourage her to develop and pursue her ideas.

Never mind about the opening lines. Never mind the various errors and infelicities that mar the sentences. I want to praise the quality of her assertions, reaffirm her willingness to see things complexly, from different sides, and push her to think further, to get even more to say. I praise several of her assertions, matter-of-factly, and ask her, through a series of open questions, to consider her ideas further:

> Nice—it goes against the grain. What makes you think so? What kept him from being happy? Was it Daisy? Would he be happy with Daisy?
>
> I like this turn of thought to the other side of things. Where can you take it?
>
> Do you think Gatsby ever comes to any recognition of this?

I try to stick with ideas that are strong and worth developing. All nine of my comments focus on ideas and development. Two of them praise her ideas, two of them moderately criticize her ideas, and six of them present open questions that are meant to push her thinking. Cherri is making gradual improvements in her thinking and writing, and I want to keep the conversation between us upbeat and positive.

In responding to these first formal essays, then, I make only a handful of marginal comments and no end comment. I want to keep my comments short and sweet. Thirty-two of my 35 comments across these three papers are focused on ideas and development. None is concerned with local matters. Over half of the comments are framed as open questions. I make at least two praise comments on each paper and only one moderate criticism. My purpose at this time is to work with what the writer already has on the page, not work against it. I try to keep students' attention on developing the content of their writing, and I try to keep my comments constructive. Presenting only a smattering of comments in the margins is also a matter of time. I don't want to put too much into these responses, given that it's still early in the course and given their limited purpose: to lead students to look to say more in their subsequent writing. I'll save more detailed comments for Essays 3, 4, and 5, after we've had a chance to get a clearer sense of what we're looking for in the way of writing that "has something to say."

Essays 2 and 3

Over the next five weeks we wrote two more papers (one exploratory writing and one formal essay) on *The Great Gatsby*, read *The Catcher in the Rye*, and wrote three papers (two exploratory writings and one formal essay) on Holden Caulfield's views toward achievement. Most of our time in class was given to discussing samples of the students' own writing and coming to terms with the key concepts of the class: working against commonplace ideas, discovering something distinctive to say, getting at ideas through precise wording and substantive detail, and talking *with* readers, not writing down to them. We also read several published essays on achievement, by students and professional writers, and discussed their ideas and the strategies they used to get at what they had to say.

I commented briefly on the fifth exploratory writing, asked students to respond to one another's sixth exploratory writing, and responded in detail to their seventh (and final) exploratory writing. Each time the focus was entirely on ideas and development. Later, I commented more fully on Essay 2 and Essay 3, concentrating again on voice and content, again with the aim of helping students see how they could develop the thought of their writing. On returning each of these papers, I'd make a point to explain what I was trying to do with my comments. I'd also ask them to respond to my responses, to see which comments they found most useful and which they found less useful or not useful at all. It was part of an ongoing effort to re-orient students to the nature and goals of my comments and underscore the importance of response in the course.

On Rob's Essays 2 and 3

Rob followed his modest successes on Essay 1 with a bold effort on Essay 2. He takes exception to the ideas in a fellow student's paper we discussed in class and forcefully asserts his views. Gatsby is no tragic hero; he's no hero at all. Gatsby, he says, is "a man that can be admired for his dedication to achievement and nothing else." In my marginal comments I praise his strong stands. I also challenge him to make a more convincing case for several of his key claims and urge him to take only as strong a stand as he can really get behind and make a case for:

> S: Gatsby hasn't donated anything to society but crime, the crime of boot-legging and other illegal activities, to achieve his wealth.

> T: On the list of criminal ways of getting ahead, though, you have to admit this one is not all that bad. Or is it? Can you convince me by your writing that you really think this is a deplorable way of advancing?

S: Gatsby's drive for success had no limitations.

T: And this you see as a flaw. OK—fine. Now how about helping us understand why you think so.

S: I believe that Gatsby never achieved any of his goals.

T: None of them? Wasn't wealth and success a goal for him?

In my end note, I try to push him to think further about his claims and
consider how they might be developed:

> I appreciate the strong stand. You seem pretty convinced that
> Gatsby is Not a Hero with a tremendous flaw. I don't question
> your views about whether he's a hero. I do wonder, though, if
> this represents fully what you think of Gatsby. Do you see noth-
> ing admirable in him beyond his drive? This may be—and that's
> fine. But how can you go back and establish this case some-
> how—perhaps by discussing how you see those things that peo-
> ple who admire him would like or appreciate. For instance, can
> you so singularly reject Gatsby when you admit that he's
> admirable for his drive, his dreaming? Can this drive be seen
> only as "ambition"? Or is there more to it? Do you think Nick is
> way off in his admiration (his qualified admiration) for Gatsby?
> You see, there are things to say here that would lead you to think
> further about Gatsby's flaws and strengths, so you might come
> to a firmer understanding of what you think, whatever that
> understanding is.

His next formal paper, on Holden Caulfield's notion of achievement,
seems to build on his last performance. The central claim of the essay is
that Holden himself is phony, adopting the very qualities he despises in
others. The writing sticks with this issue, and it is much more detailed
than his earlier writing. When he presents examples, he uses them to
develop his points, not simply illustrate them. Holden himself is a phony
because he "puts on an act to make others believe something he is not."
When he meets his classmate's mother on the train, he "gets off lying to
her." When he meets the three girls in a bar in New York, he lies. "Trying
to charm the girls would be very difficult if he was to be himself," Rob
explains, "so he becomes someone he's not." Instead of moving to a new
paragraph and a new point altogether, he pursues this line of thought:
"The difference between these two events is that Holden criticizes the
three girls but not the lady on the train only because he felt like he was
accepted by the lady. When Holden persists putting on these false acts it
is inevitable that he will be caught in a net full of phonies." But he's not
done yet. The image of Holden caught in a net of his own making

prompts another thought, one that works against a common assumption, which he pursues without introduction. Holden is not a *"catcher* in the rye" but a child who needs to be *caught.* Just like that, he's on his way. And I tell him so in my comments.

On Chris's Essays 2 and 3

On Essay 2 Chris takes to heart the concerns I expressed on his first formal essay and begins to do some of the things we'd been talking about in class. He focuses his writing right from the start, begins to go into some key statements, brings other views into his discussion, and at one point even pursues an idea through an image, something he had not done before. I responded to seven passages in the margins. Three of them praise his work and look to reinforce the moves he makes:

> I like the way you get right at a focused issue here. You seem determined to figure this out—and that can't help but engage your readers, I would think.

> I like the way you are dealing with these alternate possibilities, thinking through them.

> Hmm. I appreciate your speculation.

Three of them look to make him stretch and get more into his arguments:

> S: If Gatsby wanted to make her a possession I think he would have tried to impress her with his money and affluence.

> T: Some might argue that this is exactly what he was trying to do. What would you say in reply?

> S: Gatsby set his heart and his mind on Daisy. He went into the army and when he came out Daisy married Tom Buchanan.

> T: Do you think she grew in his mind while they were apart?

> S: Gatsby is a man to be admired. He was actually a caring man with a lot of determination.

> T: What makes you think he was "caring"? I'm interested to know.

On Writing 3 he does some more good work with providing examples and playing one view off another. I'm happy to see him doing more to get at and illustrate his points, but at the same time I want to push him to look for more from the examples he chooses. I call on him to seek better examples in one passage and congratulate him on a stronger example in another:

> S: Because Holden is not sure what he wants to do with his life, remain an innocent child or become a mature adult he often does things to act like an adult and other times like an child. For example when Holden went to the bars to get drunk that is definitely the adult side of him. Even when he tells Maurice to send up a girl to his room is an act of an adult.

> T: I am glad for the examples. Though I wonder if there aren't even better ones around—ones that get at his conflict about becoming an adult.

> S: Other times he acts like a child. With the question about the ducks and where they go for winter is something a young child would ask.

> T: Now this is an example I appreciate.

Still, his ideas lack vigor and he again runs into trouble with his focus. I challenge the quality of his assertions in a couple of places, for instance:

> S: Adolescence, the stage between childhood and adulthood, is one of the toughest stages in life that everyone goes through in their development.

> T: I know you know this, Chris, but you're not telling us anything we don't already know here.

And then, at the end of the paper, I point to the problems with his taking on so many different topics:

> You seem to be taking up these issues in the manner of answering an essay question, Chris. It seems you take up three different topics on the page, and don't really try to see them in terms of one another. I'd think you'd be more likely to engage our interest if you focused in on one of these issues and pursued it. Which one would you choose—and where would you go with it?

Chris is making some progress, and I want to let him know that I'm noticing it. But he is not making as much progress as I'd like to see. I try to be patient and wait for him to get more to work with in his writing. There's still a lot of writing ahead, and a good deal of time.

On Cherri's Essays 2 and 3

Cherri follows her success on Essay 1 with a paper that is more substantive but still in need of development. In *The Great Gatsby*, she writes, it seems as if everyone is striving for something they cannot reach. This fruitless striving makes all of them unhappy. She looks to establish these points through two examples. My responses look to turn the strengths in the paper into springboards for more insightful thinking and richer writing. I praise several of her assertions, nod along in agreement at others, and sometimes use my assent to instigate further thinking:

> Hmm. So you see Daisy as somehow only part of his dream, and a necessary limitation on it. You may be right. I'd like to see more thoughts on your view.

> So how does this relate to his ultimate goal of achieving his ideal conception of himself? What does his not being happy say about this conception? Is it related to why Gatsby is referred to (like Wilson) as a "ghost"?

> So you think he gets no sense of pleasure from the objects themselves or from having attained them? What would this say about what he is striving for? What does it say about what he expects out of Daisy?

In my end note I look to build on her ideas:

> You come to a number of provocative ideas and issues in this essay. What I like about it is the way your sentences prompt me to think about Gatsby's goals and failures, the way your statements lead to other ideas. My questions are meant to show you the kind of thinking they led me to do and to suggest areas for you to think about further.

Cherri grinds out statements that are similarly interesting but only half-realized in Essay 3, where she claims that success for Holden Caulfield means never losing the innocence of childhood. But the writing comes alive midway through the paper when she relates Holden's predicament to her own experience. That's where I start to comment:

> S: To Holden, success was simply never allowing himself to lose the innocences of childhood, to never grow up. I guess that is why I can identify with Holden's character so much.

> T: With this statement, I'm hooked. I want to know more.

> S: I can remember when I was younger I use to believe that my life would be over after graduating from high school. I never really thought passed that point in time. I remember that all my friends were so eager to grow up and all I wanted was to be young forever. They thought all their problems would be solved simply by growing up. They did not want to go to school or have to listen to their parents, but along with growing up goes lots of responsibilities such as bills, careers, and families of their own.

T: Can you see how you could really take off with this writing—
and really learn something about this issue—if you had gone
into real-life details that are important and close to you?

S: These were all things I did not want to deal with yet, but
despite my feelings, I finally realized that growing up was not
all that bad. So I decided to make the best of it. I take care of my
responsibilities such as school, work and bills first, but I try to
always remember what it was like to be young. I believe that is
what will always keep me young at heart. I think if Holden
could just learn to grasp this thought then maybe he too could
be happy.

T: What, specifically and really, were the "things" you did not
want to deal with? What bills? What career choices? What family concerns? Here's where you can make the paper yours.

S: If he would compromise a little with his feelings then he
might realize that accepting responsibility does not mean giving
up all the wonderful things about youth forever.

T: A rich idea. I'd love to hear more about it.

My comments praise her efforts and look to build on her successes. I was
taken with the way the writing takes off when she turns to her own experience, with the way it opens up possibilities for further inquiry, and I
brought it into class for a full-group discussion. At this point in the
course, seven weeks into the semester, I wanted students to start making
the move from examining their common experience about the novels to
exploring their own personal experience. I wanted them to look for even
more to say and really get behind their assertions. Cherri's paper provided a perfect case for talking about the transition. The discussion brought
out both the strengths and the weaknesses of the paper. But I was interested mainly in bringing out the *promise* in these ideas. Before I handed
the paper back, I added a note at the end that I hoped would capture the
excitement generated by our talk in class and encourage her to reach further into her thoughts:

As I hope I made it clear in my discussion in class, you've got a
number of solid ideas that you take up here and that you begin
to pursue. I think you're on the verge here of breaking this
paper, this topic, open. Can you see what it would take to do so?
Nice work.

It was a rallying cry that I hoped would have immediate pay-offs.

Essay 4

Writing 4 was assigned during the middle of week 7 and was due at the end of week 8. It was the first paper that was to be based primarily on students' own experiences. Like the earlier assignments, this one directed students to consider a general topic but left them to decide what specific subject they would explore. The prompt itself was followed by several questions that were meant to offer specific issues that they might consider:

> Identify something in your past that you wanted to achieve and use this experience as an occasion or instance for explaining how you go about striving for a goal. You may address what frame of mind you adopt in striving for such a goal or examine how you actually go about pursuing it. On the basis of this experience, what can you say about how you look at, or how you go about, striving for goals?

> Here are some questions to consider:

>> What can you say about what motivated you to pursue this goal? (Is this something you want to go into?)

>> What attitudes did you have toward the goal? Were you enthusiastic from the start? Did you feel any reluctance?

>> How would you describe how you went about the task of trying to accomplish the goal? Is there anything about your process of striving for the goal that stands out for you? Is there anything that helped you achieve it or that maybe got in the way of achieving it?

>> Is the way you looked at or went about trying to accomplish this goal the way you have typically gone about pursuing goals?

> As in our previous formal essays, use your writing to discover what you can add to our classroom conversation about achievement and share your thoughts with readers. But make an additional effort, as you are writing or as you go back over what you have already got down on the page, to form your paper into a unified essay, where each of the parts looks to achieve a certain purpose and contributes to the whole.

Now that we were half way through the course, with three formal essays and seven weeks of work behind us, I was expecting students to come up with more to say—something that was somehow distinctive, that would interest readers, and that would add to our classroom conversation. Working with a common subject matter drawn from books helped us to see how having something to say could be seen as a matter of working within and against what others have said, getting at those ideas by tying them to specific words and experiences, and making a case for our views.

Now by working with their own experiences I hoped students would have better, more accessible material to work with and come to assume a greater authority over what they said. I was looking for them, now more than ever, to reach for something to say that was in some sense original—if not new in some foundational sense, at least originally synthesized by them. I was also interested in paying more attention to the overall shape of their writing. As I told students, I wanted to consider how the quality of a writer's ideas depended to a large extent on the way they were expressed and put together. I wanted them to take greater care with how they started and ended their essays, which ideas they went into and which ones they addressed only briefly, and how they arranged their material. Over the next week we discussed several samples of Essay 3 and, in addition to talking about developing the content of their writing, we talked about shaping an essay around a single point and making each part of the paper pull its weight for the whole. I was hoping that once students began thinking more pointedly about how ideas are constructed in texts that they would be in position to make real gains in what they had to say and how effectively they shared their thoughts with readers.

Rob's Essay 4

Untitled

I feel so much like Brad in the story "Rick". I know what it feels like having a coach on your back. And to tell you from the start, its not fun.

This past year (senior year in high school) was the best wrestling season for me and the team. We accomplished many goals in the four month duration of wrestling season, not only did we go undefeated, we were District Champions, Regional Champions, and State Runner-Ups. I had also accomplished many personal goals. I was the only undefeated wrestler on the team and along with this came District Champion, Regional Runner-Up, and I had taken fourth place in the state wrestling tournament. All this may seem much, but it really isn't. I could have done much better and to know this makes me feel incomplete.

My explanation of this feeling may be confusing, so I'll try to explain carefully. When the concept "what if. . ." comes to mind, I think, "what if I had practiced harder, could I have won? Could I have done better?" This thought would run through my mind millions of times, after all of the five wrestling matches I lost during the season. Anybody could relate to this situation, even if you were involved in academics rather than athletics. This concept is so true, that it bothers me to know I could have done much better. To sooth my anger and depression, I tell myself what I've done and accomplished and say "It's better than nothing!"

Towards the end of my junior year we found out that our coach was transferring to a new school. Who was to take over? We didn't know. We heard numerous rumors of other coaches from around our district wanting to come to Northern High School and also of a wrestler just graduating from Ohio State University. It wasn't until the end of our junior year when the news came that Bret Smith, the captain of the O.S.U. wrestling team, was to be the next wrestling coach at Northern High.

It wasn't until the last week of October, during our senior year, that I had finally met Coach Smith. Standing at 5'5", 155 pounds, and built like a bull was the man that we would be calling "coach". When coach gathered the future varsity wrestlers for a meeting he told us right off the bat what our goal, as a team, was going to be: "I want a state title from you guys — nothing more, nothing less!" Once the words "state title" came out of his mouth, I knew what kind of season laid ahead.

I fortold the future! Every practice was like another day in hell and Coach was the devil. Our two hour practices would seem like eternity and from all the constant wrestling in the room the temperature would go from 65° to 85° in less than an hour. Finally, at the end of practice, exhausted and irritated from cutting weight we walk back into the locker room. These hell sessions, we call practices, would take place two hours a day, six days a week, from October to February. During these months we would wrestle thirteen dual meets and six tournaments. As a team we would place either first or second and only once placing third.

After every practice, before every match or tournament, Coach would talk to us like no other person could talk: not like a parent, teacher, nor a friend, but as a god talking to his disciples. We were his people and he was our leader. We obeyed all his commands.

Even though we've been through hell and back, everything paid off at the end. All the hard work, sweat, and pain was taken out on our opponents. To loose would be a disgrace to the team and the consequences at the next practice would be severe. I was on the mat to please Coach and myself and no one else. My reputation and Coach's reputation was on the line every match I wrestled.

I owe some of my success to coach, without him I wouldn't have been able to do all that I have done. Only if Brad (in "Rick") could understand what his coach was trying to do he would have never reacted as he did. In athletics, you need someone to push you, because sometimes you can't always rely on yourself to win.

End Comments on Rob's Essay 4

Rob—

Reading this paper, I see a lot of reason for celebration. The writing is up front, dramatic, and engaging; in it I see you trying to come to terms with your experiences and share your views with us as readers. I also see a number of areas where you might do some more work to make what is already a good paper even better—and along the way further develop some techniques I see you start to use effectively here. I think the combination of strengths and areas to work on is what led to the rich discussion we had last week in class about your paper.

One of the strengths I see in this writing is the way, in a number of places, you get at your experience concretely and specifically, in a way that will make your words *mean* something to me and other readers. For example, on page 1 you don't simply say that the wrestling team accomplished many goals; you go back over the ground and indicate what exactly you accomplished: "not only did we go undefeated, we were district champions, regional champions, and state runner-ups." You do the same kind of going over an idea but with greater detail in paragraph 5, where you describe Coach Smith's demanding, charismatic character by quoting his first words to you as a team: "I want a state title from you guys—nothing more, nothing less!" It seems that you both capture the image you want in those words. I also like the way you characterize his talk in paragraph 7, where you tell us that he "would talk to us like no other person" and then go on to say, more precisely, more emphatically, "not like a parent, teacher, nor a friend, but as a god talking to his disciples." Good way to get at his compelling style. Well done. Now that you have used your fine-point pen on passages like these, go back to the paper and note where you might have done more of this specific naming, more of this following through on your descriptions, to get at them more fully and share them with readers. Do you see what you might have done, just for one instance, with your description of wrestling practice as a day in hell?

Another strength, another thing I really like about this paper, is that you have something to say, something beyond the obvious and routine, something that you've come to through this experience as a wrestler. You describe your accomplishments, say that you did not accomplish all that you might, and then introduce your new coach as the person behind (so much of?) your success.

The stage is set. You've got me with you. But you don't return to the question raised at the start. You don't examine why all this hard work and inspired coaching did not, in the end, bring you the championship. I'm curious to know why you build up Coach so much, why you tell us all the ways he pushed and inspired you and your teammates to accept nothing short of winning, but then find yourself saying that you did not practice hard enough, did not reach your potential, and let yourself down. (The statement you make toward the end of the essay, that "everything paid off at the end," doesn't really do it. It's too easy, too worn, too pat, and it doesn't square with the disappointment you admit in the second paragraph, after you failed to win the state championship.) I sense that the paper is about more than just the dynamism of Coach Smith—that it has to do somehow with the limits of coaching. Or possibly with your limits as a wrestler. Is there anything you could do to clear this up, or to push your thinking beyond the effects that this new coach had on you and your team? You seem to have arrived at a crossroads in the paper, at a juncture in your thinking that's important but that you haven't worked out. This is the place you want to be in the kind of writing we are working on in here. Now let's see what you can learn—and share with us—by going down one of these roads and wrestling with what happened with your season of wrestling last year.

Good work in this writing. Keep at it.

Chris's Essay 4

Climbing the Mountain of Achievement

When I was little my father told me that I could do anything I wanted to as long as I put my mind to it. This advice has helped me through a lot of struggles as well as a lot of accomplishments. These are the words I took to attain many of the goals I reached.

It all started when I was old enough to understand what achievement was about. I would set a goal for myself and put my mind to it that I could reach that goal. For example, I wanted to save my allowance to buy this neat toy, a complete set of plastic military people including the enemy. I always liked the set of plastic figures because they let your imagination run wild with all the different battles you could come up with. At a price of $5.95 making $1.00 a week I thought it would be impossible. However I kept a positive attitude and with the loss off a tooth I was able to get my military set in five weeks. I was extremely happy not only because I got the toy I wanted, but also because I reached my goal.

I also set goals after that but the most significant goals I accomplished came in the eighth grade. The year before I had a rough year. I was constantly in trouble for talking, and because I would never get any of my punishments signed I ended up spending most of my time in the Dean's Office. At the end of this year my counselor, Mr. Byrd, told me that if I were to make the National Junior Honor Society that he would pay me ten dollars. The next year when I came back I asked him if the wager was still on. He respond with a yes from that moment on I focused on my schoolwork not the gossip. I now spent time in the classroom instead of the Dean's Office. The first grading period I got a 3.5. I had done this before, but my behavior had always kept me off the honor role. This time it was different. The next period I got a 4.0. I didn't think I could do it until my P.E. teacher said that I could. I set my mind to getting straight A's and I did it. I was then inducted in the NJHS, and yes Mr. Byrd stuck with his bet. This was one of the most happiest moments of my life. I was not only $10 dollars richer but I had reached another one of my goals.

This was also the year of the eighth grade trip to Washington, D. C. I wanted to go very badly the only problem was that the trip was over $400 dollars, and at that time my parents could not afford to pat for the whole trip. What they agreed to do however was to pay for half. I was excited I only had to come up with $200 dollars in two and a half months. The only problem was that I would not have the money by saving my allowance alone. So I decided to try and start washing cars. I then started to baby sit and a couple of lawn jobs came into the picture. By the end of the time period I had saved enough money to go on the trip and I even had some left over for spending money. The trip was great, but I think what made it great was because it was my trip, a trip I helped pay for.

Another one of my great accomplishments came in eighth grade when I entered the school science fair. For my science class we had to do a research paper and it was optional for us to enter our project in the fair. I figured that since I was doing all the work for the paper I might as well enter the fair and get the extra credit that was being offered. This was only the second project that I had ever done and I thought my chances of winning were impossible until I talked with my teacher. She had faith in me and thought that my earthworm project would do well in the competition. I then set out to win it all. I did not win but I came in second and my project was chosen to be entered in the County Science Fair. I had no hopes of winning. The competition was even tougher than the school fair. The next morning my science teacher called me at home to inform me that I got first place in my category. I was shocked. The girl that beat me in the school fair didn't even place in county. I then went to the State fair and I did not win. I was not upset in the least bit. Just to make it to States was an accomplishment in itself.

After I made it through the eighth grade after all the accomplishments I had I was able to do just about anything that I put my mind to, just like my father told me. I went on to have many more accomplishments and failures went along with them. I usually try to look at my failures and make the best of them and to learn from my mistakes. Anytime I set a goal I get it in my mind that I can reach that goal. An interesting technique that I learned has helped me obtain some of my recent goals. When I set out to do something I picture myself going through the events to reach that goal. After watching myself reach that goal so easily in my thoughts then it makes it that much easier to reach that goal in real life.

End Comments on Chris's Essay 4

Chris—

It seems that the point this writing and these examples are designed to make is stated in the first and last paragraphs. It goes something like this: you can do anything you want as long as you put your mind to it. Your paper is an attempt to show how you put this view to work in several goals that you achieved both as a youngster and in your early teens. You do well to help your readers see what you've accomplished in your past. Four full-length examples. I'm glad to see the detail, and I appreciate your attempts to make fuller use of your experience to illustrate your ideas. A step in the right direction. Still, as I read the essay, I find myself wanting to learn more from your examples. Even after I finish it, I feel I've discovered only a little about how, in each of these sample cases, you used your father's advice. Although you offer more examples and fuller examples than in your earlier papers, you don't really use them to help you look more closely at this idea about achievement. The examples don't quite develop or support the claim that achievement is (to a large extent?) a matter of "putting your mind to it."

I also have some doubts about the significance of your main idea, about its ability to capture what (all) was involved in achieving these goals. Can you achieve anything you want so long as you put your mind to it? Is having the right attitude all it takes to achieve? Was there something else involved in reaching these goals than "putting your mind to it"? Maybe I'm not seeing all that you mean by "putting your mind to it." Or maybe you are not seeing what's involved in these achievements as fully as you might.

Nevertheless, I like the way you start to work through these examples in order to illustrate this idea about setting your mind on what you want to achieve—and, even more than simply illustrating this point, to work with it, to consider how it contributes to your efforts.

Let's see what you can make of our talk about the examples in the paper from today's class discussion. Let's see how you can *use* your examples to greater effect in your next papers.

Cherri's Essay 4

Dancing Dreams

I always wanted to be a dancer when I was younger. I took every class I could get in to, bought the best dance shoes and tryed very hard to do my best, but unfortunately I wasn't very good. It was a real disappointment too because I really wanted to be good. I always came to class on time, and paid attention, but the harder I tryed the more frustrated I became. It seemed I was surrounded by these beautiful, long-legged girls who were just dripping with talent. They could skip class, or come in late and they never had problems with anything. My teacher would try to encourage me by telling me that I had a lot of discipline, but what good was discipline when the others could dance circles around me? I didn't want to quit, but I had become so frustrated that I was absolutely miserable.

One day after my class my teacher ask me if I would like to assist her in teaching a class of preschoolers. I was honored that she would ask me, but I terrified at the same time. How could I teach when I wasn't that good of a dancer in the first place? After my first few weeks of teaching that question was completely forgotten. I had spent so long struggling that I had realized not every one is a natural, so I broke down the steps and did them slowly the way I had always wished some one would have done with me, and once they got the basics I gave the better talented student more challenging things to keep them from getting bored. I tried to make games out of all our exercises so class wasn't all work and no play. My system of teaching worked great, and the kids seemed to be hav-

What couldn't you do—or do as well as others—that made you "not very good"? Can you give me some idea?

This sentence speaks volumes—crisp and yet rich.

"Anything" like what? One or two quick particular things would go a long way here.

How to give us something that would help us see this frustratioin better. Would a particular time do?

Was this a usual thing for her to do?

I'd love to see a sampling of how you "broke down the steps."

Now why would I underline this phrase?

Or this one? Which other phrases would you mark here?

ing fun as well as learning the basics of dance. My teacher also gave some of the other girls I danced with their own classes. They were all great dancers, but a lot of them had problems with their classes. They did things too fast, and expected the kids to get things right on the first try. They were always yelling at the kids, and complaining that their kids weren't learning anything. That is when I realized that just because I wasn't such a great dancer did not mean that I was a complete failure. My gift was not dance itself, but teaching. I was so happy when I did a good job teaching that being a great dancer did not matter as much any more. That is when I noticed another change, my dancing was actually starting to improve. I wasn't as frustrated as before and things just started to come easyer. The next year I was awarded the lead part in my dance resital and two additional classes to teach. I'm still not the best dancer in my class, but I found out that I do have a special talent which means more to me than being the best dancer in the world.

I always think of my teaching when ever I set myself a goal in life. Whenever I start striving for a new goal I try to keep an open mind. If I had been to scared to accept the teaching job, or to set in my goal of becoming a great dancer and not taken the chance then I would have never found my hidden talent. That is why I try to keep an open mind about my goals. That way if something I have my heart set on doesn't seem to be working out I can stand back before I get too frustrated and maybe see a different approach to what I'm doing, or see a different aspect of my goal that I had never really thought about before. One of my current goals is to be a fictional writer some day. Hopefully I will be able to achieve that goal, but I'm sure I'll change my mind several times along the way.

Marginal comments:

✓✓✓
See the way you begin to make the previous statement mean more by going into the next ones?

Here's an insight. I like the way you put it.

Interesting.

By now, do you know why I'm underlining this part of the sentence? Is it a strong way to say what you mean? Or a weak one?

I didn't realize you were scared. You didn't say anything to indicate that earlier.

This seems in line with what you were getting at earlier.

End Comments on Cherri's Essay 4

Cherri—

By the end of the paper, I can begin to see what you mean when you say that you try to keep an open mind about goals in order to avoid frustration and in order to keep (I suppose) other possibilities open for yourself, other goals you come across along the way. I am able to get this much from those words because of what you do by way of giving me the background of your dancing/teaching experience earlier in the paper. In fact, I can make only as much meaning of these words as the words around them allow me to make. You do a pretty good job setting up this experience, allowing me to see what happened and how you felt. I see the general pattern of events you're talking about. But I think I need to see more—and, more importantly, that you need to see more of what happened—before we can get a clearer sense of what you mean when, at the end of the paper, you make those potentially rich statements about an open mind, frustration, different approaches, and different aspects of your goals. Can you see where you might have looked more closely at some of these experiences and thereby come to see more about this frustration and open-mindedness and how you came to make them work for you and not against you?

You create a sound framework for this talk about how you achieved by letting go of one goal and taking up another, related goal. You put yourself in a position to tell us something about achievement that we might not know—or that we could not know, since it is *your* experience that you're talking about. There's a lot in here to be happy about. Now, let's see what you can do to work with these strengths and to work on developing other areas of your writing to take your efforts even further. You are on your way.

On Rob's Essay 4

Rob's topic was prompted by a published student essay that we read and discussed after I handed out the fourth assignment, a personal essay about a high-school swimming coach named Rick who drives his team to the very brink of their tolerance but in the end elicits from them their very best performance. The essay spurred a lively debate, and Rob was at the center of the talk, arguing in no uncertain terms for the effectiveness of such demanding coaches. In his paper, Rob draws on his own experience and applauds a coach who, through his passion for winning and the respect he commands, pushed his team to excel. But he doesn't just reiterate the commonplace: yes, I too know the struggles of being pushed by a coach only to come out stronger in the end. And he doesn't simply illustrate the idea through his own experience. He works with and against this idea, using it to try to make sense of what happened to him as a high-school wrestler, showing on the one hand how the team was inspired by this coach, and struggling on the other hand with the fact that he did not do his very best. Through the essay he seems to be wondering how an athlete could have such a coach, such a motivating presence, and *not* achieve all he has the potential to achieve.

In this writing, as in his last year at wrestling, Rob may not achieve all that he might. But, again, he accomplishes a lot. In it, I see him making a number of moves that I've been looking for students to make. He grounds the writing in his own ideas, views, and experiences. He works at creating a voice. He is generous with detail. He often goes back over general statements to give them substance and make them meaningful for readers. And he comes up with a number of powerful statements, among them:

> I know what it feels like having a coach on your back. And to tell you from the start, its not fun.

> All this may seem much, but it really isn't. I could have done much better and to know this makes me feel incomplete.

> Every practice was like another day in hell and Coach was the devil.

> After every practice, before every match or tournament, Coach would talk to us like no other person could talk: not like a parent, teacher, nor a friend, but as a god talking to his disciples. We were his people and he was our leader. We obeyed all his commands.

> I was on the mat to please Coach and myself and no one else.

He also plays effectively with the arrangement of the story, at the start noting his success, then revealing his regrets at not having done better, and only then taking us back to the start of the season and telling us about the arrival of the new coach and the allegiance he inspired. He does well to set a scene, something we had been talking about in class, when he first introduces Coach Smith:

> It wasn't until the last week of October, during our senior year, that I had finally met Coach Smith. Standing at 5'5", 155 pounds, and built like a bull was the man that we would be calling "coach." When coach gathered the future varsity wrestlers for a meeting he told us right off the bat what our goal, as a team, was going to be: "I want a state title from you guys—nothing more, nothing less!"

And he makes use of repetition to drive home his vision of these practice sessions as a sort of hell. Throughout the paper, in fact, he seems to be experimenting with form in order to elicit certain effects. There is plenty to be pleased with in the paper.

Still, there are things to be done with this essay—and, just as importantly, things to learn from it. The paper doesn't do as much as it might in getting at what made these practices hellish and what made Coach Smith's coaching so effective. It also doesn't follow through on the issues it raises, promisingly, about how his achievements as a senior wrestler, although substantial, really did not amount to much, why he feels he could have done much better, and what role his coach played (and perhaps could *not* play) in his accomplishments. After all the words he devotes to setting up his coach as a key force behind his success, Rob ends up with only a modest claim about his impact: "I owe some of my success to coach, without him I wouldn't have been able to do all that I have done." It's clear that Coach Smith pushed him and that Rob sees this motivation as important to his success. "I was on the mat to please coach and myself and no one else," he says. But he stops short of indicating just how important he was—and how and where he himself fell short. I want to see more on how this motivation worked. How did Coach Smith lead him to put his own reputation as a wrestler and his reputation as a coach on the line when he wrestled? I want to know what kept him from doing as well as he could, given all this prompting from his coach. It is the tension between these two reactions—my delight in seeing what he's done in this paper, my sense that there's so much more that he *can* do now that he's gotten this far—that animates my response. It is the fullest piece of writing he's done so far in the class, and I want to run with it.

I did not make comments right away on Rob's paper. I decided to work with it in our next class, and I wanted to make clean copies before marking it up. But time ran out, and I never got a chance to go back to make comments on the paper before class. We spent a whole period on the essay, identifying strengths and areas to work on, talking in detail about specific passages, and leaving a number of issues fruitfully up in the air. The discussion went so well—and I was so busy after class getting last-minute responses to other students—that I told Rob I'd get my written comments to him on Monday. It would be just as well. Rob could glory in what we'd said and think on his own for a while, without my direction or interference, about how he might address the issues we had raised in our discussion. At the same time, I could do the work I wanted to do with this writing. When I did respond, I made no marginal comments. I decided instead to turn my comments into my own sort of pep talk and challenge.

My strategy in the response is simple: to focus on two strengths in the paper and then use each of them to push Rob to work more fully with his writing. In both cases, I tell Rob what I think worked well—and make sure he knows exactly what I'm praising—and then use these strengths to challenge him to do even more. In the first half of my response, I compliment the way he goes back over and gives substance to his key statements, citing a number of examples and underscoring just what I am praising, formatted here to emphasize the depth of my responses:

> One of the strengths I see in this writing is the way, in a number of places, you get at your experience concretely and specifically, in a way that will make your words *mean* something to me and other readers.
>
> For example, on page 1 . . . .
>
> [Cite specific passage]
>
> You do the same kind of going over an idea but with greater detail in paragraph 5 . . . .
>
> [Cite specific passage]
>
> I also like the way you characterize his talk in paragraph 7 . . . .
>
> [Cite specific passage]
>
> Good way to get at his compelling style. Well done.

Then I urge him to go back to the paper and see where he might do more to follow through on other key statements, leaving the bulk of the work up to him:

> Now that you have used your fine-point pen on passages like these, go back to the paper and note where you might have done more of this specific naming, more of this following through on your descriptions, to get at them more fully and share them with readers. Do you see what you might have done, for instance, with your description of wrestling practice as a day in hell?

In the second half of the response, I praise the rich ideas he is starting to get at in the essay and play back my reading of the text:

> Another strength, another thing I really like about this paper, is
> that you have something to say, something beyond the obvious
> and routine, something that you've come to through this expe-
> rience as a wrestler. You describe your accomplishments, say
> that you did not accomplish all that you might, and then intro-
> duce your new coach as the person behind (so much of?) your
> success. The stage is set. You've got me with you.

Then I point to the main conceptual problem he comes up against in the
essay, in a negative evaluation; try to explain how the ideas he already
has on the page do not adequately get at all that he seems to set out to say,
in several reader-response comments and interpretations; and call on him
to pursue these ideas, using an open problem-posing question, a hortatorical comment, and a piece of advice:

> But you don't return to the question raised at the start. You don't
> examine why all this hard work and inspired coaching did not,
> in the end, bring you the championship.

> I'm curious to know why you build up Coach so much, why you
> tell us all the ways he pushed and inspired you and your team-
> mates to accept nothing short of winning, but then find yourself
> saying that you did not practice hard enough, did not reach
> your potential, and let yourself down. . . . I sense that the paper
> is about more than just the dynamism of Coach Smith—that it
> has to do somehow with the limits of coaching. Or possibly with
> your limits as a wrestler.

> Is there anything you could do to clear this up, or to push your
> thinking beyond the effects that this new coach had on you and
> your team? You seem to have arrived at a crossroad in the paper,
> at a juncture in your thinking that's important but that you
> haven't worked out. This is the place you want to be in the kind
> of writing we are working on in here. Now let's see what you
> can learn—and share with us—by going down one of these
> roads and wrestling with what happened with your season of
> wrestling last year.

Seven of my 37 comments offer praise; another 10 explain or elaborate on
this praise in follow-up comments. Just as many comments point to matters he might take up in revision and ask him essentially to see what he
can do to develop and extend his main ideas. I'm too interested in taking
advantage of these ideas to give other, lesser matters much play. I don't
call him on the contradiction in the first two paragraphs about going
undefeated. I don't ask him to establish how much the team had

improved. I don't ask him if there was anything beyond Coach Smith's style that made him an effective coach. And, in spite of the many errors and infelicities that slip into the paper now and again, I make no local comments. I'm happy with acknowledging the progress he has been making and directing him to work with developing and extending his ideas. Rob, it may be clear by now, thrived on incentive. I want to keep him focused and looking to make some gains.

On Chris's Essay 4

Chris's fourth essay presents a tough case. He is getting more words, ideas, and examples in his writing. He is working with material that is more concrete and accessible. He is more focused in this writing than in any of his earlier pieces. And he probably expects a more approving response than I will give. On the one hand, I want to praise his efforts, let him know, as before, that I see some progress. Part of me, in fact, wants to focus entirely on praising what he does do well here. On the other hand, I don't want to ease the pressure just yet. I want to push him to look for more substantive content and richer ideas. I gamble.

Essentially Chris is trying to run one general idea through a series of similar incidents, each one illustrating the same idea and nothing more: how he has benefited in his pursuits from his father telling him that he could do anything he wanted as long as he put his mind to it. He offers four instances in which he set out to attain a goal and reached it. The fact that he offers such full illustrations is not lost on me, but neither is the fact that all of them take place in or before the eighth grade. He's playing it safe, too safe to come up with anything more than a broad outline of what happened. In an early example, he recounts how he improved his grades and earned his way into the junior honor society, but he never really uses the example to explain or develop his key point. What exactly did he do differently than he was doing before? How did his father's influential advice play a part in the change? In the next instance he tells us how he earned enough money to go on his trip to Washington. And the details help. They suggest how much he was willing to do in order to make enough money to go on the trip. But he never tells us what it took to maintain his drive to earn the money or how his father's advice helped him in his pursuits. How did he "put his mind" to this goal, and how did that help him get the jobs, keep at the jobs, and get the money he needed to go on this trip? Again, he tells us nothing of the mechanics of this goal seeking. The same thing happens with the next example. What impact did his father's advice have on how he went about putting together his science project? Tellingly, we never see any mention of his father or his father's advice until the last paragraph. We get no real talk about his influence, much less any investigation into it. Did it become easier, for instance, to put his father's words into practice after it worked the first few times? Chris is aware that he needs to do something more with this main idea. He deals with it briefly in his last paragraph when he talks about envisioning what it will take to achieve a goal. But it's too little too late, and I leave the essay thinking I've got to ask him for more than he has given us here.

I decide to write all of my comments in an end note so I can monitor which of my reactions Chris reads before others. I'm in no hurry to hit him with my criticism. I want to compliment his move toward citing examples and ease into my concerns:

> Four full-length examples. I'm glad to see the detail, and I appreciate your attempts to make fuller use of your experience to illustrate your ideas. A step in the right direction. Still, as I read the essay, I find myself wanting to learn more from your examples.

While I want to let him know that I appreciate his moving to examples, I also want to let him know that, more than simply *citing* examples, he needs to *use* his examples to explain his ideas and perhaps even develop them further. To underscore my point, I restate my response more directly as a criticism: "The examples don't quite develop or support the claim that what it takes for you to achieve is . . . a matter of 'putting your mind to it.'"

Only then, with this issue behind us, do I address the more delicate problem of a main idea that may be too obvious to be of any real interest to a reader—or that cannot account, by itself, for his success. I avoid telling him straight up that the idea is not significant or that it's simplistic. For one, it would be too harsh, leading him to think that his ideas are simply no good. More importantly, it's not that the point is insignificant, it's that he doesn't *make* it significant. He doesn't go beyond this statement itself, doesn't use it to examine how he was able to achieve these goals or what is involved in "putting his mind to it." I want him to see the problem as a failure to get into an idea and offer something more than the obvious to readers. I present my response as a qualified evaluation:

> I also have some doubts about the significance of the statement, about its ability to capture what was really involved in your achieving these goals you tell us about.

From here, my comments look to encourage him to consider how he might use his examples to get at a point *and* develop other, related points. I close my comment on an upbeat note, exhorting him to look to do the kind of work with examples that we hadtalked about in a recent in-class discussion of another student's paper.

I waited to see what impact the comments might have.

On Cherri's Essay 4

More than likely, I turned to Cherri's fourth essay with great expectations, and she didn't disappoint. The paper is a real step ahead, both in the content of the writing and in her sense of forming an essay to have certain effects at certain times. There's more careful thinking, a fuller, more focused treatment of the subject, and more reaching to find something to say. She contrasts her modest abilities as a dancer with those of her more talented fellow students and supplants her dreams as a dancer with her new-found potential as a dance teacher. In doing so, she puts herself as a writer in a position to make something *of* her experience: to say something about it that goes beyond this narrative of what happened. She starts with—and at first it seems she will rely on—a couple of ready commonplaces:

> Different people have different talents, and we have to be flexible if we are to find the goals that are best for us.

> People who love an activity but have a hard time doing it well are in a better position to teach it.

But then, pursuing these ideas, she comes to two notable insights into her experience, one after the other: "I was so happy when I did a good job teaching," she says, "that being a great dancer did not matter as much any more." She considers the statement and then comes to an even richer statement: "That is when I noticed another change, my dancing was starting to improve. I wasn't as frustrated as before and things just started to come easier." When she was less intent on attaining a certain level of performance and more content to enjoy what she was doing, she was able to relax and, by relaxing—and, notably, by allowing herself to enjoy dancing once again—was able to improve. By shifting the lens and looking beyond her frustration, she defines a more complex way of seeing the experience and discovers something more to say. The idea is all the stronger, the impact even greater, because the turn of events is unexpected (and because it comes up unexpectedly is all the more pleasurable) and, we see, has been set up from the start.

I want to praise her richly for these ideas and for the way she makes her statements *mean*. But, as with Rob, I also want to capitalize on these successes. I want her to do more to look into these experiences, get at her key ideas, and give them substance. How frustrated had she become with her dancing? When she "broke down the steps" (to an exercise or a dance?), what kind of steps did she break them into and how did she present them to her students? What "more challenging things" did she give the more talented students to do? She says her system worked great. How could she establish this claim by talking about how her students were learning "the basics of dance"? When she began dancing again for enjoyment, how did she "actually start to improve" and how did things start to come easier? By looking more closely at these experiences she might come to an even better sense of how these events came together to act on her as they did—and find even more to say.

In my marginal comments I call attention to the lines that stand out in the essay and praise her for them:

> This sentence speaks volumes—crisp and yet rich.
>
> Here's an insight—I like the way you put it.
>
> Interesting.

But most of my marginal comments focus on places where I'd like to see her get at her ideas more clearly or give greater substance to her claims:

> What couldn't you do—or do as well as others—that made you "not very good"? Can you give me some idea?
>
> How to give us something that would help us see this frustration better. Would a particular time do?
>
> Anything like what? One or two quick particular things would go a long way here.
>
> I'd love to see a sampling of how you "broke down the steps."

In the second paragraph I string together a series of open problem-posing questions to lead her to consider how she might go back over her statements and make them more meaningful:

> S: I gave the better talented students more challenging things.
>
> T: Now why would I underline this phrase?
>
> S: My system of teaching worked great.
>
> T: Or this one? What others would you mark here?
>
> S: Things just started to come easier.
>
> T: By now, do you know why I'm underlining these passages? Is it a strong way to say what you mean?

I want to help Cherri conceptualize this principle, get better at recognizing these places in her own writing, and give her practice at going back over her key statements at a lower level of generality. To provide some motivation, I show her that she can do this substantiating, that she already does it in the paper when she goes back over and explains her assertion that her fellow student-teachers had problems teaching: "See the way you begin to make the previous statement mean more by going into the next ones?" To lead her to attend more carefully to her proof-reading, I place a dash next to lines in which there are errors. As I told the class when I returned their papers, students whose papers were minimally marked in this way should go back and correct the problems on their own, talk with me if they had any questions, and be more vigilant about these kinds of errors in their future writing.

In my end note, I emphasize the positive and build on it, turning the praise into a lesson. I tell her *what* I understand her to be saying in the paper and *how* I am able to come to that understanding because of the details she provides and the way she uses detail to establish a context and make her statements stand up:

> I am able to get this much from those words because of what you do by way of giving me the background of your dancing/teaching experience earlier in the paper. In fact, I can make only as much meaning of these words as the words around them allow me to make. You do a pretty good job setting up this experience, allowing me to see what happened and how you felt. I see the general pattern of events you're talking about.

Having laid this foundation, I push her to do more to get at and possibly extend her ideas:

> But I think I need to see more—and, more importantly, that you need to see more of what happened—before we can get a clearer sense of what all you mean when, at the end of the paper, you make those potentially rich statements about an open mind, frustration, different approaches, and different aspects of your goals. Can you see where you might have looked more closely at some of these experiences and thereby come to see more about this frustration and open-mindedness and how you came to make them work for you and not against you?

I close the response with two hortatorical comments and a note of praise, another attempt to encourage Cherri to keep up the good work. Overall, 12 of my comments offer praise for her ideas and her work here. Ten present open questions about supporting, developing, and extending her ideas. Three offer advice for continued work and revision. Another nine comments go back over and elaborate on previous comments. It was a rich paper to work with—the kind of paper that, if it is worked with well, can teach as much as weeks of classroom instruction or a dozen textbook lessons.

Essay 5

On Essay 5 we continued our inquiry into the subject of achievement, this time looking into the downside of striving to attain some goals, the line that separates accomplishment and ambition, and the drawbacks of a life bent on pursuit. The assignment, once again, pointed students in a certain direction but left the specific route and destination up to them:

> Explore one idea or set of related ideas on the downside of striving for goals, being ambitious, or devoting oneself to a goal. We are told, for example, to give ourselves completely to our tasks. But we know we can't always give ourselves fully to our goals. What are we to do in the face of such conflicting demands? How do we decide to give ourselves to one thing or another? What are the gains and losses of a life given to constant striving? Given to a certain kind of striving?

> Or examine a popular attitude, view, or saying about achievement and modify or work against the idea. Look at the claim in light of your own experience and test it, turn it over on itself, or qualify it in some way. Is there a better way to see achievement or ambition? Is there something more to see than our everyday views might lead us to see?

> Use your writing as a means of discovery and pay attention to how you shape the writing so that you get at your ideas and share them with your audience, the members of this class. Look to form your paper into a unified essay, where each of the parts contributes to the effect of the whole. Construct the essay around a central issue or idea, be selective about your introductory and concluding paragraphs, and arrange your writing in a way that will best get at your views and enable your readers to understand them.

The paper was assigned at the end of week 8. Students were to complete a sophisticated rough draft during week 9, return to the paper over the weekend, and put together their final draft for Monday of week 10. In between, we discussed several samples of Essay 4 (including Rob's paper on his wrestling coach), looking at statements we saw as distinctive or interesting, pointing to places we wanted to hear more, and indicating where the writing wasn't working as well as it could. We spent a good deal of time talking about how writers might go about deciding which matters to take up in a piece of writing, which ones to emphasize and elaborate on, and which ones to just deal with briefly—all on the basis of the writer's central idea and purpose. We reflected, in an in-class writing, on how our work in the class was going. And then we met, one-on-one, in a 15 to 20 minute conference about their work in the course thus far. Students would identify the strengths and weaknesses in their writing up to this point, indicate what they had been working on over the past few weeks, and then define one or two areas they looked to work on in the weeks ahead. I would talk mostly in reply to what they said. As our time in the meeting drew to a close, I would ask them to assess their progress in the course, and then I would give them my evaluation of their work, identifying their strongest papers, assessing their progress on the key concerns of the course, and then giving them a sense of how I graded their overall performance up to that point. The idea was to have them articulate the course concepts, use them to read and evaluate their own writing, and focus their work for the second half of the course. My hope was that the discussion would also motivate them to redouble their efforts in the work ahead.

When I read Essay 5, I would be looking for how well the writers were creating a casual voice, getting something to say, and going back over the ground of key statements so that they would be clear and meaningful for others. I would give more attention to how well they shaped their writing around a single point and made each part of the paper pull its weight for the whole. At this point, when their individual progress in the course permitted, I also wanted to start attending more to the flow of their paragraphs, the structure of their sentences, and matters of correctness. If a student had reached a point where he was really saying something in his writing and developing his key statements, I would indicate ways to strengthen a sentence or perhaps deal somehow with any recurring mechanical problems. If a student had not yet reached this point, I would defer this kind of sentence-level work for Essay 6 or Essay 7. The foundation of the course had been laid over the past seven or eight weeks. I was now looking to see where students would go with their writing. This was the heart of the course.

Rob's Essay 5

It's More Than a Drawback

Along with the accomplishments I've made during wrestling season, drawbacks seem to evolve. After all I've accomplished, you would wonder, "what kind of problems could possibly happen?" Well, your not the only one!

Ever since wrestling season had started and to this day, I stay up late at night, laying in my bed, thinking about all that I've been through. I think about every match I've wrestled since 5th grade to my last match in the state tournament. I think about all the matches I've won and lost. I think about all the times I screwed around in practice and got in trouble for doing so. I think about every damn thing I've done wrong and wished I could have done better. All these feelings of pain and grief will never leave until the day I die.

I like this way of going into what you think about. Can you see how it'd be even better with specific things you remember—e.g., losing that last state final when you missed the last pin by a slip of the hand?

As an athlete, I'll tell you what achieving goals has done to me. It has scarred me mentally, but not physically. Growing up in a family of wrestlers is what probably caused this problem. My Dad, who wrestled all through high school and two years at the University of Iowa, had supported me from the first day I mentioned I wanted to wrestle. As soon as I joined a local wrestling club, he was there to coach me. For three years he was in the corner of the mat coaching me. For three years I felt like I was put on earth to wrestle and that's it. Through middle school and high school, my Dad wasn't the coach anymore, he was just a fan in the crowd, but he was the only fan I could hear. Over those three years I was conditioned to block out all the noise that went on during a match and concentrate on listening to my father's voice. So during some of my matches, all I could here is my Dad and not my other

A strong voice here—you're talking directly to us.

Strong

Whew—what a statement. And I love the way you follow through on it and extend the idea.

coach. After every match I wrestled he would come down from the stands and shake my hand, no matter if I won or lost, and congradulate me on a good match.

My older brother was also a wrestler. He started wrestling about the same time I had started. Ever since we began wrestling together, we would be persistent on competing with each other. He wanted more trophies than I had and nothing would stop him from accomplishing his mission. The only trophy I wanted to win was the trophy of respect from my father. The only trophy my brother wanted was the one that said "I CAN KICK THE CRAP OUT OF MY LITTLE BROTHER." I never enjoyed having my brother wrestle, because he felt like had to prove something to me and the other wrestlers on the team. If I was able to take him down and our coach tells me it was a good move, my brother would get mad and intentionaly hurt me. I couldn't understand what made him do that. Because of those past events, I wanted to hurt all my opponents. I didn't care if I was disqualified for unsportsman-like conduct or if someone cut both of my legs off because I purposely hurt my opponent, as long as I did it, because someone did it to me. All the pressure, wether good or bad, from my family was an obstruction in achieving one of my goals of being a great wrestler.

Another product caused by wrestling was my bad attitude. It's a coaches' saying that you should be tough both mentally and physically. It is possible to become too mentally tough . . . I should know (this shouldn't be a surprise to you by now). It was a problem for me because it got in the way of numerous things. It got in the way of wrestling most of all. During my last year of wrestling, our coach would pound into our heads the thought of "only the strongest will survive" practically every practice. My mind would get extremely tired thinking about wrestling while I was in practice, causing me to daydream about

Whew—another killer statement. This sentence rings with conviction.

Strong, revealing.

Your details on this page help you earn this generalization. I can really begin to see the pressure, and imagine it.

What else would he do or say?

Thanks for the details. Again, though, can you see how you could get at this point by specifying a particular TV show, Algebra homework, or whether you were thinking of having ham or steak for dinner?

other things which have no relation to wrestling, like TV shows, homework assignments, or what will probably be for dinner.

Always having to win and keeping the team's reputation my top priority, things were getting a little hard to handle. Towards the end of January I developed stomach pains which made it hard for me to run or wrestle. After a few doctor appointments I was told that I had an acute — ulser. All the worries, difficulties, and stress I had with wrestling was burning a hole in my stomach. A few days later everything returned to normal. The stress was still there, but it wasn't as bad as it was before I went to the doctor.

This is sad and irritating to read. Sorry to hear about it—but you talk about it so straight to me that I sense that you've hardened yourself to it— or maybe have just gotten over it or are getting over it . . . .

Did you just change your attitude? Or what? Did the time off help? What led to the change?

All I wanted was to win and please everybody, to show them that I had it in me. For some reason I wasn't doing it for myself. Somewhere, in my eight years of wrestling, I had lost the concept of wrestling and sports being fun and turned it into a vital necessity of life. Anything that involves competition is a sport to me. — Whether its academics or athletics, I'll do anything to come out on top. When I win, I'll be satisfied until the next chance of competition approaches.

I love the way you extend your thinking here, how you say more about your experience.

I've seen some of that hard-nosed effort and redoubled effort in your work in this class—and it's paid off.

— Over the years I've been transformed into a machine, whether or not it was self-inflicted, <u>I can't resist the opportunity of a challenge</u>. These reasons I've given are not my drawbacks to achievement, they're my losses to what I once loved ...... wrestling.

Even though you've become so aware of these circumstances? Interesting.

A strong closing—a real pin.

Rob—

The writing you do on this paper is worth all your work in the course, and reflects the work you've been doing over the past several weeks. You do an amazing job with this paper, capturing your experience, revealing your feelings and attitudes and pain, and coming to terms with it yourself and sharing it effectively—strongly—with your readers. It is a triumph. One of the best papers I've received this semester, perhaps even the best.

Chris's Essay 5

The Ups and Downs of Achievement

To achieve is one of the greatest feelings any person can have. We all like to achieve and we constantly strive in our lives to continue achieving. Along with the great sense of accomplishment when you reach your goal comes a lot of hard work and sacrifices. No matter what it is that you are trying to achieve the hard work comes with it. If that means that in order to get an A on a test you have to study over the weekend and miss all the fun and excitement that goes on while you are studying, then you have to do it. The next time you need to save money for a big expense that is coming up you might be limited to going without your weekly music purchase. If you want to become better fit, the results will not appear just sitting on the couch watching T.V. You have to get out and bust your butt. These examples show that in order to achieve, no matter what your goal is, you have to make sacrifices. The bigger the goal the greater the sacrifice that it will take to reach that goal.

How would you take it if I said you sound a bit like a presidential candidate here—or some kind of army commercial? Is this behind your strategy in the paper, this way of sounding? Do you want to sound so . . . official?

This seems true enough. The problem is, it may be too much of a truism. How much will it say to us?

I can remember when I was fifteen years old and I had gotten my restricted licence. The next step was to get my regular licence and then a car. I had a lot of lofty ideas of what kind of car I wanted. A nice used Ford Mustang 5.0 convertible, black with all the exciting extras. This car ran around $6,000.00. I then talked to my dad and told him of the car I wanted to get. He laughed and told me that he would let me get what ever I could afford. At my current allowance I would have been able to get the car I wanted when I turned twenty-seven.

!

The only choice I had was to get a job. I went out and searched the local job market and I got a job at a fancy fast food restaurant called Rudy's Sirloinburgers. I was started out at $4.00 an hour, which was pretty good considering that minimum wage was $3.35. Working twenty hours a week during school, forty hours during the summer, and a personal savings of $1,000.00 I would be able to get the car of my dreams before my junior year in high school. I told my dad of this great plan. The only problem was that I had forgotten about good old Uncle Sam, insurance, and my social life, which was not cheap. I then recalculated my income situation and realized I was about $3,000.00 short. This really upset me. I could no longer get the car of my dreams and I felt that I was working for nothing. My father and I talked and he told me that we would work it out.

I went on working and shortly after I turned 16 I got my driver's licence. I was very excited because I had a new freedom, | my father looked at it as more leverage if I were to screw up. The next step was to get a car. My father and I discussed the situation and we decided that the best car for me would be an early 80's mid-size car manufactured by GM. This decision was based primarily because of cost, safety, and insurance. The search then began. Newspaper classifieds became a part of my daily reading. My budget was $2,000.00. This way I would have enough to pay for insurance and still have money left over in my account, so I wouldn't be on empty. I can't tell you how many Buick Regals, Chevy Monte Carlos, Oldsmobile Cutlass Supremes, and Pontiac Grand Prixs I looked at with my father. The ones that were in my price range were real pieces of junk. The ones I liked were outrageously overpriced. I was able to talk one salesman down to $2,100.00 for the 1981 Buick Regal he was trying to move off his lot. I checked with my dad and we decided to buy it. This was one of the most happiest days in my life. I now had a set of wheels, more leverage for my father.

Thanks for the specifics here.

This story is perfect <u>example of the sacrifices a person has to make</u> in order to reach a goal. Not only did I have to give up a lot of my free time to work, my social life also had to take budget cuts. I was not able to go out every weekend like I had done before and blow all of my money. I had to make some <u>great sacrifices</u> to save the money that I did. My basesball card collecting hobby took the biggest cut. Instead of buying baseball cards, I put the money towards my car. I also<u> had to get a car that wasn't my first choice</u>. When my father and I started looking at cars I was upset that I couldn't get what I wanted. Everything I looked at was nothing compared to the car of my dreams. After I bought the car I put a lot of time and effort into the car to make it better than it was. I got the windows tinted, put in a good stereo, washed it every two weeks, and maintained the car overall. But to tell you the truth, I was more than happy in the end because it was my car, not the salesman's, not the guy's down the street, not even my father's. What I am trying to say is that in order to reach a goal it may be tough as hell, but don't give up because achieving that goal is one of life's greatest achievements.

You haven't given us much of this sacrifice in the story above.

I'm not sure these are __great__ sacrifices. But I can see how they are sacrifices. I was ready for more talk about them.

There's that heightened voice again from the beginning. Do you think it works? Would you change anything?

Chris—

I see some signs of your working on your writing here. I especially like the way you __use__ your example to talk through your point about the sacrifices needed in order to achieve. I must admit, though, that I'm not all that taken with the key point you spend your time talking about. It seems like a pretty standard idea—one that would not really add much to our understanding of sacrifice and achievement. Do you see how you might take this idea, plunge into it further, and come up with an idea that might be more distinctive, something that might interest us and enlighten us more?

Cherri's Essay 5

Downfalls of Achievement

When most people think of achieving a goal they think of a pleasant experience, but this is not always true. Most of the more desirable goals in life are reached only by <u>sacrificing</u> other things such as time, money, and effort. Sometimes you give up something that does not seem important at the time, but later on you realize that what you had was better than what you got from your goal. I believe that if we choose our goals carefully and make ourselves aware of the <u>consequences</u> before hand then the goals we reach will be well worth the trouble.

You started by talking about "sacrificing" things in order to reach your goals, and now you're talking about "consequences." Will you be talking mainly about sacrifices or consequences? The consequences of what?

One of my major goals in life is to become a fiction writer. That has been one of my goals since I was twelve years old. My childhood was <u>not exactly pleasant</u>, and I have always had a wild imagination so <u>reading books was my escape</u> from reality for a little while. When I was in junior high I realized that I was <u>a pretty good writer</u>, and I have been <u>writing</u> ever since.

Do you see how each of these passages has all kinds of experience and ideas buried within? Try to uncover some of them, to help us see what you mean. What kind of books did you read to escape? Escape from what? What made you think you were "a pretty good writer"? How much writing have you been doing? What kinds?

I know that there are a lot of draw backs to this little dream of mine. I realize that there are thousands of other people with same dream as me, and relatively few ever get anything published, much less make it big. Also writing takes up a lot of time. You can't just sit down at a computer and start writing. You have to research your subjects thoroughly. I've read about writers who spent years just doing the research for their work before they ever started to write. Then, of course, there is the worst draw back of all, having a publisher reject your writing after all that work, or having some book critic tear your work apart. Despite

I appreciate the examples you provide here. They help to show that you realize what you'd be getting into. What else can you tell us about the drawbacks (or obstacles)?

all the down falls and disappointment that can be involved in this line of work I still want to do it. I honestly believe that the <u>achievement</u> of this goal will far out way the <u>sacrifices</u> that I will have to make to get there.

The <u>achievement</u> of this goal or the <u>satisfaction</u> from achieving the goal?

I don't get a good sense of what these "sacrifices" might actually be.

End Comments on Cherri's Essay 5

Cherri—

I think the main point you're driving at here is that we ought to be aware of the difficulties involved in trying to reach our goals. You tell us briefly about the origins of your interest in becoming a fiction writer. You indicate that you are aware of the difficulties (you call them "drawbacks") of achieving this goal. And you go on to say at the end that the goal would be worth the sacrifices.

But it takes me some time to figure out just what you are saying in the essay, to understand exactly what this paper is about. I think the problem comes from the many different key terms you use. You start the paper by talking about "sacrificing" in order to achieve some goal, and you return to the idea of sacrificing at the end. But you also get into other key terms in these first and last paragraphs that muddy the water for me. You mention something about assessing the potential "consequences" of achieving goals in paragraph 1. You talk in paragraph 3 about the "drawbacks" of pursuing a writing career—and the "disappointment" that can be involved in it. It seems as if you are using these terms interchangeably, as if they are all synoymous. Yet there are clear differences between making sacrifices for a goal, seeing drawbacks (or difficulties?) in pursuing a goal, dealing with disappointments along the way, and making yourself aware of potential consequences of achieving (or failing to achieve) a goal. Ultimately, I think you are most interested in talking about making yourself aware of the difficulties or obstacles you would have to overcome before setting out in pursuit of a far-off goal. I'd go back and decide just what I was really interested in talking about, and then try to figure out which of these other terms to address and which ones to take out. Then I'd try to see if I have done enough to *get at* these key terms and ideas and figure out how they all fit together.

I like the general idea you're working with here: doing some careful consideration before taking on a difficult goal. I like your using your own experience to illustrate the idea. The path to a career in writing is certainly full of obstacles, many of which you recognize. As it stands, though, there's much more to say, much more that needs to be clarified and elaborated—about your interest and motivation for becoming a writer, your sense of the difficulties of writing, and your willingness to make the necessary sacrifices and put up with the likely disappointments in order to reach your goal and be a published writer. What can you do to get more of your ideas down on the page and shape them more clearly? What else can you tell me about considering the difficulties of achieving a significant goal or making sacrifices in order to reach it?

On Rob's Essay 5

By Essay 5, Rob had hit his stride. His fourth paper was good. This one was better. It's not writing that is especially insightful or distinctive. He doesn't say anything that most of us in class haven't heard or don't already know. The central idea is fairly commonplace: how one's family can get in the way of success. The essay draws its strength from two sources: the voice of the writing and the way he gets behind what he says and infuses his words with feeling. Rob cuts the distance between writer and audience and talks to us as readers. His words are attached to things, and they seamlessly give way to ideas that are not just asserted but felt. Statements like the following enable him to get at his experience, construct a mood, and give local habitation and a name to this idea of how others' expectations can get in the way of one's goals:

> I think about every damn thing I've done wrong and wished I could have done better.

> My Dad wasn't the coach anymore, he was just a fan in the crowd, but he was the only fan I could hear.

> The only trophy I wanted to win was the trophy of respect from my father.

> All I wanted was to win and please everybody, to show them that I had it in me.

Much of this voice and feeling are the result of sharp naming and good old careful crafting. Notice how he uses parallel structure in the following sequences to elicit emotion and drive home his point:

> I stay up late at night, laying in my bed, thinking about all that I've been through. I think about every match I've wrestled since 5th grade to my last match in the state tournament. I think about all the times I screwed around in practice and got in trouble for doing so. I think about every damn thing I've done wrong and wished I could have done better.

> As soon as I joined a local wrestling club, [my dad] was there to coach me. For three years he was in the corner of the mat coaching me. For three years I felt like I was put on earth to wrestle and that's it.

And notice how the writing loses some of its impact, for instance, when he gets lackadaisical with his naming and sentence structure and doesn't look to talk with his readers:

> Ever since we began wrestling together, we would be persistent on competing with each other.

> Another product caused by wrestling was my bad attitude.
>
> It was a problem for me because it got in the way of numerous things.
>
> Somewhere, in my eight years of wrestling, I had lost the concept of wrestling and sports being fun and turned it into a vital necessity of life.

Even potentially strong assertions suffer at times from vague language and loose structure:

> Because of those past events, I wanted to hurt all my opponents. I didn't care if I was disqualified for unsportsman-like conduct or if someone cut both my legs off because I purposely hurt my opponent, as long as I did it, because someone did it to me.
>
> Always having to win and keeping the team's reputation my top priority, things were getting a little hard to handle.

Rob is at the point in his work where he needs to give more time, more consistently, to such forming, but he is putting into practice our talk in class about structuring for effect and making real strides in developing the content of his writing. He is developing a nice repertoire of strategies for getting at his assertions, playing one thing off another, and extending his ideas. In a nice use of metaphor, he compares the "trophies" his brother vied for and the only one that he set his sights on: the respect of his father. He makes a couple of nice distinctions: in the middle of his paper seeing his father no longer as a coach but as a fan in the crowd, the only fan he could hear, and at the end seeing the family pressures not as drawbacks to his striving after his goals but as lost opportunities. There's a lot more he could with this writing, to get at what happened and extend these ideas. But I'm delighted with the effort I see him putting forth and the progress I see him making. These reactions, no doubt, set the tone for my response.

My comments are a celebration. I write 18 praise comments, more than half of my response, complimenting everything from his content to his voice to his conclusion to his essay as a whole to his overall work in the class. Seven comments praise his assertions, among them:

> Strong.
>
> Whew—what a statement.
>
> Whew—another killer statement. This sentence rings with conviction.
>
> I love the way you extend your thinking here, how you say more about your experience.

Four praise the way he goes back over assertions to give them greater substance:

> I like this way of going into what you think about.
>
> I love the way you follow through on [this statement] and extend the idea.
>
> Your details on this page help you earn this generalization. I can really begin to see the pressure and imagine it.
>
> Thanks for the details.

We tend to be not as enthusiastic about our praise as we are insistent about our criticism, but I want to be lavish in my praise here. More than boost his ego or compliment him on a job well done, this praise is meant to recognize his improvements, reinforce the key terms of the course, and encourage continued work in these areas in future writing.

I'm not so taken by what he's done well, however, that I don't see opportunities to push him further, because the most fruitful time for instruction follows immediately on some success, I try to take advantage of several opportunities to lead him to consider where he might have put these same strategies into practice elsewhere and made this paper even better. I follow two positive comments about his use of detail with questions designed to lead him to consider how he might have made even better use of concrete naming:

> I like this way of going into what you think about. Can you see how it'd be even better with specific things you remember—e.g., losing that last state final when you missed the last pin by a slip of the hand?
>
> Thanks for the details. Again, though, can you see how you could really get at this point by specifying a particular TV show, Algebra homework, or whether you were thinking of having ham or steak for dinner?

I also ask him on two occasions for more information—about how his coach would pound his convictions into their heads and what it was that eased the stress that led to his ulcer.

The comments, nevertheless, remain tightly focused. Twenty-five of my 33 comments attend to ideas and extratextual concerns. I think now that he's come this far with his content, he's ready to start giving more attention to sentence structure and error, but I don't see any need to spend time on them here. Right now I want to be positive. I want Rob to feel good about his work and take this success to his next writing. I make no comments about the local matters. I just minimally mark a handful of minor problems, placing a dash in the left-hand margin next to lines that have errors in mechanics, spelling, or punctuation. I'll note in class when I return the essays that these dashes mark places where there are certain errors, and I'll ask students to identify and correct them on their own. I'll also remind them that I'll be giving more attention to such matters during the rest of the course.

Rob says at the end of this essay that any form of competition is a sport to him. "Whether its academics or athletics, I'll do anything to come out on top." This paper—and his work in class over the past four weeks—is a case in point. He is doing what it takes to be on top, and I am thrilled with the effort and progress.

On Chris's Essay 5

Chris's Essay 5 presents another difficult case. He continues to work on focusing his writing on a single idea. He gives fuller treatment to the experiences he is writing about. And he provides more specific details here than in his earlier papers. Yet if the essay is longer and more detailed, it's not a lot more substantive, or interesting. Chris focuses his writing better, but he's not looking to get beyond the obvious and find something to say. His main idea—that you have to sacrifice in order to reach your goals—is the kind of idea that is easy to illustrate but hard to take beyond the commonplace. He runs his ideas through examples, but he is not looking to make the examples really work for him, to help him establish and develop his key ideas. The two middle paragraphs of the essay, where we expect him to develop and pursue his key claim, have little to do with the sacrifices that were needed to reach his goals. They deal more with how he worked toward the goal, made compromises, was persistent, or made adjustments in his goals. He offers more detail, but he's still leaving large gaps around his key statements. What was said when he and his father came to decide that a five- or six-year-old car would be best? What were his reactions to this decision? How long did he search for the car—and how did he feel along the way? He is not yet developing a sense of how to regulate his discussion according to the importance of a point and its function in the essay as a whole. If he is trying to engage the principles of the course, he is not quite able to really put them into practice in more than a perfunctory way. I want to let him know that there is still much to do.

Looking back, I'm not satisfied with my response. The comments are rather aggressive, even grumpy. It may be late at night. I may be far into the stack of papers. I may be running short on time. I may be unhappy with the idea he's dealing with. Or I may just be irritated that Chris is not doing more. At any rate, I'm vexed, and at times this vexation shows:

> How would you take it if I said you sound like a politician here—or a commercial for the army? . . . Do you want to sound so official?

> There's that official voice again from the beginning.

> I must admit . . . that I'm not all that taken with the point you spend your time talking about.

Preoccupied by what he's not doing, I don't notice what he does accomplish or look to find ways of improving the paper. I don't really define the problem with his main idea. I don't see that this lengthy recounting of his quest for a car doesn't really advance his claim about making sacrifices. And I don't help him see how he might develop his point or get more to say by looking at this example more closely. The question I raise at the end of my final comment may very well leave too much for Chris to deal with on his own: "Do you see how you might take this idea, plunge into it further, and come up with an idea that might be more yours and something that could interest us and enlighten us more?" The response as a whole seems terse and too undeveloped to provide Chris with the kind of help he probably needs.

Of course, we shouldn't expect to make responses that always say what we would optimally say. It's not easy responding to stacks of 20 or 25 student papers, much less when you're mainly concerned with leading students to develop the content of those papers. As Peter Elbow likes to remind us, writing was not meant to be read *en masse* and responded to one after another. Still, I wish I'd done something more for Chris here. And as I think about what I might have done, I come up with some ideas. Here is a revised response (pp. 230-32) that looks to do what I didn't have the presence of mind, the patience, or the time to do when I first read Chris' paper.

The revised set of comments still have a critical edge to them. I want Chris to know that I'm not happy with the ideas he's floating in the essay and that he has to get something more to say. Nine of my 45 comments make firm or moderate criticisms of his voice and content. Some of this criticism is presented directly, with little if any qualification:

> . . . I have to say that I was hoping to see more—more distinctive thoughts, more substance, more progress.

> You don't really offer us much as readers when you stake your entire paper on the idea that you have to make sacrifices in order to achieve.

> Yet the example as you present it across prghs 2, 3, and 4 seems an illustration of how you had to compromise or modify your goals more than of the sacrifices that you had to make.

Chris's Essay 5 with Revised Comments

The Ups and Downs of Achievement

To achieve is one of the greatest feelings any person can have. We all like to achieve and we constantly strive in our lives to continue achieving. Along with the great sense of accomplishment when you reach your goal comes a lot of hard work and sacrifices. No matter what it is that you are trying to achieve the hard work comes with it. If that means that in order to get an A on a test you have to study over the weekend and miss all the fun and excitement that goes on while you are studying, then you have to do it. The next time you need to save money for a big expense that is coming up you might be limited to going without your weekly music purchase. If you want to become better fit, the results will not appear just sitting on the couch watching T.V. You have to get out and bust your butt. These examples show that in order to achieve, no matter what your goal is, you have to make sacrifices. The bigger the goal the greater the sacrifice that it will take to reach that goal.

Here you sound like a keynote speaker at a graduation ceremony. Is this the way you want to sound here, for us?

Sounds pretty generic. How much is this telling us that we don't already know?

This seems true enough. The problem is, it may be too much of a truism. How much will it say to us?

I can remember when I was fifteen years old and I had gotten my restricted licence. The next step was to get my regular licence and then a car. I had a lot of lofty ideas of what kind of car I wanted. A nice used Ford Mustang 5.0 convertible, black with all the exciting extras. This car ran around $6,000.00. I then talked to my dad and told him of the car I wanted to get. He laughed and told me that he would let me get what ever I could afford. At my current allowance I would have been able to get the car I wanted when I turned twenty-seven.

Hah! Well done.

The only choice I had was to get a job. I went out and searched the local job market and I got a job at a fancy fast food restaurant called Rudy's Sirloinburgers. I was started out at $4.00 an hour, which was pretty good considering that minimum wage was $3.35. Working twenty hours a week during school, forty hours during the summer, and a personal savings of $1,000.00 I would be able to get the car of my dreams before my junior year in high school. I told my dad of this great plan. The only problem was that I had forgotten about good old Uncle Sam, insurance, and my social life, which was not cheap. I then recalculated my income situation and realized I was about $3,000.00 short. This really upset me. I could no longer get the car of my dreams and I felt that I was working for nothing. My father and I talked and he told me that we would work it out.

I went on working and shortly after I turned 16 I got my driver's licence. I was very excited because I had a new freedom, | my father looked at it as more leverage if I were to screw up. The next step was to get a car. My father and I discused the situation and we decided that the best car for me would be an early 80's mid-size car manufactured by GM. This decision was based primarily because of cost, safety, and insurance. The search then began. Newspaper classifieds became a part of my daily reading. My budget was $2,000.00. This way I would have enough to pay for insurance and still have money left over in my account, so I wouldn't be on empty. I can't tell you how many Buick Regals, Chevy Monte Carlos, Oldsmobile Cutlass Supremes, and Pontiac Grand Prixs I looked at with my father. The ones that were in my price range were real pieces of junk. The ones I liked were outrageously overpriced. I was able to talk one salesman down to $2,100.00 for the 1981 Buick Regal he was trying to move off his lot. I checked with my dad and we decided to buy it. This was one of the most happiest days in my life. I now had a set of wheels, more leverage for my father.

How did this talk go?

How hard did you have to look before you found something? Did you ever waver in your decision to go with a cheaper car— or get teased by a nicer one than you could afford?

Thanks for the specifics here.

This story is perfect example of the sacrifices a person has to make in order to reach a goal. Not only did I have to give up a lot of my free time to work, my social life also had to take budget cuts. I was not able to go out every weekend like I had done before and blow all of my money. I had to make some great sacrifices to save the money that I did. My baseball card collecting hobby took the biggest cut. Instead of buying baseball cards, I put the money towards my car. I also had to get a car that wasn't my first choice. When my father and I started looking at cars I was upset that I couldn't get what I wanted. Everything I looked at was nothing compared to the car of my dreams. After I bought the car I put a lot of time and effort into the car to make it better than it was. I got the windows tinted, put in a good stereo, washed it every two weeks, and maintained the car overall. But to tell you the truth, I was more than happy in the end because it was my car, not the salesman's, not the guy's down the street, not even my father's. What I am trying to say is that in order to reach a goal it may be tough as hell, but don't give up because achieving that goal is one of life's greatest achievements.

Here you get into the sacrifices. After all your talk above, I was expecting more about these sacrifices.

Is this a sacrifice or a compromise? I suppose it can be seen as a sacrifice, since you gave something up. Still, I wonder if it's best put in the category of a "sacrifice."

Here again is that voice of the speech-maker at graduation. How do you think others would react to it?

Revised End Comments on Chris's Essay 5

Chris—

I see some signs of your working on your writing here. I like that you provide a lengthy example about a goal you sacrificed for, along with some specific detail along the way. I also like the way you start to use specific examples to get at your point about the sacrifices you made in reaching for this goal. You seem to be getting more generous with examples and details in your writing. Good to see.

At the same time, I have to say that I was hoping to see more—more distinctive thoughts, more substance, more progress. You don't really offer us much as readers when you stake your entire paper on the idea that you have to make sacrifices in order to achieve. It seems like a pretty standard idea, one that most of us would readily agree with and that would not add much to our understanding of the subject. The question is: How to make this experience with getting a car give you more than just that broad generalization? Maybe if you looked more closely at the experience you could find something to tell us *about* making sacrifices to achieve some goal. You might see not just *that* you made some sacrifices but *what* was involved in making them or *how* you felt about having to make them. How were you able, for instance, to get over having to give up making additions to your baseball card collection? When you visited car lots and came across cars that were really nice but beyond your budget, did you find that you had to keep reminding yourself of your goals? Did you learn anything about having to adjust your goals according to your circumstances? Or maybe you could reconsider the terms you use to get at this experience. You seem to see your dreams and your search for a car as "sacrifices" you had to make in order to achieve your goal. Yet the example as you present it across prghs 2, 3, and 4 seems an illustration of how you had to *compromise* or *modify* your goals more than of the *sacrifices* that you had to make. (You get to the sacrifices, it seems, only in the last paragraph: what you had to give up in order to get your goal of having a car.) If you looked to make these kinds of distinctions you might discover a lot more to say about sacrifices and achievement.

There's plenty to work on—I'd like to see you push yourself more and see what you can come up with by way of saying more in your writing. Now's the time to throw yourself into high gear.

At times, the criticism is followed, for better or worse, by a closed question which, coming after a negative evaluation, serves both to intensify the criticism and explain it:

> Here you sound like someone giving a speech at a graduation ceremony. Is this the way you want to sound here, for us?

> Sounds pretty generic. How much is this telling us that we don't already know?

> The problem is, it may be too much of a truism. How much will it say to us?

At other times, I follow my criticism with explanations:

> You don't really offer us much as readers when you stake your entire paper on the idea that you have to make sacrifices in order to achieve. It seems like a pretty standard idea, one that most of us would readily agree with and that would not add much to our understanding of the subject.

Notably, this criticism is only a part of the response. Because a teacher's criticism can be only as useful as it is made to constructively lead the student to look back on his writing and try to make improvements, I look to offset some of this criticism by acknowledging the things that he does well:

> Hah! Well done.

> Thanks for the specifics here.

> I see some signs of your working on your writing here. I like that you provide a lengthy example about a goal you sacrificed for, along with some specific detail along the way. I also like the way you use examples to get at your point about the sacrifices you made in reaching for this goal. You seem to be getting more generous with examples and details in your writing. Good to see.

The main difference between the two sets of comments, though, is the way, in the revised comments, that I more clearly define the problem with his main idea and then try to help him revise. I offer two suggestions about how he might examine this experience more closely and develop his ideas:

> Maybe if you looked more closely at the experience you could find something to tell us about making sacrifices to achieve some goal.

> Or maybe you could reconsider the terms you use to get at this experience.

I follow up this advice with questions that are meant to clarify my suggestions and offer Chris some specific ways of pursuing these options:

> How were you able, for instance, to get over having to give up making additions to your baseball card collection?
>
> When you visited car lots and came across cars that were really nice but beyond your budget, did you find that you had to keep reminding yourself of your goals?
>
> Did you learn anything about having to adjust your goals according to your circumstances?

I also raise specific questions in the margins that are meant to lead him to think more fully about his experience:

> How did this talk go?
>
> How hard did you have to look before you found something? Did you ever waver in your decision to go with a cheaper car— or get teased by a nicer one you couldn't afford?
>
> Is this a sacrifice or a compromise?

Both sets of comments, it is worth emphasizing, concentrate on the content of the writing and resist getting into matters of sentence style and correctness. I don't even minimally mark the errors with dashes in the margins. In my view, Chris is not ready for such sentence-level editing. He still has too much work to do on developing the overall content and shape of his writing to give much time to these concerns. As time at the university is always limited, for students no less than teachers, every chunk of time he spends on fixing up minor problems is time taken from work he might more usefully put toward making his writing a way of thinking and learning and sharing his thoughts with others. However, the revised comments are sharper, more directive (even though they are less critical), and ultimately more helpful. I think they would help Chris better understand the problems I see and give him the direction he needs to work on them productively and make his writing better.

You can't hit the nail on the head with every response—and, in fact, there are many nails to hit, many opportunities to do something useful and constructive in any given response. Nevertheless, it seems a good practice always to respond as if the student will break through on the very next writing and make the kind of progress you hope he might make. That's what I'm trying to do—and do better on my second try— with Chris.

On Cherri's Essay 5

Most of the stories we publish about our classrooms are stories of success. We hear the story of the good student who meets our every expectation and garners our every approval. We hear the rags-to-riches narrative of the mediocre student who, through trial and perseverance—and some deft innovative teaching—has miraculously turned into an A writer by the end of the semester. But instruction only rarely proceeds in such straight ascending lines. More stories need to take on a middle course and look to capture the slow advances, the modest gains, the signs of development, the sudden slips, the sudden gains, and generally the unpredictable, difficult-to-see progress that students make in their work as writers.

All of which is to say that Cherri's fifth essay was not what I was hoping for. After steady improvement, she slips on this assignment. She surveys the territory, but she never plots it out or hammers in the stakes. She's simply not sure about her subject. Is it the "downfalls" of achievement, as her title suggests? And by that does she mean the drawbacks of *achieving* a goal or the drawbacks of *trying* to achieve a goal? Is she concerned with the difficulties of achieving? The sacrifices one has to make in order to achieve? Or is she concerned with the consequences, the after-effects, of having achieved (or not achieved) something? She moves from one sense to another and never settles on her subject—or notices the ambiguities she is running into. As if this were not enough, the essay is short. It appears she doesn't ever really get into the writing at all.

The assertions she makes are undistinguished and remain at a general level. She offers no substantiation for her claims that her childhood was "not exactly pleasant." She provides no substance for her claim that she began reading and writing in order to escape from a childhood that "wasn't exactly pleasant," and she does nothing to show what made her see herself as a "pretty good writer" in junior high school or what kind of writing she has done since. She seems only faintly aware of the difficulties of a career in writing, and she never really establishes the allure that a career as a writer would have for her. Would the satisfaction come only after publication? Does she find a career in writing appealing because it would allow her to do a lot of reading, decide her own hours, and work at home? Does she still find that writing helps her, as she suggests, to deal with personal challenges? Or is she attracted to writing because she thrives on a life given to the imagination? There are many questions left unaddressed, a lot of territory untraversed, in the essay.

Nevertheless, I don't want to over-react in my comments. It would be easy to rear back and criticize this writing or speak of Cherri's performance as a setback. But I don't feel any need to give her the kind of wake-up call that I felt it was necessary to give Chris. I want to respond with

the long view in mind, making comments that aren't just critical but helpful, comments that will re-engage her work as a writer. It might even be
a good idea, I think, to just let her slide on this one. Chalk it up as an
assignment she just couldn't get into and not make any more of it. Present
only a couple of comments and see what she does on her next paper. But
I decide instead to write a lot of comments and try to turn this writing
into another lesson on looking more closely at one's experience, getting
something more to say, and sharing it with readers. There's a lot of good,
I think, that can come from having Cherri work on (or even just consider) the possibilities in this writing.

I write detailed comments in the margins and an elaborate note at the
end. The marginal comments concentrate almost entirely, once again, on
ideas and development. The final comments also concentrate on the
content, but they deal, in addition, with the overall shape and focus of the
writing. I try to remain upbeat and constructive throughout the response.
In the margins I present several interpretive comments, reader responses,
and praise comments, looking to playback how I read the text and pointing out strengths in the writing:

> You started by talking about "sacrificing" things in order to
> reach your goals, and now you're talking about "consequences."

> I'm glad to hear it.

> I appreciate the examples you provide here. They help to show
> that you realize what you'd be getting into.

I make only one criticism in the margins, and it is a qualified evaluation:
"I don't get a good sense of what these 'sacrifices' might actually be." I
also present a couple of comments in the form of closed questions:

> Do you see how each of these passages has all kinds of experi-
> ences and details wrapped up in them?

> The achievement of this goal or the satisfaction from achieving
> this goal?

Almost all of the other marginal comments are open questions. One leads
her to consider her focus in the essay: "Will you be talking mainly about
sacrifices or consequences?" The others are meant to help her develop her
ideas:

> What kind of books did you read to escape? Escape from what?

> What made you think you were a pretty good writer?

> How much writing have you been doing? What kinds?

> What else can you tell us about the drawbacks (or obstacles)?

The end comment is more critical and offers more direct help. I start by playing back what I think she is saying in the essay: that we ought to make ourselves aware of the difficulties involved in our goals before we plunge head-long into pursuing them. Then I intersperse several critical comments (in italics) with a number of interpretive and explanatory comments:

> *But it takes me some time to figure out just what you are saying in the essay, to understand exactly what this paper is about.* I think the problem comes from the many different key terms you use. You start the paper by talking about "sacrificing" in order to achieve some goal, and you return to the idea of sacrificing at the end. *But you also get into other key terms in these first and last paragraphs that muddy the water for me.* You mention something about assessing the potential "consequences" of achieving goals in paragraph 1. You talk in paragraph 3 about the "drawbacks" of pursuing a writing career—and the "disappointment" that can be involved in it. It seems as if you are using these terms interchangeably, as if they are all synonymous. *Yet there are clear differences between making sacrifices for a goal, seeing drawbacks (or difficulties?) in pursuing a goal, dealing with disappointments along the way, and making yourself aware of potential consequences of achieving (or failing to achieve) a goal.*

After dramatizing the trouble I have following her ideas, I offer advice about how she might clarify the focus of the essay and make her key terms and ideas work together:

> I'd go back and decide just what I was really interested in talking about, and then try to figure out which of these other terms to address and which ones to take out. Then I'd try to see if I have done enough to get at these key terms and ideas and figure out how they all fit together.

I then try to encourage her to define and elaborate on these ideas, which will need a lot more substance if they are going to be interesting and meaningful for readers:

> As it stands, though, there's much more to say, much more that needs to be clarified and elaborated—about your interest and motivation for becoming a writer, your sense of the difficulties of writing, and your willingness to make the necessary sacrifices and put up with the likely disappointments in order to reach your goal and be a published writer.

I close by asking her to think about what she could do to clarify, shape, and develop her ideas more fully.

Across the response, I'm counting on the fact that Cherri has steadily progressed and that the paper lies close to home and might well be something she'd like to work with. Just how effective my comments will be depends on how invested she is in this writing—and how willing she is to go back and at least consider how she might work through these ideas. Even if she doesn't return to this writing and revise it, I think the comments will have a positive effect on her upcoming work as a writer.

Conclusion

I don't believe students' written products can improve dramatically in 15 weeks. As a teacher I've come to expect more modest gains in my students' writing, looking for it to improve in certain restricted ways, along certain lines, while not necessarily expecting a demonstrable improvement in overall writing quality. Growth in writing tends to proceed slowly, the writer making only modest gains gradually, with practice, over time. It is more important to expose students to principles and strategies of writing that may eventuate in broad gains over the long-term than try to make immediate improvements in overall quality. My teaching is not so much geared to the completion of individual texts as it is strategic and developmental. When I read student writing, I look for certain signs of development, evidence that students are trying to employ the techniques we've been working on in the course. My object is to push students to push themselves to look more fully at their experience, discover ways to turn their thoughts into text, and learn to say more in their writing. The comments I make on their writing are the most important thing I do as a writing teacher. So I take care in deciding when I respond, what I respond to, and how I respond to their papers, and I look always to make my comments responsive to the particular needs of the individual student.

During the six-week stretch of time between their first and fifth formal essays, I looked to orient students to writing as a way of thinking, a way not simply to argue a point or transcribe commonplace ideas but to discover something anew, something they could get behind as writers, something they believed worthwhile, and in doing so perhaps get something interesting to say to readers. The exploratory writings were designed to encourage students to write, as James Britton would have it, at the point of utterance, trying to figure out what they had to say by literally coming to terms with their experience. The first two formal essays were meant to give students practice in finding something more distinctive and interesting to say and making a case for their key claims. On the next several assignments—Essays 3, 4, and 5—students were asked to bring these principles to bear on their writing and, in addition, shape their ideas and materials more purposefully into a text, to get at their vision more clearly for themselves, their own understanding, and communicate better with readers. Essay 4 and Essay 5 were the heart of the course. They were also where I provided my most intensive response. I wrote only a few comments on the exploratory writings, if I responded at all. I wrote an average of 12 comments on Essay 1 and 21 comments on Essays 2 and 3. On Essay 4 and Essay 5, I wrote 31 comments apiece—by far the most I wrote on any papers across the semester. After the fifth essay, I reduced the number of comments on each paper. In fact, I wrote a letter combining my responses to Essay 6 and Essay 7 in which I compared their work on the two papers, evaluated them against their earlier writing, and, in anticipation of their last final assignment (a self-evaluation of their work in the course), guided them to review their work across the semester. I devoted my comments on Essay 8 to areas I liked. Then on Essay 9 I left it up to students to comment on one another's rough drafts and revisions and, in the end, grade one another's writing.

My responses through this key stretch of the course are marked by certain patterns. Seventy-four percent of my comments focus on ideas and development. I am particularly drawn to commenting on the extent to which the writer's content works against commonplaces and becomes somehow original and distinctive. I have a special bias for writing that is grounded in the writer's first-hand knowledge, and I like to encourage students to experiment with certain textual strategies such as going back over their ideas at a more specific level, extending their ideas, using repetition, and playing one voice or view dialogically off another. I place a premium on explicit, concrete detail and elaboration. Like Francis Christensen, I believe student writing has to grow thick and wild before it can be usefully trimmed. An additional 16 percent of my comments focus on extratextual concerns, especially the writer's voice, the relation of the ideas in the text to the student's own ideas and experience, and the student's ongoing work in class. I routinely look at the writing in terms of its exploratory purpose and its potential impact on readers. My comments tend to be full, even elaborate. I write an average of 24 comments per paper. I write an average of 14 words per comment: eight words per marginal comment and 17 words per end comment. My end notes average 350 words.

Across these three papers under study, my dominant modes of response are praise, open questions, and explanatory comments. Twenty-four percent of my comments are presented as praise. Twenty-two percent are framed as open questions. Seventeen percent are explanatory comments, especially those that look to explain and follow up on earlier comments. Another 14 percent are given to playing back the student's text, in interpretive comments or reader-responses. Only 10 percent are given to criticism and only 5 percent make requests for revision. (Even these evaluative and directive comments tend to take the more moderate forms of qualified evaluations and advice.) My comments tended to be open-ended at the beginning of the course. They became more directive (and, not coincidentally, fuller and more detailed) in the middle of the course. In the last few weeks of the semester, I placed more and more emphasis on peer response. I responded less, and when I did respond I concentrated on praising their strengths, noting their progress, and raising questions. When I had the chance, I tried to provide careful editing and proofing on at least one of each student's last papers, usually restricting myself to one or two pages of the text and leaving the rest for the writer to work with on her own.

Although the same general tendencies can be found in my responses to all three case-study students, my comments change in discernible ways from student to student, shifting according to the strengths and weaknesses in their papers and my sense of their evolving needs as learning writers. I call attention to extratextual concerns on Rob's papers twice as much as on Chris' and Cherri's papers, especially our work in class and his ongoing work as a writer. Rob had a slow start in the course, but when he stepped up his efforts his writing showed immediate gains. These extratextual comments were intended to show how his writing was improving. I also focus slightly more in Rob's writing on matters of organization. His content was more fully realized and was ready for such additional attention on arrangement. I was also able to address local matters in his writing earlier than in the other two students' writings. It should not be surprising, then, that I also write significantly more praise comments on Rob's papers: 33 percent as compared with 20 percent on Chris' writing and 19 percent on Cherri's. The high percentage of praise is, no doubt, a function of the quality of his writing, but it is also a result of my attempt to capitalize on his improvements.

I write the fewest comments on Chris' papers and more tightly limit their scope. I write 18 comments per paper on his writing, compared to an average of 28 comments on Cherri's and Rob's. Most of my comments are focused on his voice, the quality of his assertions, and his use of examples. Chris was having more trouble than the others getting something substantive to say, and I was wary of giving him too much to deal with at a time. I make more criticism on his papers, but I also provide a fairly high proportion of praise—one out of every five comments. Although I want to point to areas that aren't working as well as they might, I also want to be constructive. The criticism I make does not outweigh the praise.

My attention on Cherri's papers veers more toward matters of development. On all three papers she had some difficulty getting at her ideas and making them stand up. She tends to leave key terms undefined or underdefined, and she doesn't do enough to go back over her key statements and give them substance. Yet I was always led to feel that Cherri was giving herself to her writing. She was not yet able to realize her ideas as much or as consistently as Rob, but she clearly had something to say and was more comfortable with her writing than Chris. She seemed more into the class and more motivated to work on her writing, and I was content to gently guide her along. I make only a handful of criticisms on her three papers. I offer several pieces of advice on Writing 4 and Writing 5, to give her some direction for revision. But most of my comments—one-third of all my comments on her three papers—are framed as open questions designed to lead her to think along specific lines about how she might develop her ideas.

My comments, then, are geared to the individual student as well as the goals of the course. Notably, though, the "student" I was responding to was a construction, a self construed from the student's work in the course, especially his writing, with little information about the real person behind the text, about the person's interests, knowledge, values, background, and attitudes. Almost all I knew about these students was based on their writing and inferences I might have made about them as a result of how they behaved in class and what they did in their writing. I was not, then, responding so much to the student behind the text as I was to the implied author that I created on the basis of his or her work and writing. Everything I needed to know as a responder about these students, I assumed, was contained here, in their texts.

Overall, my style of response is constructive, elaborate, and fairly directive. It is constructive in its voice and my frequent use of praise. It is elaborate because I work in detail with the issues I raise, playing back how I read the writing, tying my comments to the words of the student's text, and explaining my primary comments. It is directive inasmuch as I write a lot of comments, with a clear agenda, and it is only fairly directive inasmuch as I am guided by and work with the student's own choices. I push students to make their writing exploratory and pursue the choices they've made as writers, but I also try to encourage them to choose their own specific topics and determine the course they'll take in their writing. If my comments are not (overly) directive, if I don't take over the student's text, I do provide certain direction. My style is also conversational in the sense that it highlights the content of their papers and looks to engage writer and reader in a mutual inquiry about their writing. As these sample case studies suggest, I try to make comments that talk with students in a casual voice, engage them in an exchange about their writing, build on their strengths, and push them to continue to work at their writing.

As recent scholarship has increasingly reminded us, teacher response is only as good as it fits into the larger work of the class and responds to the needs of individual students. To be effective, teacher comments must look beyond the student's text and consider the writing in terms of the assignment, the type of writing, and the stage of drafting. But in order to be really successful they also have to reflect and reinforce the principles and criteria that are valued in class, address the writing in light of the student's ongoing work, and advance both the immediate and long-term goals of the course. When the comments are at their best, they don't simply provide students with an assessment of their writing and they don't simply turn students back to their text for revision. They dramatize how their texts are being experienced by a reader. They bring key principles of the course to life by grounding them in the students' own writing. They build on the larger classroom discussion and feed back into it, one propelling the other along the path of learning. They motivate. And they teach.

Sources Cited

Britton, James. *Language and Learning*. London: Allen Lane, 1970.

Christensen, Francis, and Bonniejean Christensen, eds. *Notes toward a New Rhetoric: Nine Essays for Teachers*, 2nd ed. New York: Harper, 1978.

Elbow, Peter. "Options for Responding to Student Writing." In Richard Straub, ed. *A Sourcebook for Responding to Student Writing*. Cresskill, NJ: Hampton, 1999; 197-202.

5

Guidelines for Responding to Student Writing

Offering advice about responding to student writing is like offering advice about playing chess. You can learn how each piece moves, a number of gambits, and some general strategies. But the game has to be played—and learned—on the board, amid a hundred shifting factors. The moves you make depend on the board in front of you, the ground you want to hold or seize. It's only after you've played a while—only after you've gotten an idea of all the choices and the way contingency must be reckoned with at every turn—that you're in a position to really learn the game. Learning how to respond is a bit like learning to use your pawns wisely or knowing when to put your queen into play. You try to follow certain principles. You look for certain keys. You watch for certain warnings. In this chapter, I'd like to offer a fairly detailed set of strategies for responding with the aim of helping new and experienced teachers get some bearings on how they might best respond to their students' writing. I'll offer advice not only about making comments themselves but about situating comments within the larger work of the writing classroom.

Teacher response, I am assuming here, is integral to effective writing instruction—as important as any other activity or responsibility we take up as writing teachers. The comments we make instantiate what we really value in student writing. They offer an opportunity to make the key concepts of the class more meaningful to students. And they enable us to give substance to the claims we make about their roles as writers, our roles as teachers, and the work of writing. If we claim to be facilitators in the classroom, our comments should be noticeably encouraging and helpful. If we claim to give students practice in making their own choices and developing their authority as writers, our comments should allow them room to decide which comments they take up and which they pass up in revision. If we claim to emphasize the content and thought of writing, our comments should deal mostly with the author's ideas.

Running through all of the advice below is the belief that careful, thoughtful commentary can make a real difference in the immediate and long-term development of student writers. Never mind claims that teacher commentary doesn't make a difference. Never mind the easy skepticism that students don't even read the comments; all they're interested in is the grade. Give students sincere, well-designed comments, comments that give them thoughtful feedback about what they have to say (not just how they say it or whether it's correct) and how they might work on their writing, in a classroom that is charged with a belief that students can learn to write better, and they will read the comments, appreciate them, and get something out of them—if not on the next draft, then on the next paper or the one after that, or perhaps when they write again next semester.

Bringing the Class into Your Responses

1. Response begins with the course description. It begins with the assignment and the work in class. It begins with your values and expectations. It begins with what the students write. You read the writing, but you read the writing both as a reader and with the reader in mind. You read with an eye to the assignment, to the work you've done in class and the work you hope to accomplish. You read with an eye to the writer in the text and the student behind the writing. Before you even pick up the pen or open a file, much about how you'll respond has already been determined. So it makes sense as you invent the class, day by day, in the assignments, the lessons, the class discussions, and the things you say about writing, that you also consider how these choices will ultimately come to bear on the way you read and respond to what your students write—and how your responses, in turn, might help you shape your instruction.

2. Before you start to read a set of papers (optimally even as you put together the assignment and talk with students about the writing they are to do), consider the aims of the writing. Try to get a sense of what you are looking to accomplish with this writing right now, in the short term, and over time, in the long term. What do you want to accomplish through your reading and your comments? What is the one thing, above all others, you'd like these comments to do? How does what you are looking for here go with what you have been working on or what you intend to work on in the class? Decide what your main focus will be—and what you will generally *not* deal with in these papers.

3. Decide how long you'll take with each paper—and how many you'd like to have finished in an hour or two. Do all you can to stick to the plan. You may not be able to keep up, but you've got a goal in mind.

4. Once you start actually looking at the papers, you have two choices: reviewing the paper first, before you make any responses, or responding as you read the first time through. Both options have their strengths and drawbacks. The first method: Read the paper over once quickly and select the focuses of your response. Put a line next to key passages and jot down a list of your concerns as you go. Then, after you've gone through the paper, decide your major points, work up a general strategy, and compose your response. This might seem at first to take more time, but it probably ends up being more efficient because it allows you to focus better when you comment on the paper. The second method: Just comment as you read the first time through the paper, and cast your comments in terms of a reader's moment-by-moment responses. Whenever something strikes you as worthy of a comment (based, if you're smart, on priorities you've established), you write it down. This method is more risky: it can take a lot of time, it can lead to some erasing and recanting, and it can easily lead to commentary that ranges far and wide and fails to provide adequate direction to the writer. But it does provide an opportunity to provide fuller responses to specific passages (and, when it's well done, perhaps greater guidance and stronger control).

Viewing Response as an Exchange

5. Look to engage students in an inquiry into their subject, by treating what they have to say seriously and encouraging them, in turn, to take their own ideas seriously. Turn your comments into a conversation with students, a real dialogue that encourages them to read the comments and respond to your responses. Write out your comments, especially your most important comments, in full statements. Short, cryptic comments, abbreviations, and a lot of editorial symbols may too readily be taken as the hasty marks of an editor or critic . . . or the pouncing corrections of a teacher. Fuller comments help create an exchange between reader and writer, teacher and student. They dramatize how you are reading and making sense of the text, and they construct you as someone who is intent on helping them improve their writing.

6. Write your comments as much as you can in nontechnical terms, tying the comment to specific concerns in the writing and using the language of the student's text. The goal here, again, is to enact an exchange. The more you address the content of the writing, tie your talk to the student's language, and refer to specific issues and passages in the writing, the more likely you'll engage the student and bring her into a discussion.

7. Try to link your comments to the key terms of the larger classroom conversation. It's important to establish a vocabulary for talking about

writing—one that may very well go beyond the language that students bring into the course. Yet, at the same time, keep this talk grounded in your students' own writing.

8. Add follow-up comments that explain, elaborate, or illustrate your primary comments. Comments that explain other comments will be construed as help.

Responding as Selecting

9. Focus your commentary on no more than two or three concerns in a set of comments, making sure that your comments reflect your priorities and advance the goals of the course. Students do best when they can work on a couple areas of writing at a time.

10. There's no need to address every instance of a problem—or, for that matter, every success. Select key instances and build your response on them. Leave the rest for the student to identify and work out on her own.

11. Don't overwhelm the writer with comments. Look to address 5 to 10 passages per paper. Look to write somewhere between 12 to 25 comments (i.e., statements) per paper, including marginal and end comments. It's not the number of comments that distinguish informed teachers' responses from uninformed teachers'; it's what you do in the comments you provide. Instead of being comprehensive, try to cover less ground and be more effective with what you do take up.

12. Be respectful of the student's space: be careful about crossing through sentences or writing indiscriminately between the lines of the text. You expect students to be neat and orderly; try to be so yourself.

13. Look for ways to limit what you take up and try to accomplish in a given set of comments. Not every paper that you read needs to be commented on extensively—or, for that matter, commented on to the same extent. Write more comments on papers that seem more open to fruitful revision. Write more comments for students who need more help or students you want to challenge to do even better work.

Focusing on First Things First

14. Emphasize matters of content, focus, organization, and purpose. Work on these concerns until the writing achieves some reasonable level of maturity. If you're working on early drafts or even immature final drafts, feel free to deal exclusively with matters of content. There is no sense in getting into shaping and refining a paper that has nothing yet to say.

15. Address local matters in detail only after the writing is doing more or less what it sets out to do in content, focus, and organization. Unless you have good reason, don't emphasize matters of correctness either too early in the drafting of a paper or too early in the course. Asking students to serve several masters can lead only to their serving none of them very well.

16. Employ minimal marking for errors: punctuation, grammar, spelling, and other local conventions. Instead of marking and explaining every error, just put a tick mark in the margin next to the line where the error occurs. Leave it up to the student to locate and correct the error. Have students meet with you if they have trouble, or check their work after they've had a chance to make corrections. (Another option: when you return the papers with your comments, have a 15-minute workshop in which students find and correct the errors you've minimally marked in the margins.)

17. Keep an eye always on the next work to be done: the next draft, the next paper, the next issue of writing that the class or this student writer will take up. Make comments that are geared toward improvement, not simply the assessment of a finished text.

18. Experiment with ways of focusing your comments on certain issues at certain times in the course. Sequence your comments across the semester, taking up issues that are most important to you at the start of the course and adding other areas as you go. On early papers, for example, present only positive comments or restrict yourself to commenting only on the content and development of student writing. On some papers, or some drafts, just deal with the voice and tone of the writing. On final drafts late in the semester, abandon work on developing the content and focus exclusively on sentence structure or the pacing within paragraphs.

Shaping Your Comments to the Larger Context of Writing

19. Read the student's text in terms of its (stated or assigned) rhetorical context. Does the writer construct a persona that is appropriate to the occasion? How well does the writing address the intended audience? Does it achieve the purposes it sets out to achieve?

20. Tie your talk on the page to the work you've been doing in class, and your immediate and long-terms goals. Use the key terms of the class in your responses—again, to give them local habitation and a name.

21. Decide how closely you are going to hold students to following the exact demands of the assignment—or how much room you are going to

allow them to develop their own topics and their own purposes in their own ways.

22. Shape your comments according to the needs of the individual student. It's not the paper in front of us, after all, that we're teaching. Work on what the student would do best to work on.

Creating a Give-and-Take Relationship with Students

23. Learn the uses of both directive and facilitative forms of commentary. Without criticism and calls for changes there'd be less direction in your responses. Without comments that play back the text, ask questions, provide reader responses, and offer explanations, there'd be less help and encouragement in your commentary.

24. Look to take advantage of the many uses of praise: to recognize a job well done, to teach a principle, to underscore successful strategies, and to encourage students to continue working on their writing. Use praise in one area or in one passage to build confidence in tackling others. Write at least as many praise comments as criticisms. Be supportive and encouraging. Yet also be demanding. Look to move the student, wherever she is now in her development as a writer, forward.

25. Frame your comments in forms that modulate the control you exert over students' writing. Instead of relying on commands, shape your calls for changes in the form of advice. Instead of using only direct criticism, present some of your criticisms as qualified evaluations or reader responses, forms that highlight the subjective or contingent nature of commentary. Ask questions—and real, open questions, not simply questions that disguise some criticism or command. Too many directive comments can close down interaction and take away the authority a writer needs to develop as an author, a writer with something to say. Students do best when they are involved in an exchange, not in a battle of wills. More than a critic pointing out problems or an editor dictating changes to be made, look to create yourself in the role of a reader, a guide, a helpful teacher, a challenging mentor, or some kind of coach.

26. Try to make at least occasional use of comments that simply play back your reading of the student's text, without overtly evaluating, questioning, or advising the student about the writing. Comments that provide your interpretations will let the writer know how his writing is being understood. They will also let her know you are reading the writing first of all for its meaning.

27. Fit your comments to your own strengths and style as a teacher, and along the way look to add to your strengths as a responder. No one way of responding will work, or work the same way, for every student. It is necessary, then, to develop a repertoire of responding strategies, to meet the demands of different students and different settings.

Using Marginal Comments or End Comments

28. There's no necessary difference between putting comments in the margins or in a separate response, in end notes and letters. Marginal comments allow for greater immediacy and specificity. They allow you to deal directly with specific issues in relation to specific passages. They also lend a ready concreteness to your responses. End comments encourage you to provide a fuller context for your comments and carry on a fuller discussion about them. They also give you a chance to lend some perspective to the various issues you raise in the margins. In end comments, generally speaking, start with some piece of praise or a general overview of what you see the student doing in the writing. Direct the student's attention to your key concerns. Elaborate and explain your comments and tie them back to the student's text. Look to make your end comments somehow complement your marginal comments. The end note may highlight and elaborate the key marginal comments. It may focus on one key area that is addressed in the margins. It may take up areas that are not treated in the marginal comments but that you now want to focus on. The over-riding idea here, as in response in general, is to find ways to involve students in an exchange about their writing, with the aim of leading them to work further on developing themselves as writers.

Integrating Responses into the Class

29. As teachers, we show what we value by spending time on it in class. If all we do after we've spent hours making comments is hand the papers back in a rush at the end of a class, while students are packing their books away, we make the statement that the comments are not important, that they are not to be taken seriously. We allow the comments to be seen as a matter of course: students write papers and hand them in, the teacher comments on the papers and hands them back, we all move on to the next paper, checking another thing off the list of things to do. Develop a different habit. Whenever you're about to hand papers with your comments back to students, take time to talk about the responses you've made. Indicate any important patterns you've seen in their papers, note the key concerns of your responses, and discuss the purposes behind your comments. Let students know what they are to do with the comments now that they are in their hands.

30. Make response a two-way street—or, better yet, a free-flowing highway. When the students hand in their papers, encourage them, in a separate note attached to their writing, to direct your attention to special concerns they have about the writing. Read the paper in light of these concerns, or use them in discussing your own responses to the paper. At different times in the course, have students react to your responses, identifying any questions or confusions they might have and pointing out those they find the most and least useful.

31. Concentrate most of your work with response in the first half of the course. Gradually have students take on greater responsibility for responding to one another's papers. The more students see you modeling your own ways of reading, evaluating, and responding to writing, the more adept they will be when it comes time for them to respond to one another's writing. The more you put into your responses early on in the course, the more you will be able to establish a firm foundation for your work to come, and the more you can rely on students to provide feedback to one another's writing later on.

32. Make self-evaluation a part of the course: Have students periodically evaluate their own strengths, progress, and areas for improvement as writers. Such work will lead them to develop a keener sense of what you are looking for, and what they might look for, in their writing.

These, then, are some principles to follow, some guidelines to help you find your way. Ultimately, of course, if responding is indeed like playing chess, you finally have to develop a feel for it on your own. Discover your own strengths. Find your own best strategies. Develop your own style. The best comments, finally, do not focus on one area or another. They do not provide just a little criticism or a lot of help. They are not directive or facilitative. The best comments take on what is most important in this paper, for this student, at this time. They encourage students to look back on their choices and consider their options. They pursue. They apply pressure. They offer incentive. They teach. And they challenge the student to make the next move.

6

Managing the Paper Load,
Or Making Good Use of Time

At the 1998 Conference on College Composition and Communication in Chicago, at the end of a late-afternoon session on responding to student writing, a middle-aged woman in a print dress stood up to ask a question. I had seen her at two or three other sessions on response, but she made no comments and asked no questions. Now she leaned forward, gripped the chair top in front of her, and looked straight into the eyes of the panelists. "I have been to sessions all day on this topic. I've heard one idea after another about what I can try and what I should be doing when I respond to student writing. It all makes sense. It all sounds very good. But . . . I teach four classes a semester. A hundred and twenty students. I spend my nights and weekends marking student papers. Everything I've heard up to now will take even *more* time. I am overwhelmed. Exhausted. What I came here to find out, what I want to know—and what nobody is telling me—is: How can I do it in *less*?"

A hard question. Really no question at all, but a request, a complaint—a plea. She has come looking for relief, a way out. What can a teacher do just to keep up with what she has to do when she has such a course load, when she has so many students, when week in and week out she has so many papers to deal with? How could she do the kinds of things she was being asked to do with response? What would I do if I had 100 students a semester, most of them in writing classes?

I want to tell her that she can put these contemporary principles of response into practice in no more time than she now takes in responding to her students' writing. She can deal more fully with the student's content, look at the writing in terms of its larger contexts, write out her comments in full statements, elaborate on her key comments, and write comments that are constructive, taking no more than 15 or 20 minutes a paper. I want to encourage her, to tell her that our response to student writing is the most important thing we do in a writing course, the activity that has the greatest potential to make a difference in the ways students write and look at themselves as learning writers. There are no timesavers. There are no ways to cut corners and do a good job. I want to hold out a belief that whatever time we do spend reading and responding to student writing is time well spent—and will show itself, in time, in student writing. And yet, I know I am asking a lot, maybe asking too much. Quick counterclaims will not work. Pep talks will not do. She is standing there ringing the top of the chair, and she is feeling overwhelmed. *What can I do?*

Still, when I get the chance to respond, I go with my first thoughts. I remember trying to concede, on the one hand, that the principles of response she had been hearing about would probably take more time, not less, and trying, on the other, to convince her that they could be put into practice in no more time than she was now spending. I remember suggesting that it wasn't simply a matter of cutting back; it was a matter of making good use of whatever time we did spend—could spend—responding.

Now I'd like to take another shot at the issue and offer some practical suggestions for how we might make comments that are detailed, substantive, and constructive but won't require more time than we usually have to give to response—and, if they are taken up imaginatively, might even take less time, at least some of the time. First I'll offer advice for approaching response strategically across the semester. Then I'll offer advice for approaching response to individual papers. Finally, I'll offer specific strategies for commenting fully yet efficiently.

Planning Comments Across the Course

Let me begin with two basic principles that when ignored, lead to a lot of purposeless commentary and a lot of wasted time, for teachers and students alike, and then go on from there.

1. You don't have to respond, much less respond fully, to all assignments. Not all writing assignments need to be graded, marked up, or even read in order to be valuable, and not every paper that we read needs to be commented on, or commented on extensively. Some writing requires only a quick read-through and a nod here and there. Some only a well-placed question or two, a couple acknowledgments, or a few reader responses. Some can be read by peers in class. Some writing doesn't have to be read at all: its value can lie in the fact that it has been composed, and in being composed has helped compose the writer. It all depends on what you're trying to accomplish.

2. You don't have to provide equal time or make the same type of response for every student or every paper. Not all papers merit the same depth of response. Some papers and some students require more response, some less. It is not only okay but beneficial to give only as much response as the individual paper merits or the individual student needs or can make use of productively.

3. So get creative with your assignments and be selective about which assignments you read more (or less) fully, and what issues you deal with (and don't deal with, or don't yet deal with) in your comments. The more assignments, the more room you have to be selective with the comments you do make. You can free yourself from having to address a range of concerns on every paper, across every page. You can focus on only certain concerns at certain times. Instead of reading every writing from top to bottom, for content, arrangement, style, and correctness, decide ahead of time on one or two key concerns for the writing and write comments only on those areas.

4. Establish a sequence of concerns you will emphasize in your reading and responding across the semester. What will you be most concerned with on the first paper? On the second and third papers? On the papers that come in at the end of the course? Again, address only certain concerns at certain times. Decide whether you will address targeted concerns on every paper or whether you will read papers according to criteria that develop incrementally across the term. A good principle is to deal extensively with the content and thought of students' writing in the first half of the course and hold off on doing more with sentence structure and correctness until the second half. Let students know what you are and are not addressing at a given time, in your assignments, in your classwork, and in your responses. Then set your priorities and stick to them.

5. Decide where in the course you will provide detailed sets of comments and where you will provide only brief commentary. For instance, respond only briefly in the first two or three weeks, and save your most elaborate responses for the early-middle segment of the course. As the semester progresses and you've built a foundation for your work, place more and more responsibility on students to respond to one another's writing and maybe even help grade completed essays. Use more inclusive comments only in the second half of the course or only at the end of the semester. Also, do more and more self-evaluation as the course goes on. Any writing class that is going to have more than a minimal effect must help students become independent learners.

Planning Comments Before Each Set of Papers

6. Before you begin reading—or, better yet, after you've glanced through the stack of papers—get set in your mind what your main concerns will be on this set of papers. The more you know what you are looking for, the better your response and the more efficient your work.

7. Decide which modes of commentary you will be most inclined to use—and why. Are you going to emphasize praise and open questions, to give students a sense of what you are looking for but keep them firmly in charge of their own writing? Are you going to look mainly to play back the text in interpretive and reader-response comments? Or, in an effort to provide more direction, are you going to point out problems and direct the writer to make certain revisions?

8. To cut back dramatically on the time you give to response, divide the stack of papers in half. Read half of the students' papers more fully this time, the other half more fully next time, according to the criteria established for the paper. Or skim through the stack of papers quickly and place them in two stacks—papers that you'll respond to in detail this time, papers that you'll respond to only in brief. To take it a step further, have students themselves select two or three (or four) of their papers on which they want full comments. Assume that they will get the most out of comments on papers that they are most interested in looking back on and revising. Why spend time making a full set of comments on a paper that the student acknowledges is not ready for such full response? Keep a record of those students whom you've responded to in detail and those you have not, and try to respond more or less fully accordingly on the next assignment.

Responding to Individual Papers

9. Read through the paper once quickly without stopping to make any comments; as you go, somehow identify (with checks and minuses, dashes, or penciled-in words) the concerns you'll take up in your response and select the key instances where these problems occur. This double reading might seem at first to take more time, but it doesn't. In fact, it may save time in the long run. The time you put in on a preliminary reading will help you get a sense of and sort through the papers to come, decide what you'll focus on in your comments, and make the time you spend responding more directed and purposeful.

10. Limit the scope of your responses. Focus on two or three priorities and give students certain things to work on at certain times. Put other matters on hold—they aren't going anywhere. If it's a rough draft, concentrate especially, say, on content, focus, and purpose. Deal only briefly, perhaps in a general comment or two at the end, if at all, with matters of wording, sentence structure, and correctness. If it's one of many papers to come in during the semester, just deal with its content or voice. If it's a draft that's already gone through a revision or two and needs now to be polished up and readied for readers, devote yourself to commenting on sentence-level

matters. This is the time to address problems with wordiness and punctuation. Save full-length marginal and end comments for papers that are going to be revised—or papers that are ripe for instruction. When you're about to hand the papers back, let students know what you have—and haven't—dealt with.

11. Instead of dealing with every instance of every concern you take up in a paper, concentrate on only two or three places where these issues arise. Leave the rest for students to work with on their own.

12. If you address fewer issues, you can deal more fully with the comments you *do* make. Play back your reading of the text, offer some evaluation or advice, and then follow up the comment with an explanation or some helpful questions. By making fewer comments but writing them out more fully, you can help students better understand the comments and use them more effectively to improve their writing and develop their practical understanding as writers. In doing so, you will make better use of the time you spend and earn better dividends for your efforts.

13. Get creative with your marginal comments. On selected assignments, focus on one or two concerns in the margins and write fewer but fuller comments. Several well-developed marginal comments will take less time than a full end note, yet they can go far in directing the student to specific issues and leading her back into the writing. Save the end comment for presenting a larger perspective on the writing. On other assignments, make only marginal comments and no end note at all. Commenting in the margins requires less contextualizing than end notes and can be done more quickly. Make the marginal comments on a couple areas only, so you won't have to use an end comment to clarify points or indicate priorities. Such comments are especially useful when you are highlighting certain areas of writing in class or after you've made fuller comments on earlier papers or on earlier drafts. This earlier work will prepare students for the kinds of comments you make.

14. Get creative with your end notes. Don't fall into the habit of always responding in detail in the margins and then providing a full overview in your closing comment. On selected assignments, provide only a brief end note to the student and deal only with one or two concerns (for this assignment, for this point in the class, for this paper, or for this student). This method is especially useful on papers that have a considerable problem with one key issue of writing that gets in the way of any other successes, say, a draft that leaves its key points undeveloped, a draft that has a lot of material but is poorly arranged, or a paper that is well-developed and effectively arranged but needs work on sentence structure. When you focus your end note on only one or two areas of writing, you can then

do a little bit more with each of these areas, making whatever comments you *do* make clearer and more useful. Never mind about covering the remaining territory. Or, just make a quick general statement about one of these other concerns and leave it at that: "You have a lot of minor errors in usage and punctuation on these two pages—look to clean them up on the next draft." There will be time for these matters, if not on the next draft of this paper, then on the next paper; if not this semester, next semester. Make a habit of doing whatever you do *well* rather than always trying to address all there is to address. Less is more.

15. If you limit your comments to one or two areas and still want to give the student more information about other areas of the writing, use a grid or scoring guide, indicating with a quick check or number how she has done along a two-point scale (satisfactory/unsatisfactory) or three-point scale (exceptional/good/fair).

16. Use minimal marking to indicate (but not necessarily correct or even explain) errors. Instead of circling, correcting, and explaining the student's mistakes, just place a dash or a tick mark (no need to write any words) in the margin next to the lines in which the errors occur. Leave it to the student to find and correct. Moreover, instead of minimally marking all errors, minimally mark only one or two selected types of errors: say, comma splices and commas or misspellings and usage problems. To make up for not explaining the problems in your comments, plan a short workshop on one or two of the most frequent problems for the class as a whole. Copy and hand out samples of the error taken from the papers. Discuss the problem and illustrate it through several samples. Have students go through the rest of the handout and make corrections and then, when you hand back their papers, have them go through their writing, find any places where they have made such errors, and correct them.

17. Extend the use of minimal marking to indicate selected sentence-level problems that students can address on their own, either with the help of a handbook or, better yet, in in-class workshops that acquaint them with the problem and give them practice at making improvements. This strategy is especially useful, for instance, with working on shaping the beginnings and ends of sentences for clarity and emphasis. On a given paper or set of papers, minimally mark sentences that don't get orientational information and transitional phrases up front and out of the way of the main idea. Or mark sentences that don't end (and/or that successfully end) on a strong note, a point of emphasis. Leave it up to the writer to note the strength or revise the weakness in the marked sentences.

18. Make use, selectively, of other abbreviations and symbols. On selected papers, mark—without necessarily putting any words on the page—

ideas or passages you like, ideas that you'd like to hear more about, places where you had trouble understanding the writing or had questions, sentences that were sharp or fuzzy. Peter Elbow uses straight underlines to indicate passages he likes and wavy underlines to indicate passages he found difficult to read. Glynda Hull sometimes asterisks samples of a given problem across a student text and holds off commenting on them until her end note. I like to draw a box around key terms or statements that are left undefined or undeveloped, a backward-pointing arrow to note places where I see the student going back over her earlier writing to give it substance, and brackets to indicate passages that the student might consider deleting. If you're doing intensive work with voice or defining key terms, use an abbreviation to call attention to these concerns. The key to using such abbreviations and symbols is to keep them limited to a couple of concerns and make sure students know what they are meant to signify. Using more than a few symbols or abbreviations is asking for trouble. The less your comments engage and communicate with students, the more the time you've spent responding is wasted.

Making the Most When You Hand Back Your Responses

19. Before you hand back a group of papers, take time to go over what you've done in the comments and why you've done it. Then give students time to read the comments in class. Identify what you were looking for, what you were trying to do in your responses, and what kind of comments you usually made. If you spend so much time making comments on a set of papers, why would you want to hand them back in a hurry after class, as students are rushing to get out? We make time in class for what we most value. If we really value our responses to student writing and want students to value them too, we have to set aside time in class for reading and talking about our responses.

20. Make a regular practice of having students respond to your responses. Encourage them to ask questions, play back how they understand what you are saying, and identify the responses they find most and least helpful. From time to time, make copies of your comments and discuss them in class. Connect what you are doing in your comments with the larger work of the course.

21. Instead of requiring every formal paper to be revised or reworked, have students decide themselves whether or not they will pursue a revision for a better grade. The fewer perfunctory revisions you have to read, the more time you will have to give to students who are giving themselves to their work.

I can't assure beleaguered teachers that these strategies will enable them to significantly reduce the time they now spend responding to student writing. The fact is that substantive, constructive teacher response is going to take time. But I believe these strategies can be employed without spending any more time than they now spend with response, and I promise that they'll make whatever time they do spend more worthwhile.

7

Students' Perceptions of Teacher Comments

Up to this point, we have been examining response from the teacher's perspective, looking at the strategies informed teachers use in responding to student writing. The natural question is, of course, do they work? Do they result in better writing or help students become better writers? No simple matter. What works, of course, depends on what students are able to *do* with the comments. What works in one class, on one assignment, for one student, might very well not work for another. Further, what constitutes "good writing" or "improvement in writing" may be different from teacher to teacher, class to class, and program to program. Are we looking to improve the next draft? Get clean, clear prose? Improve the student's composing processes? Improve the student's understanding of writing? Help students develop critical thinking or a critical literacy? In order to determine what works we have to decide what we are assessing and how we are going to assess it. All this and we haven't even begun to consider the difficulties in isolating the effects of certain kinds of comments on student performance—and seeing them in terms of the larger contexts of instruction.

I'd like to pursue a simpler question. Instead of examining how students actually make use of teacher comments and whether the responses make any demonstrable difference in their writing, I'd like to focus on how students *perceive* our comments: which kinds they appreciate and find useful and which ones they feel they do not get much out of.

I asked 172 students from nine first-year writing courses at Florida State University to respond to a 40-item questionnaire, indicating their preferences for a range of teacher comments. The comments were selected from responses that 20 different teachers made on a sample student paper—a first rough draft of an argumentative essay, "What If Drugs Were Legal?" (see pp. 11-12). Students were asked to read the essay and then respond to the questionnaire. They were to assume that they were getting the draft back with teacher comments and were going to do a revision. They were asked to indicate their preference for each comment, using a four-point scale: definitely prefer, prefer, do not prefer, definitely do not prefer. To better understand their preferences, students were asked on 10 items to explain the reasons for their choices, giving as much detail as possible. One hundred and forty-two students completed the survey.

The questionnaire was designed to investigate students' reactions to three variables of teacher response: the focus, the specificity, and, especially, the mode of teacher comments. I had a long list of questions. Which areas of writing do these students want us to address in our comments? Do they appreciate comments on the content of their writing? Do they value comments about organization? Do they appreciate comments on local matters? Do they prefer lengthy comments or brief comments? Do they prefer responses that present direct criticisms of their writing and explicitly call on them to make changes in their texts? Or do they prefer suggestions and questions—that is, forms of commentary that are less directive? What do they think of qualified criticism, reader responses, and praise?

The students, as it turned out, were quite adept at making distinctions among different types of comments and had sound, well-articulated reasons for the comments they found most useful. They seemed to be influenced far less by the *focus* of teacher comments than by the *degree of specificity* of the comments and the *modes* of commentary. Below, I'll outline the findings of this study, using the four-point scale employed in the questionnaire: the lower the number rating, the more the students preferred the comment under question. The comment that earned the best rating averaged 1.3; the worst-rated comment averaged 3.2. (For a detailed account of the study, see "Student Reactions to Teacher Comments.")

Specificity

First and foremost, the students wanted comments that were clear, specific, and understandable. They did not respond favorably to any comment that they saw as vague or difficult to follow. (The sample comments were typed up in the questionnaire, but if they weren't, the students would no doubt have expected comments to be legible too.) The 12 most general comments on the survey, which averaged six words per item, received an overall rating of 2.5, among them the following:

> Don't just generalize. Support your ideas with evidence and facts. (item 1)

> Good material—but it needs to be tightened up. (item 8)

Many students were baffled or put off by these comments:

> *We've been told this since 8th grade. The problem must be stated more in depth—it's a generalization.* [item 1]

What evidence and facts? Don't generalize your comments either. [item 1]

Tightened up? The teacher should be more specific. This does not tell me anything. [item 8]

What do you mean by tightened up—if you want us to explain and be specific, you must be also. [item 8]

The students showed an overwhelming preference for comments that addressed specific matters in their writing, in specific ways. The more specific, the more elaborate, the more they liked them. The nine items that were specific but unelaborated (averaging 19 words per item) were rated at 2.3, among them the following comments:

> You must show, in more specific terms, exactly what damage society suffers from drug users. (item 7)

> Are there other things that are bad for the body that most members of society do not consider wrong? (item 12)

Far and away, they most preferred—and enthusiastically expressed their appreciation for—comments that were specific *and* elaborate, for instance:

> Perhaps there is something that you could use to your advantage in the behavior of other sorts of addicts: smokers, gamblers, shoppers? (item 20)

> Your paper might be clearer if you state, point by point, your opponent's view, as clearly and objectively as you can. Then you can deal with each of his arguments and show the weaknesses in his position. (item 24)

> In your next draft try to focus on developing more convincing arguments against legalized drugs. For instance, what can you do to show how drugs like marijuana and cocaine would be more dangerous if they were legal and therefore more available? (item 40)

The nine most detailed comments in the study (averaging 30 words per item) were rated at 1.8. (In more practical terms, every difference of .5 between two comments means that 60-70 students—half of the total respondents in the study—rated a comment one point higher or lower than the other.) These comments stood among students' favorite responses on the survey.

Students made no bones about it: they wanted comments that they could understand and that pointed specifically to issues in their writing. There is no substitute for comments that are clear, specific, and tied directly to the language of the student's text.

Focus

The students seemed to appreciate comments on all areas of their writing. They were as interested in getting comments on global matters of content and organization as comments on sentence-level concerns. Within these two groups, however, they showed a greater preference for some types of comments than others. Students gave comments that acknowledged the ideas on the page a favorable rating of 2.0, among them the following:

> Good—you've defined the particular issues with which you do not agree and summarized the author's argument. (item 23)

> In the last paragraph, you say that "LeMoult's points are good and true but I believe he is approaching the subject in the wrong manner." What of LeMoult's points are "good and true"? How is he "approaching the subject"? Why is he approaching the problem "in the wrong manner"? (item 38)

As one student explaining his response to item 38 put it: "It's taking the author's idea and trying to develop it, not change it." Not surprisingly, they were wary about comments that looked negatively on or somehow worked against the ideas that were already down on the page. The following comments in particular were rated poorly:

> I don't think we'll get anywhere with the circular argument that drug use is criminal and should not be legalized. (item 13)

> These arguments are not convincing. (item 17)

> You've missed his point. (item 18)

Many seemed to believe that their right to have their own opinions make null and void all questions about the content of their writing. It was not up to the teacher to assess what they said, these students seemed to be saying, but only how (well) they said it, suggesting a view of writing as essentially a matter of transcribing thought, not a way of thinking and shaping thought.

Students appreciated comments on organization and development, and they did not seem to mind criticism when it dealt with sentence structure and correctness, that is, local matters that could easily be fixed. They seemed decidedly less favorable toward comments on wording. Perhaps whereas they saw judgments about grammar and sentence structure as matters of right and wrong, they saw comments asking for a reconsideration of word choice as reflecting the idiosyncratic preferences of the teacher. They seemed genuinely appreciative when a comment made it clear that the teacher read the paper closely and acknowledged their ideas.

Mode

Students recognized differences in the ways comments were presented—and they were aware of the attitudes, roles, and power relations created by different modes of commentary. Three-fourths of the students noted in their follow-up remarks that their preferences were influenced by how a comment was presented or how it made the teacher come across as a responder. They spoke of how some comments sounded helpful and encouraging, whereas other comments sounded harsh and critical. They noted how some comments made the teacher come across as thoughtful and caring and how others made the teacher come across as judgmental or sarcastic. They indicated that some comments helped the writer develop her ideas and that others forced the teacher's views on the writer. Some students were able to make even finer distinctions, distinguishing between comments that "offer suggestions" and those that "tell the student what to do" and between comments that "only criticize the student" and those that, though they may criticize, "show the writer how the writing can be improved."

Students most favored comments in moderate modes, responses that provided direction but did not insist on a certain path for revision and that came across to them as help. Most of all, they appreciated comments in the form of advice and explanations. They liked all praise—even if it was only presented barely in the single-word comment "good" or presented in tandem with criticism. The best praise, as other researchers have indicated, was that which also provided reasons for something being good. Students also seemed to like comments in the form of open questions, especially when they were expressed in specific terms and presented in a helpful voice.

They did not prefer—and in many cases balked at—comments framed in highly directive modes, responses that stated in no uncertain terms how the writing should be done and that pushed the teacher's views on the writer. They did not appreciate straight or harsh evaluative comments—especially those dealing with content and those presented in general terms. They were able to detect subtle evaluations that were presented indirectly in reader-response comments and preferred these modes slightly more than straight evaluations. They gave a mixed review to commands and to closed questions. They appreciated comments that pointed to problems that needed to be addressed, but they did not like any comments that were presented in a harsh, judgmental, authoritative tone. Overall, the students preferred comments that offered some direction for improvement but asserted only moderate control over the writing. Their favorite modes of commentary by far were advice and explanations—comments that typically are specific, offer direction for revision, and come across as helpful.

On a scale of 1 to 4, with 1 indicating the comments they most preferred, students gave the following ratings to the modes of commentary:

Explanations	1.56
Advice	1.76
Praise	1.93
Open Questions	2.08
Closed Questions	2.24
Commands	2.28
Criticism	2.70

In the sections below, I'll explain and assess the ways this group of students perceived the sampling of teacher comments.

Advice

Hands down, the students most preferred comments presented as advice
and comments that offered explanations. As a group, the eight advisory
comments averaged 1.76 on the 4-point scale. Five of the comments in the
category were among the nine items that were the most preferred across
the survey. Students saw advisory comments as positive and
helpful—the comments of an encouraging teacher or guide rather than
the comments of a critic, as they noted in explaining their reactions to
item 2, "In your next draft try to focus on developing more convincing
arguments against legalized drugs":

> It identifies the problem in a way that makes the teacher seem like they
> care.

> Offered help for the next draft, not putting down.

They also saw the advice presented in item 2 as preferable to the imperative presented in item 1 ("Don't just generalize. Support your ideas with
evidence and facts"), because, as a number of students explained, it was
more positive:

> This is a better approach than [the first comment]. It's just plain advice
> to help.

> This is a more positive statement that gives the writer options of what
> to change.

Students were unanimous in seeing the same strengths in item 16:

> Before writing the next draft, you might try listing as many
> things you can think of that are legal *and* that are also danger-

ous—like cigarettes, firearms, skydiving, and over-the-counter drugs—and consider how these things are different from illegal drugs. Then choose the best arguments and work them into your essay.

Some appreciated the helpfulness of the comment:

> *Gotta like the help!*
>
> *This is very helpful advice. The writer now knows how to approach the next draft.*
>
> *Very helpful—shows the writer what it is they are lacking and helps them by triggering the ideas.*

Others liked the way the advice established a softer tone than directive modes of commentary and left them in greater control of their writing:

> *Suggestions are given instead of gripes.*
>
> *The teacher gave a sound suggestion that would probably be very helpful without criticizing the author in any capacity.*
>
> *It'll help them think more and write the paper better. They don't tell him/her how to write it.*
>
> *May offer some ideas and material, but this comment is an "offered suggestion," not a command.*

Some appreciated the response because, beyond the suggestion, it provided detailed help:

> *Gives examples on how to make the paper better. Teachers are for guidance in the subject, not to rip everything apart.*
>
> *This tells me how to support my thesis rather than saying I'm not supporting it.*
>
> *The detail is what is important.*
>
> *[I give it a "1"] because it gives the student ideas to explore. The teacher could have just said the first part [before "like cigarettes"] which would have been no help.*

One student summed up in a word her sense of all that is good about this comment: "Perfect."

Tellingly, the comments that fared best with students were those that offered advice, followed up this advice with an example or explanation, and worked with the ideas the student already had down on the page, as in the following comments, which received 1.4 and 1.3, the best ratings in the study:

> Your paper might be clearer if you state, point by point, your opponent's view, as clearly and objectively as you can. Then you can deal with each of his arguments and show the weaknesses in his position. (item 24)

> In your next draft try to focus on developing more convincing arguments against legalized drugs. For instance, what can you do to show how drugs like marijuana and cocaine would be more dangerous if they were legal and therefore more available? (item 40)

Every comment framed as advice in the study was met favorably. None was rated over 2.1, the average for the 40 items on the survey.

Explanations

The students gave the responses with added examples and explanations a rating of 1.56, better than any other type of commentary in the study.

> Before writing the next draft, you might try listing as many things you can think of that are legal and that are also dangerous—like cigarettes, firearms, skydiving, and over-the-counter drugs—and consider how these things are different from illegal drugs. Then choose the best arguments and work them into your essay. (item 16; rated 1.6)

> Perhaps there is something that you could use to your advantage in the behavior of other sorts of addicts: smokers, gamblers, shoppers? (item 20; rated 1.8)

> Good—you've defined the particular issues with which you do not agree and summarized the author's argument. (item 23; rated 1.7)

> In your next draft try to focus on developing more convincing arguments against legalized drugs. For instance, what can you do to show how drugs like marijuana and cocaine would be more dangerous if they were legal and therefore more available? (item 40; rated 1.3)

Just how much students appreciated such explanatory comments is further indicated by how they reacted to items 11 and 24. Both responses offered the same advice, but whereas one made the suggestion and stopped, the other went on to offer an explanation for the advice:

> Your paper might be clearer if you state, point by point, your opponent's view, as clearly and objectively as you can. (item 11)

> Your paper might be clearer if you state, point by point, your opponent's view, as clearly and objectively as you can. Then you

> can deal with each of his arguments and show the weaknesses
> in his position. (item 24)

The students appreciated both responses, but they overwhelmingly preferred item 24 (1.4), rating it almost a full point better than item 11 (2.1).

Praise

The students liked praise. The comments that offered positive evaluations were among the most well-received in the study. They preferred praise accompanied by an explanation of what the teacher saw as good (item 23) slightly more than the simple, unelaborated evaluation "Good" (item 39). These students were not particular about where they found praise—they appreciated it wherever it turned up. Although they were not taken with item 8 as a whole ("Good material—but it needs to be tightened up"), they did respond well to the simple praise comment that leads into the call for revision. Students who rated the response favorably explained their reasoning this way:

> *It offers positive approval, but also gives positive motivation.*
>
> *Gives positive comment first and then offers a bit of advice to help the paper.*
>
> *Lets me know they like the idea I'm presenting but I need to rework it*

Students seemed to want to know when they were doing something well in their writing. Many may even be hungry for praise.

Questions

These students were generally receptive to questions, but they were particularly receptive to open questions. They seemed to appreciate the freedom and control over their writing that comments framed as questions offered. They appreciated questions that provided direction or help more than comments that implicitly criticized their writing or challenged them to make revisions. The average rating for open questions was 2.08—the third most preferred mode of commentary in the study behind advice (1.76) and explanations (1.56). The average rating for closed questions was considerably less favorable: 2.24, only a notch better than commands.

The students responded especially well to open questions that were elaborate and tried to lead them to develop the ideas they already had on the page:

> How can you explain and support these views so they will be
> more convincing to readers of the publication? (item 21)

> In the last paragraph, you say that "LeMoult's points are good and true but I believe he is approaching the subject in the wrong manner." What of LeMoult's points are "good and true"? How is he "approaching the subject"? Why is he approaching the problem "in the wrong manner"? (item 38)

They liked item 21 because it offered direction even as it allowed them room to decide which changes, if any, were to be made:

> *The question allows the writer to come up with ideas of his own, without being backed into a corner by a specific suggestion.*

> *Leaves the writer open to answer and think about what he/she has written. Poses a challenge to correct the paper. Very constructive.*

> *The teacher is trying to help without giving the information to you.*

Those who did not like this question said they wanted more direction and a clearer sense of what the teacher wanted:

> *Leaves you in the air about what the teacher wants.*

> *Could you say it another way? More explicitly perhaps?*

> *I'd rather be given suggestions.*

Item 38, the most detailed open question in the study, was their favorite comment in the form of a question and the third most preferred comment on the overall survey, earning a rating of 1.5. They appreciated the specificity of the comment as well as the open-ended help provided by the questions, as the following reactions suggest:

> *This makes the writer examine themselves without the teacher having to tell them what is wrong. The writer can answer these questions— see for himself if the paper makes sense.*

> *These questions that the reader poses leave the writer to reflect and then creatively and uniquely fill in missing sections.*

> *Very detailed, gives writer sense teacher really read it and was therefore interested.*

> *Specific places to look, not generalities.*

The students were less enthusiastic about, but still were favorable toward, comments 12 and 28, which were shorter and more general:

> Are there other things that are bad for the body that most members of society do not consider wrong? (rated 2.2)

> Is this important to your argument? (rated 2.2)

The students gave closed questions a mixed review, and finally preferred them only to criticism and commands. They were most receptive
to closed questions that, even though they might have implied the
teacher's criticism, seemed to offer help or direction more than simply
confronting the student with a problem:

> Do we? All drugs? (item 37; rated 2.05)

> Can you break up these sentences so I can follow your ideas
> more easily? (item 6; rated 2.2)

They were least receptive to questions that they saw as more critical than
helpful:

> Is this your only and most important argument? (item 14; rated
> 2.3)

> What, then, of alcohol and tobacco. They are "legal." Would you
> make use of them criminal? (item 26; rated 2.6)

These closed questions, in fact, received the most mixed reactions in the
survey, with some students finding them harsh and critical and others
finding them useful and positive:

> *The teacher sounds like he is attacking the student. The teacher should
> only suggest and make positive remarks that would help the paper.*

> *Sounds so sarcastic, the student would most definitely be offended.*

> *The teacher points out something that the writer may have not thought
> about but does not wrong her for not doing so.*

> *I like this because it helps you think more about revisions to be made
> without making you feel ignorant.*

The students found questions most useful, then, when they provided a
clear sense of direction for revision and left room for them to act on the
comment on their own. They did not appreciate questions that were
framed in harsh or critical ways or that implied some criticism of their
writing.

Commands

The students had mixed reactions to another form of traditional response:
imperative comments that call on them to make some change in the writing. On the one hand, they appreciated that the comments pointed out
problems that needed to be addressed. As one student explained in
response to item 1, "Don't just generalize. Support your ideas with evidence and facts": "Even though it's telling him/her how to write the

paper, it's basic info that would make the paper more effective." On the other hand, they did not like the harshness of the commands, as the following students noted, again in explaining their reactions to item 1:

The teacher is too harsh in getting her point across.

The teacher is being abrupt. The student would think she is terribly wrong.

The students seemed more receptive to commands when they were presented precisely and specifically—and, perhaps as a result, came across more positively. Only three of the imperative comments received poor ratings—and these may have been rated poorly because they are stated in terms that are not only vague but also blunt and critical:

Your second argument. Now develop this one. (item 34; rated 2.6)

[Good material–] but it needs to be tightened up. (item 8; rated 2.6)

You need to tighten up your thinking <u>as well as</u> your expression. (item 22; rated 3.1)

More likely than not, the ubiquitous teacher term "tighten" did not make the last two comments any more appealing. As one student, speaking for many, put it, "What the hell does 'tightened up' mean? The comment is a good one, but it is very very unclear and helpless."

Criticism

The students least preferred comments that they were probably most familiar with, the staple of traditional commentary: criticisms. Four of the five comments they rated as the least preferable in the study were terse, negative evaluations:

You've missed his point. (item 18; rated 3.2)

I don't think we'll get anywhere with the circular argument that drug use is criminal and should not be legalized. (item 13; rated 3.1)

These arguments are not convincing. (item 17; rated 3)

Not so. See above. (item 25; rated 2.8)

These students were not against having problems in their writing pointed out; they were against having them pointed out in highly judgmental ways. They felt that there were better ways to present these responses. As one student put it, "I prefer comments that don't necessarily come right out and say it is bad but objectively try to give advice to the writer."

The students viewed qualified criticisms and reader responses in slightly more favorable terms:

> I hear LeMoult saying something different—that drugs are so dangerous to society largely because laws make them illegal. (item 32; rated 2.5)

> I find the statements that we all know drugs are wrong less than convincing. (item 35; rated 2.4)

A number of students seemed to prefer these comments, in which the teacher filters her response through her subjectivity as a reader, to straight criticisms. They felt these comments had a softer tone, and they appreciated the way the comments offered an individual reader's perspective on the writing:

> *The reader stresses that this is his opinion.* [item 35]

> *Gives a viewpoint he/she should consider—it doesn't tell how to write the paper.* [item 35]

> *The teacher points out a possible problem in reader interpretation and does it in a polite way.* [item 10]

But a number of students still felt the comments were more critical than they had to be:

> *I don't like the way it is stated. It sounds extremely too critical.* [item 35]

> *Maybe this comment is true but the teacher doesn't need to say "less than convincing." Don't slam the student.* [item 35]

These reactions indicate that these students may not have seen qualified comments as the teachers may have intended—as statements that are more open, subjective, and tentative than standard criticisms, the responses of a teacher in the role of a reader more than that of a critic or judge. Perhaps they had little experience with these nuanced criticisms and saw them simply as criticism regardless of the qualifications. At any rate, students generally seemed uninspired by critical comments and put off by criticisms with a sharp judgmental edge. It is not, according to their reports, that they don't expect or want teachers to identify problems in their writing; they do. They simply don't like or respect—or seem interested in addressing—comments that talk at them or down to them, not with them.

Conclusion

This study shows that students want and appreciate teacher comments. They also find some types of comments better than others. Students did not mind being told what was wrong or not working in their texts, and they even welcomed comments that pointed out problems and indicated ways to improve their writing—*if* the comments identified specific concerns, were presented clearly, and were written out in specific terms. In fact, students expected teacher comments to tell them how they had done on the writing and what they could do to improve it. They especially appreciated comments that, in addition, were cast as guidance or help.

Teachers' written comments, the study indicates, can be understood and received well—and, consequently, taken up and used effectively in revision—if teachers are careful about the ways they present them to students. The specific form of teacher comments counts. The rule of thumb: if you are going to make a comment, make it well. Rather than spray the paper with various notes and abbreviations, take your time, select which areas of writing are most important for this student, at this time, and write out more fully each of the comments you do make. Try to cast your comments in ways that will engage and inform students, in terms that will connect your comments to the larger conversation of the class. Try to give them the kind of comments they will be interested in reading and working with. Response to a large extent is nothing more—and nothing less—than interpersonal communication, a matter of talking respectfully with someone else.

This is not to say that we should simply give students the kind of comments that they like. That we should look only to please. Just because students are not going to welcome comments that question their word choice, challenge them to think further or more deeply, or don't tell them exactly what we want does not mean we should refrain from making such comments. Teaching requires resistance almost as much as it depends on cooperation. Whatever comments we make, whatever changes or challenges we decide to present, we should make in the name of helping students learn.

The study also suggests we pay greater attention to whether our comments will likely be taken in the ways that we intend—and to take time in class to talk about our strategies of commentary and the goals behind them. If "successful" comments are, by definition, those that engage students' consideration, turn them back into their writing, and lead them to make better, more informed choices as writers, we need to develop a keener sense about how students view different types of comments and how we can make responses that encourage and push them to work more productively on their writing.

8

A Selected Bibliography on Teacher Response

Books and Collections

Anson, Chris, ed. *Writing and Response: Theory, Practice, Research*. Urbana: NCTE, 1989.

Elbow, Peter, and Pat Belanoff. *Sharing and Responding*. New York: Random House, 1989.

Freedman, Sarah Warshauer. *Response to Student Writing*. Urbana: NCTE, 1987.

How to Handle the Paper Load. Classroom Practices in Teaching English 1979-1980. Urbana: NCTE, 1979.

Judine, Sister I. H. M., ed. *A Guide for Evaluating Student Composition*. Urbana, IL: NCTE, 1965; ERIC ED 033 948.

Lawson, Bruce, Susan Sterr Ryan, and W. Ross Winterowd, eds. *Encountering Student Texts: Interpretive Issues in Reading Student Writing*. Urbana: NCTE, 1989.

Sorcinelli, Mary Deane, and Peter Elbow. *Writing to Learn: Strategies for Assigning and Responding to Writing Across the Disciplines*. San Francisco: Jossey-Bass, 1997.

Straub, Richard. *A Sourcebook for Responding to Student Writing*. Cresskill, NJ: Hampton Press, 1999.

Straub, Richard, and Ronald F. Lunsford. *Twelve Readers Reading: Responding to College Student Writing*. Cresskill, NJ: Hampton Press, 1995.

Reviews of Scholarship

Griffin, C.W. "Theory of Responding to Student Writing: The State of the Art." *College Composition and Communication* 33 (October 1982): 296-301.

Horvath, Brooke. "The Components of Written Response: A Practical Synthesis of Current Views." *Rhetoric Review* 2 (Janurary 1984): 136-56. Rpt. in Gary Tate, Edward P.J. Corbett, Nancy Myers, ed. *The Writing Teacher's Sourcebook*, 3rd ed. New York: Oxford UP, 1994.

Jerabek, Ross, and Daniel Dietrich. "Composition Evaluation: The State of the Art." *College Composition and Communication* 26 (May 1975): 183-86.

Knoblauch, C.H., and Lil Brannon. "Teacher Commentary on Student Writing: The State of the Art." *Freshman English News* 10 (Fall 1981): 1-4. Rpt. in Richard Graves, ed. *Rhetoric and Composition: A Sourcebook for Teachers and Writers.* Upper Montclair, NJ: Boynton/Cook, 1984.

Assigning and Responding to Student Writing

Elbow, Peter. "High Stakes and Low Stakes in Assigning and Responding to Writing." *Writing to Learn: Strategies for Assigning and Responding to Writing Across the Disciplines,* 5-13. See Sorcinelli and Elbow, 1997.

Larson, Richard L. "Making Assignments, Judging Writing, and Annotating Papers: Some Suggestions." *Training the New Teacher of College Composition,* 109-16. Ed. Charles W. Bridges. Urbana: NCTE, 1986.

Larson, Richard L. "Writing Assignments: How Might They Encourage Learning?" *Twelve Readers Reading: Responding to College Student Writing,* 375-85. See Straub and Lunsford, 1995.

Lindemann, Erika. "Making and Evaluating Writing Assignments." *A Rhetoric for Writing Teachers,* 2nd ed., 191-223. New York: Oxford UP, 1987.

White, Edward M. "Using Scoring Guides to Assess Writing." *A Sourcebook for Responding to Student Writing,* 203-12. See Straub, 1999.

Young, Art. "Mentoring, Modeling, Monitoring, Motivating: Response to Students' Ungraded Writing as Academic Conversation." *Writing to Learn: Strategies for Assigning and Responding to Writing Across the Disciplines,* 27-38. See Sorcinelli and Elbow, 1997.

Responding Theory and Practice

Anson, Chris. "The Artificial Art of Evaluating Writing." *Journal of Teaching Writing* 1 (Fall 1982): 159-69.

Anson, Chris, Joan Graham, David Jolliffe, Nancy Shapiro, Carolyn Smith. "Responding to Student Writing." *Scenarios for Teaching Writing: Contexts for Discussion and Reflective Practice,* 34-62. Urbana: NCTE, 1993.

Auten, Janet Gebhart. "Power and the Teacher's Pen: Talking about Teacher Response to Student Writing." *The CEA Forum* 28 (Summer 1998): 1-4.

Auten, Janet Gebhart. "A Rhetoric of Teacher Commentary: The Complexity of Response to Student Writing." *Focuses* 4 (1991): 3-18.

Baumlin, James, and Tita French Baumlin. "Paper Grading and the Rhetorical Stance." *Encountering Student Texts,* 171-82. See Lawson, 1989.

Bazerman, Charles. "Reading Student Texts: Proteus Grabbing Proteus." *Encountering Student Texts,* 139-46. See Lawson, 1989.

Berkenkotter, Carol. "Student Writers and Their Sense of Authority over Texts." *College Composition and Communication* 35 (October 1984): 312-19.

Brannon, Lil, and C.H. Knoblauch. "On Students' Rights to Their Own Texts: A Model of Teacher Response." *College Composition and Communication* 33 (May 1982): 157-66.

Chiseri-Strater, Elizabeth. "Evaluation as Acts of Reading, Response, and Reflection." *Nuts and Bolts: A Practical Guide to Teaching College Composition*, 179-202. Ed. Thomas Newkirk. Portsmouth, NH: Boynton/Cook, 1993.

Connors, Robert J., and Andrea Lunsford. "Teachers' Rhetorical Comments on Student Papers." *College Composition and Communication* 44 (May 1993): 200-24.

Connors, Robert J., and Cheryl Glenn. "Responding to and Evaluating Student Essays." *The St. Martin's Guide to Teaching Writing*, 3rd ed. New York: St. Martin's, 1995.

Daiker, Donald. "Learning to Praise." *Writing and Response: Theory, Practice, Research*, 103-13. See Anson, 1989.

Danis, M. Francine. "The Voice in the Margins: Paper-Marking as Conversation." *Freshman English News* 15 (Winter 1987): 18-20.

Elbow, Peter. "Options for Responding to Student Writing." *A Sourcebook for Responding to Student Writing*, 197-202. See Straub, 1999.

Flynn, Elizabeth. "Learning to Read Student Papers from a Feminine Perspective." *Encountering Student Texts*, 49-58. See Lawson, 1989.

Fuller, David. "Teacher Commentary That Communicates: Practicing What We Preach in the Writing Class." *Journal of Teaching Writing* 6 (Fa/Wi 1987): 307-17.

Haswell, Richard. "Minimal Marking." *College English* 45 (October 1983): 600-04.

Hodges, Elizabeth. "Negotiating the Margins: Some Principles for Responding to Our Students' Writing, Some Strategies for Helping Students Read Our Comments." *Writing to Learn: Strategies for Assigning and Responding to Writing Across the Disciplines*, 77-89. See Sorcinelli and Elbow, 1997.

Hodges, Elizabeth. "The Unheard Voices of Our Responses to Students' Writing." *Journal of Teaching Writing* 11 (1992): 203-18.

Johnston, Brian. "Non-Judgmental Responses to Students' Writing." *English Journal* 71 (April 1982): 50-53.

Kehl, D. G. "The Art of Writing Evaluative Comments on Student Themes." *English Journal* 59 (1970): 972-80.

Knoblauch, C.H., and Lil Brannon. "Responding to Texts: Facilitating Revision in the Writing Workshop." *Rhetorical Traditions and the Teaching of Writing*, 118-50. Upper Montclair, NJ: Boynton/Cook, 1984.

Krest, Margie. "Monitoring Student Writing: How Not to Avoid the Draft." *Journal of Teaching Writing* 7 (Sp/Su 1988): 27-39.

Lees, Elaine. "Evaluating Student Writing." *College Composition and Communication* 30 (December 1979): 370-74.

Lunsford, Ronald F. "When Less Is More: Principles for Responding in the Disciplines." *Writing to Learn: Strategies for Assigning and Responding to Writing Across the Disciplines*, 91-104. See Sorcinelli and Elbow, 1997.

Mandel, Barrett John. "Teaching Without Judgment." *Ideas for English 101: Teaching Writing in College*. Ed. Richard Ohmann and W. B. Coley. Urbana: NCTE, 1975.

Moxley, Joseph. "Responding to Student Writing: Goals, Methods, Alternatives." *Freshman English News* 17 (Spring 1989): 3-4, 9-10.

Moxley, Joseph. "Teachers' Goals and Methods of Responding to Student Writing." *Composition Studies: FEN* 20 (Spring 1992): 17-33.

Murray, Patricia Y. "Teachers as Readers, Readers as Teachers." *Encountering Student Texts*, 73-85. See Lawson, 1989.

O'Neill, Peggy, and Jane Mathison Fife. "Listening to Our Students: Contextualizing Response to Student Writing." *Composition Studies* 27 (Fall 1999): 39-51.

Onore, Cynthia. "The Student, the Teacher, and the Text: Negotiating Meanings through Response and Revision." *Writing and Response*, 231-60. See Anson, 1989.

Phelps, Louise Wetherbee. "Images of Student Writing: The Deep Structure of Teacher Response." *Writing and Response*, 37-66. See Anson, 1989.

Podis, Leonard A., and Joanne M. Podis. "Improving Our Responses to Student Writing: A Process-Oriented Approach." *Rhetoric Review* 5 (Fall 1986): 90-98.

Probst, Robert. "Transactional Theory and Response to Student Writing." *Writing and Response*, 68-79. See Anson, 1989.

Purves, Alan. "The Teacher as Reader: An Anatomy." *College English* 46 (March 1984): 259-65.

Robertson, Michael. "'Is Anybody Listening?': Responding to Student Writing." *College Composition and Communication* 37 (1986): 87-91.

Rothgery, David. "'So What Do We Do Now?' Necessary Directionality and the Writing Teacher's Response to Racist, Sexist, Homophobic Papers." *College Composition and Communication* 44 (May 1987): 87-91.

Schwegler, Robert. "The Politics of Reading Student Papers." *The Politics of Writing Instruction: Postsecondary*, 203-26. Ed. Richard Bullock and John Trimbur. Portsmouth: Boynton/Cook, 1991.

Searle, Dennis, and David Dillon. "The Message of Marking: Teacher Written Responses to Student Writing at Intermediate Grade Levels." *Research in the Teaching of English* 14 (October 1980): 233-42.

Smith, Summer. "The Genre of the End Comment: Conventions in Teacher Responses to Student Writing." *College Composition and Communication* 48 (May 1997): 249-68.

Sommers, Nancy. "Responding to Student Writing." *College Composition and Communication* 33 (May 1982): 148-56.

Sperling, Melanie. "Constructing the Perspective of Teacher-as-Reader: A Framework for Studying Response to Student Writing." *Research in the Teaching of English* 28 (1994): 175-207.

Straub, Richard. "Teacher Response as Conversation: More than Casual Talk, An Exploration." *Rhetoric Review* 14 (1996): 374-98.

Straub, Richard. "The Concept of Control in Teacher Response: Defining the Varieties of 'Directive' and 'Facilitative' Commentary." *College Composition and Communication* 47 (May 1996): 223-51.

Welch, Kathleen. "Sideshadowing Teacher Response." *College English* 60 (April 1998): 374-95.

White, Edward M. "Post-Structural Literary Criticism and the Response to Student Writing." *College Composition and Communication* 35 (May 1984): 186-95.

Zak, Frances. "Exclusively Positive Responses to Student Writing." *Journal of Basic Writing* 9 (1990): 40-53.

Alternative Methods of Teacher Response

Anson, Chris. "In Our Own Voices: Using Recorded Commentary to Respond to Writing." *Writing to Learn: Strategies for Assigning and Responding to Writing Across the Disciplines*, 105-13. See Sorcinelli and Elbow, 1997.

Carnicelli, Thomas. "The Writing Conference: A One-to-One Conversation." *Eight Approaches to Teaching Composition*, 101-31. Ed. Timothy Donovan and Ben McClelland. Urbana: NCTE, 1980.

Harris, Muriel. *Teaching One-to-One: The Writing Conference.* Urbana: NCTE, 1986.

Hawisher, Gail, and Charles Moran. "Responding to Writing On-Line." *Writing to Learn: Strategies for Assigning and Responding to Writing Across the Disciplines*, 115-25. See Sorcinelli and Elbow, 1997.

Lauer, Janice. "Interpreting Student Writing." *Encountering Student Texts*, 121-28. See Lawson, 1989.

Murray, Donald. "The Listening Eye: Reflections on the Writing Conference." *Learning by Teaching.* Montclair, NJ: Boynton/Cook, 1982.

Newkirk, Thomas. "The First Five Minutes: Setting the Agenda in a Writing Conference." *Writing and Response*, 317-31. See Anson, 1989.

Rose, Alan. "Spoken versus Written Criticism of Student Writing: Some Advantages of the Conference Method." *College Composition and Communication* 33 (October 1982): 326-31.

Sommers, Jeffrey. "The Effects of Tape-Recorded Commentary on Student Revision: A Case Study." *Journal of Teaching Writing* 8 (Fall/Winter 1989): 49-75.

Sommers, Jeffrey. "The Writer's Memo: Collaboration, Response, and Development." *Writing and Response*, 174-86. See Anson, 1989.

Tobin, Lad. "Responding to Student Writing: Productive Tension in the Writing Conference." *Writing Relationships: What Really Happens in the Composition Class*, 40-56. Portsmouth, NH: Boynton/Cook, Heinemann, 1993.

Rule, Rebecca. "Conferences and Workshops: Conversations on Writing in Process." *Nuts and Bolts: A Practical Guide to Teaching College Composition*, 43-65. Ed. Thomas Newkirk. Portsmouth, NH: Boynton/Cook, Heinemann, 1993.

Effects of Teacher Comments

Burkland, Jill and Nancy Grimm. "Motivating Through Responding." *Journal of Teaching Writing* 5 (Fall 1986): 237-46.

Dohrer, Gary. "Do Teachers' Comments on Students' Papers Help?" *College Teaching* 39 (1991): 48-54.

Dragga, Sam. "The Effects of Praiseworthy Grading on Students and Teachers." *Journal of Teaching Writing* 7 (1988): 41-50.

Ferris, Dana. "The Influence of Teacher Commentary on Student Revision." *TESOL Quarterly* 31 (1997): 315-16.

Gee, Thomas. "Students' Responses to Teacher Comments." *Research in the Teaching of English* 6 (Fall 1972): 212-21.

Lynch, Catherine, and Patricia Klemans. "Evaluating Our Evaluations." *College English* 40 (October 1978): 166-80.

Sperling, Melanie, and S.W. Freedman. "A Good Girl Writes Like a Good Girl: Written Responses to Student Writing." *Written Communication* 4 (1987): 343-69.

Straub, Richard. "Students' Reactions to Teacher Comments: An Exploratory Study." *Research in the Teaching of English* 31 (February 1997): 91-119.

Ziv, Nina. "The Effect of Teacher Comments on the Writing of Four College Freshmen." *New Directions in Composition Research*, 362-80. Ed. Richard Beach and Lillian Bridwell. New York: Guilford, 1984.

Reading and Evaluating Student Writing

Coles, William E., Jr., and James Vopat. *What Makes Writing Good: A Multiperspective*. Lexington, MA: Heath, 1985.

Cooper, Charles R., and Lee Odell, eds. *Evaluating Writing: Describing, Measuring, Judging*. Urbana: NCTE, 1977.

Crowley, Sharon. "On Intention in Student Texts." *Encountering Student Texts*, 99-110. See Lawson, 1989.

Elbow, Peter. "Ranking, Evaluating, Liking: Sorting Out Three Forms of Judgment." *College English* 55 (1993): 187-206

Gere, Anne. "Written Composition: Toward a Theory of Evaluation." *College English* 31 (1980): 44-58.

Knoblauch, C.H., and Lil Brannon, "The Development of Writing Ability: Some Myths about Evaluation and Improvement." *Rhetorical Traditions and the Teaching of Writing*, 151-71. Upper Montclair, NJ: Boynton/Cook, 1984.

Thompson, Thomas. "Understanding Attitudes Toward Assessment: The Personality Factor." *Assessing Writing* 2 (1995): 191-206.

Winterowd, W. Ross. "The Drama of the Text." *Encountering Student Texts*, 21-33. See Lawson, 1989.

Grading

Corder, James. "Asking for a Text and Trying to Learn It." *Encountering Student Texts*, 89-98. See Lawson, 1989.

Elbow, Peter. "Grading Student Writing: Making It Simpler, Fairer, Clearer." *Writing to Learn: Strategies for Assigning and Responding to Writing Across the Disciplines*, 127-40. See Sorcinelli and Elbow, 1997.

Freedman, Sarah Warshauer. "Why Teachers Give the Grades They Do." *College Composition and Communication* 30 (May 1979): 161-64.

Irmscher, William F. "Evaluation." *Teaching Expository Writing*, 142-78. New York: Holt, Rinehart, and Winston, 1979.

Tobin, Lad. "Responding to Student Writing: What We Really Think About When We Think About Grades." *Writing Relationships: What Really Happens in the Composition Class*, 57-74. Portsmouth, NH: Boynton/Cook, Heinemann, 1993.

9

Sample Papers for Response

This chapter presents 10 student essays, without comment, to provide cases for practicing response. Each of the essays is accompanied by information about the classroom context—including the assignment, the work in class, and the student writer—in order to simulate the circumstances that inform and animate our reading and response. The first three papers were written in the same course, for the same assignment. The last six papers were written in the freshman writing course that is examined in Chapter 4, two by students whose work is highlighted in this earlier chapter, the rest by other students from the same class. The aim here is to present sample writings from a setting that readers would already be familiar with, so that the writings could somehow be read within a certain context and with the added benefit at times of knowing something about the student's earlier work in the course.

Sample 1: Argumentative Response Essay

Sample 2: Argumentative Response Essay

Sample 3: Argumentative Response Essay

Sample 4: Speculating about Causes Essay

Sample 5: Personal Essay: Heather's Writing 4

Sample 6: Personal Essay: Heather's Writing 5

Sample 7: Personal Essay: Amy's Writing 5

Sample 8: Personal Essay: Kandi's Writing 5

Sample 9: Personal Essay: Rob's Writing 7

Sample 10: Personal Essay: Cherri's Writing 7

Teachers learn to respond effectively by looking at how other teachers respond. They develop a repertoire of responses by studying the use of various strategies in different contexts. But they learn to develop their own response style only through practice and reflection. These sample response scenarios are meant to provide opportunities for such practice and reflection.

Samples 1 and 2
Paper 3: Argumentative Response Essays
Drafts

BACKGROUND

The two following essays were written in the same class, for the same assignment. It is the third writing of the course, the first of three argumentative essays students are to write. (The first two papers were summaries of articles.) All three essays are to be written in response to an article that students select from a list of options, all of which have been discussed in class. These two students have chosen to write on a newspaper article arguing against continuing the practice of dissecting animals in high-school biology courses, "It's Time to Cut Out Dissection." This is the second draft of the assignment. Students have already written and received peer responses on a discovery draft. They are required to hand in a substantive revision of the essay one week after they get their draft back with your comments. After this revision, they may choose to close their work on the project or make one more pass at revising and proofing the paper.

Melinda got off to a shaky start in the semester, missing several classes and handing in several exercises late. But she has recently gotten back on track and proven herself a dependable student and a capable writer. She always is participating in class, and her writing, while not exceptional, has clearly been above average. Nevertheless, you feel that she has been holding back, not really applying herself in her writing. Her rough drafts have been promising, but her revisions have not been as substantive as you would like them to be. Evan is a good student and seems to be a nice guy. He is easy-going. He is polite, yet not so polite that he is not willing to be assertive. He is professional in his work. He is eager to talk in class, and when he talks he usually has something to say. Since early in the course, you have noted his facility with language and have come to regard him as one of the strongest writers in the class. In fact, you told him in the second week of the semester that you would be challenging him not to rest on his laurels but to raise his writing to the next level, a cut above merely fluent, competent writing.

In class discussion, you've reviewed the argument of "It's Time to Cut Out Dissection," and you've made a point of calling on students to go beyond simple counter claims and make a case for their arguments. You noted, in particular, for example, that it wasn't enough to say that something would be lost without hands-on dissection of real specimens: one had to specify what would be lost. Arguments have to be built on evidence.

ASSIGNMENT

Write an argument in response to one of the following articles, in an academic essay where you take a stand and try to convince others of the reasonableness of your views: "It's Time to Cut Out Dissection," "Wired for the Bottom Line," or "Should You Make Elizabeth Dole President?" Your final essay should be 3-4 typed pages.

*   *   *

Some advice on how to go about this project: Select an issue in one of the articles, optimally an issue in which you have some interest or experience. Identify an idea or view that you would like to counter, qualify, or augment. Look carefully at what the author is arguing, making sure you are being fair to his or her claims and the spirit of those claims. Study the author's arguments, note your responses, and come up with ideas and evidence to develop your take on the issue. Draw up a plan for approaching the paper or maybe do some freewriting to get your ideas out on the page. Then try to compose a rough draft where you articulate your main ideas and consider how they might best be put together.

In your essay, somewhere near the start, indicate the issue(s) at stake, identify the author and article you are responding to, and summarize the author's position. Then present your stance and develop and support your arguments with reasoned evidence. Across the essay, look to construct a sense of yourself as a knowledgeable, fair, and authoritative writer. Remember: your job is not to persuade others that your view is right or that it's better than the author's; your job is to convince your readers—let's say, others who have read this article or who are interested in the subject—that you have a view that is just as valid and merits consideration.

Here is the schedule of due dates:

Discovery draft	Wednesday, October 13
Full Draft	Monday, October 18
Revision	Monday, November 1
Additional Revision (optional)	Friday, November 12

Editor's Note: This classroom context and these papers come from a writing class taught by Kelly Tompkins at Florida State University.

It's Time to Cut Out Dissection

By Neal D. Barnard and Karen M. Pirozzi

We're lucky today. We know plenty about hearts. We know how they pump blood, and we understand the intricate pattern of muscle activity that sends oxygenated blood from the heart around the body. Sometimes doctors can even fix hearts that aren't working right. We're also lucky to have pictures, videos, plastic models and computer models of hearts to help teach about them in schools. So now there's no excuse to kill animals for dissection so students can acquire this knowledge about the heart and the rest of the body. But many grade schools and high schools still use dissection as a means of education. Experts estimate about 6 million cats, dogs, frogs, sharks and other animals are killed each year to this end. Truly, dissection may induce more hardening of the heart than learning about the heart among students. Cutting open an animal just to see what's inside teaches that life is disposable and that self-interest rules.

Many educators have come to recognize the strong link between violence against animals and later violence against humans, particularly highlighted in the wake of the recent spate of school shootings. With that in mind, examining the subtle messages we send each day as educators, parents and citizens becomes critical. When we use alternatives to dissection, we support quality biology instruction. And we also model respect for living beings. And changing teaching practice provides a wonderful opportunity to discuss the need for compassion and the tremendous wealth of resources we have to learn about life, rather than death.

Old-school teachers may argue that nothing can compare to seeing the "real thing," yet the fetal pig or frog is being used as a substitute for a human. Computer simulations of human anatomy come amazingly close to the "real thing." Much more than a damp, dead animal. Even highly respected medical schools such as Harvard, Yale, Columbia and Stanford have eliminated animal labs that were once used for teaching. If a doctor can graduate from a top-notch medical school without cutting up a cat, 10th-graders hardly need the experience.

Dissection telegraphs students the message that life is cheap. However, dissection itself isn't.

A school with five biology classes, for example, will spend about $1,300 to buy 35 bullfrogs per class every year. By contrast, the "Digital Bullfrog" CD-ROM requires a one-time outlay of just $200. Of course, CD-ROMs and other virtual models also expose students to the latest learning technology. Their use combines the teaching of biology and computers, a potent pairing for students' futures.

Studies have shown that students learn just as well with models as with animal dissections. Other studies have shown many children find dissection troubling. While few have the nerve to dissent or even question their elders, these compassion-oriented youngsters nonetheless find the experience upsetting, a circumstance that may turn them off from pursuing medical or science careers. These children, and most caring adults, would be even more upset if they knew the details of how these animals come to be embalmed with formaldehyde.

Investigations have shown that many frogs and sharks come from the wild, causing serious depletion of natural populations in some areas, not to mention disruption of the ecological balance of which they were part. Many of the 100,000 cats killed each year for dissection come from animal shelters, breeders and pet stores. Sometimes they are family companion animals who have been stolen by dealers' minions from neighborhoods and yards. Even though legislation exists prohibiting pet stealing and abuse, the practices remain widespread. Investigators tell stories of witnessing still-living cats deliver kittens en route to the gas chamber.

While no educator would condone these practices, many unwittingly support them through their purchases. But we're lucky. Today's children can learn about biology, technology and respect for life all at the same time, simply by taking advantage of what modern science has made available.

Neal D. Barnard, is founder of the Physicians Committee for Responsible Medicine. Karen M. Pirozzi is a graduate student in education and school psychology at the College of St. Rose in Albany, N. Y.

—Tallahassee Democrat, September 12, 1999

Melinda Chou
ENC 1102
Paper 2 Draft

Dissections When Appropriate

In the article "Dissections in Leon County," Brian McClain, district science education coordinator, states that "animal dissection is . . . a 'valuable learning experience'." I agree with his point that hands-on dissection experiment is a vital part of a student's education, but only when it is done at an appropriate age. Many students of the middle school age are required to dissect an animal as part of their science class curriculum. It is at this age where a child is generally too immature and playful to actually retain any of the intended information from the experiment. However, in later years of high school where a student has more control over his or her class schedule, dissection in upper level biology or natural science classes would be more beneficial because the student has chosen to be in a class where the experiment is part of the curriculum.

As a seventh grader, I was required to dissect a frog in class. There were about 36 kids in my class and I think that maybe two of them actually got anything out of the experiment, neither of those two being myself. Most of the girls squealed at the sight of a dead animal or made a huge production over the fact that it was an innocent creature whose life had been stolen from him and so they refused to do it on "moral grounds," or in my opinion, to create drama and look for attention. On the other hand, the boys saw this as a prime opportunity to play surgeon, or do such things as cut out the frog's eyeballs and throw them at each other; or even, and this was my personal favorite, cut a limb or two off of the frog's body and hide it in one of the previously mentioned drama queens lunch bags. Amidst all this goofing off, the probability of a teacher being able to control that many 12 and 13-year old students while trying to teach about anatomy is extremely low. What is more, the chances of any of those students actually retaining any of the information about the mass of "goo" that they just cut out of "Sparky" their pet frog is even lower.

When students are about four to five years older and in their last years of high school, they have come a long way since their first encounter with the dissection process. Those few years have a huge impact on their maturity level because that is one of the most crucial growth stages in life, both mentally and physically. By the time one is a senior or junior in high school, he or she has started thinking about future plans such as college, or for some, even a career. It is also at this time when students have more freedom of choice in which courses they will take. So if they want to take a class where dissection will be part of the curriculum, then they can, and they will probably be surrounded by other students who are actually interested in doing the experiment and will benefit from the lesson it teaches. These classes will probably have less people so there can be a controlled learning environment and no time wasted on those students who do not wish to dissect.

It is said in the article "It's Time to Cut Out Dissection" by Neal D. Barnard and Karen M. Pirozzi that schools should look to new advances in technology such as cd roms and virtual programs as alternatives to dissection because they are not only cheaper, but eliminate the need for the expenses used to buy the animals for dissection. This makes no sense because the amount of money it would cost to buy enough computers to make the experiment beneficial for all the students in the class severley outnumbers the cost of buying animals for a better hands-on procedure. Furthermore, these new advances seem to be getting newer and better every year, which would require massive amounts of funding to keep the technology updated. It is also hard for teachers to teach the student using a computer because their attention can't be focused on all the screens at once, and as sad it may sound, not everyone in the country is computer literate.

With the massive overcrowding of schools today, class sizes are increasing and there is not as much money provided for schools as there used to be. This is one of the main reasons why dissection should be saved for students in upper level science classes, who have chosen to be there and are actually willing to do the experiment. It can help a student who may be interested in furthering a career in medicine by providing a solid background in anatomy. On the other hand, those students who know that they want nothing to do with the biology field can concentrate more on taking classes more beneficial to them. The amount of money that could be saved by eliminating dissection for inappropriate ages and unnecessary classes could then be used on more important problems such as the shortage of books in the American school systems. Dissection should be kept where it can be fully appreciated by students who want to learn about anatomy, and not wasted on those who would rather play around.

Evan Olsen
ENC 1102
Paper 2 Draft

No Dissection? No Way

What is dissection? According to Webster's Dictionary dissection is "dividing into parts especially for examination and study." It is not the killing of animals for no purpose. Dissection has been a much-utilized learning tool for many years throughout high schools in America, and should not be taken out of the high school curriculum. Dissection is necessary to give future doctors, veterinarians, and scientists the practice and experience needed when it comes time to perform the real thing. I know that as a past surgery patient, I felt more comfortable and confident with my doctor knowing that they had been practicing on real animals since Freshman Biology and not just looking at models.

There are some people, however, who feel dissection is no longer necessary in high schools. Authors Neal Barnard and Karen Pirozzi, who wrote the article "It's Time to Cut Out Dissection," feel that "cutting open an animal just to see what's inside teaches that life is disposable and that self-interest rules." This connection is hardly plausible when speaking about high school students. Most high school students are mature enough to understand why dissections are preformed and what purpose they serve. This is something most instructors explain before the lab. So a student that still associates violence with dissection is probably going to have bigger problems than Freshman Biology and there is nothing anyone can do to prevent that. However, I don't think that we live in a world where scientific exploration in high school creates mass murderers.

A large portion of Pirozzi and Barnard's article tries to explain that there are models and computer programs that can entirely replace dissection. This would be the equivalent of saying a professional race car driver could receive his training in a video arcade. Most people know it takes a lot of practice to be any kind of professional. I would like to think that doctors were considered professionals and held to the same standards of "practice makes perfect" that Jeff Gordon is held to. Jeff

Gordon did not become one of the best by looking at models of race-tracks and car engines or playing NASCAR Nintendo games. He probably started by riding his bike as a child, then racing with go carts, then progressing to real 200 mph race cars, just as today's doctors probably started with a frog or worm then progressed to a cat, and then worked with actual cadavers.

Although models and computer programs could not fully take the place of dissection, they are a great compliment to the actual procedure. These programs can be a precursor to help students get an overview and prevent some students from becoming lost. A computer simulation of the dissection would help teach proper cutting techniques as well as showing a clear view of what they are to examine. This idea does not occur to Pirozzi and Barnard in their article as they feel the computer program would be a financially sound *replacement*. Not to be confused with an *addition* to the curriculum that would boost the quality of learning for high school students.

As a high school student, I preformed a couple dissections. I didn't personally find the process too exciting and I didn't move on to pursue a medical career. However, as I sat picking at the chicken wing, which was one of our dissection projects, I looked around and noticed that half the class was completely engulfed in the dissection. It's no coincidence that many of the same people I noticed in that class of mine are pursuing careers in the medical field right now, one at Harvard University. Did dissection make them all want to be doctors? Some of them it did, but for the others it did offer the training and practice necessary to be in the best possible position to pursue a medical career. Isn't that one of the primary goals of our educational system?

Would it be too radical not to make money such a priority in these matters? Unfortunately money does play a big factor, but how much cheaper would it be to replace dissection with equivalent learning aides? Some sort of three-dimensional model must be present to allow students get a closer look into how the parts fit together. Also, the computer program would need to be installed, which according to the article, is a one time outlay of $200. However, every student must have access to a computer for the dissection, which in most high schools is very difficult. Computer labs that are generally in the library would be the only place possible and they would not provide the atmosphere necessary for real dissection. Unfortunately for Pirozzi and Barnard money and the quality of learning are very proportional in this case. The more money invested in scientific education, the better the quality of education.

Imagine that you are a surgery patient and your doctor is a young, but intelligent man who graduated from Harvard (a college, according to the article, that has completely done away with animal labs that were once used for teaching). Had dissection not been available for him since high school, you could very well be his first "real" patient . . . ever! Medical malpractice would skyrocket if this were the case. Dissection is needed to train, elevate experience, and give confidence to the future doctors and scientists that most need it, for their sake and ours. We have had the knowledge to replace dissection for a long time and yet it still stands as a staple in scientific education. This is exactly how it should stay, not for the politicians, or the activists, or even the school board, but for the students it will benefit.

Sample 3
Paper 3: Argumentative Response Essay
Draft and Revision

BACKGROUND

The following writing was done in response to the same assignment as Samples 1 and 2, by a student from the same class. In this case, however, both the student's (Todd's) rough draft and his revised draft are included. You may respond to the rough draft, in combination with the two earlier papers, or you may read the revised version of the essay in light of Todd's earlier draft.

It is the third writing of the course, the first of three argumentative essays students are to write. All three essays are to be written in response to an article that students select from a list of options, all of which have been discussed in class. This student has chosen to write on a newspaper article arguing against continuing the practice of dissecting animals in high-school biology courses, "It's Time to Cut Out Dissection."

Todd has seemed, let's say, reluctant about the course. He has not talked in class; he has even declined to respond when he's been called on. He has been visibly unimpressed with the prospect of getting into groups to work with other students in class workshops. And, though he has handed in all the assignments on schedule, the first few writings he submitted were lean in content and noticeably short: they were typed in a large font and framed by nearly two-inch-wide margins.

In class discussion, you've reviewed the argument of "It's Time to Cut Out Dissection," and you've made a point of calling on students to go beyond simple counter claims and make a case for their arguments. You noted, in particular, for example, that it wasn't enough to say that something would be lost without hands-on dissection of real specimens: one had to specify what would be lost. Arguments have to be built on evidence.

ASSIGNMENT

Write an argument in response to one of the following articles, in an academic essay where you take a stand and try to convince others of the reasonableness of your views: "It's Time to Cut Out Dissection," "Wired for the Bottom Line," "Should You Make Elizabeth Dole President?" Your final essay should be 3-4 typed pages. (For more details on the assignment, see pp. 284-86.)

Todd Langford
ENC 1102
Paper 2 Draft

Dissection: There Is Still a Need

With the loss of hands on experience with dissection in the labora-
tory to computer simulated programs our society will lose out on many
benefits that come along with this learning experience. Who knows the
high school kid that is dissecting the cat in anatomy class might like it
enough to pursue a medical career as a brain surgeon, and develop new
ways to operate on the human brain successfully. Doing something like
dissection over the computer will not give the same effect that it would
doing the real deal. Dissection will also provide a better learning experience with the tools involved and the higher interest factor.

Dissection in high school and higher level education can be a great
learning experience due to the hands on experience that computer simulations do not give. If the dissection labs are designed correctly people
can get a much better grasp of the organs and their position in the body
rather than looking at a two dimensional computer screen that does not
provide the student with the same visual effect of the animal. When I
took anatomy in high school my labs were designed to make it nothing
but a learning experience. My teacher made us do various incisions on
a cat and take out certain organs. This process took about 6 weeks dissecting once a week. We would dissect the animal and have to write a
report on what we did and how we did it. It gave me a great learning
experience on where things are really located in the body. So when one
says that dissecting in high school is nothing but a joke I beg to differ.
If the structure is right and the teacher is serious about making the student learn, then it can be a successful dissection. The hands on experience can give the student the ability to make the decision if they are
capable of dissecting an animal or if not, maybe that will alter the persons choice of study in the future.

Dissecting an animal can aid in the persons choice of a particular
field in college. For example, if someone liked it when they were dissecting it might open up a new idea for them to think about when choos-

ing a field of study in college. If a person did not like it, that would close a few options so that they do not waste their precious time and money studying medicine. When that person finally comes to the dissecting part and does not like it, that is when they decide that it is not the thing for them. By this time that person has lost time and money on something that is not what they want to do. With this example, dissection has actually aided a person in choosing a career path that best fits the person or has shown them that the medical field is not for them. Computer simulation could not give a person the effect of seeing it in real life and making a decision if it interests the person or not.

When dissecting in high school I was made to learn all the tools that were involved in doing the dissection. Ms. Hess, my anatomy teacher, taught us about the dangers and the proper ways of using the scalpel, tongs, tweezers, and various other tools that aid in a successful dissection of a animal. A person is also getting the hands on experience not only with the animal but with the tools also. For example, the scalpel can be very dangerous if a person cuts the wrong way. Doing the dissection also can aid in a person using these various tools with precision and accuracy. Cutting just deep enough and just long enough are very important when dissecting.

Dissecting can also get most peoples attention a little more than a computer simulated dissection. Students will be more attentive just for the mere fact that there is something real in front of them. A person will be more interested in something that is not in everyday life. A computer is nothing new to hardly anyone today. When a person in high school gets to dissect for the first time its a whole different experience than they have ever been through. When your dealing with high school kids for the most part getting their attention and interest is not as easy as it is thought to be. I know when I was in high school it was tough to get my attention for a full class.

Dissection should be kept in schools today. If taken away the student would lose out on many things addressed earlier in the paper. Dissection also is a valuable tool for students to use in determining their future. Without it their is a major loss, and it should remain in schools.

Todd Langford
ENC 1102
Paper 2 Revision

Dissection: There Is Still a Need

People are arguing that dissection today is outdated. With the loss of dissection to computer simulated programs students are going to miss out on the many benefits that come along with it. Who knows, the high school kid that is dissecting the cat in anatomy class might like it enough to pursue a medical career as a brain surgeon, and develop new ways to operate on the human brain successfully.

Dissection in high school and in higher level education can be a great learning experience due to the hands-on experience that computer simulated programs cannot offer. If the dissection labs are designed correctly people can get a much better grasp of the organs and their position in the body. The computer cannot offer this type of visual even though it is three dimensional. Your still looking at something on a flat screen which is taking away a lot of realistic features about it. When I took anatomy in high school my labs were designed to make it nothing but a learning experience. My teacher made us do various incisions on a cat and take out certain organs. This process took about 6 weeks, dissecting only once a week. We would dissect the animal and have to write a report on what we did and how we did it. It gave me a great learning experience on where things are located in the body and how they really look and feel. The computer could not give me this same experience because feeling can not be done through the computer and also the art of cutting the animal. Bill Berlow stated in a article titled Dissections in Leon county that "if students learned anatomy only on CD-ROM, are you dealing with nature or are you dealing with the virtual world? We as science educators would hate to think that all work could be done on a computer screen".* If the teacher makes the kids do the experiment correctly and make them study what exactly they are removing from the animal then the structure is right and the class will have a successful dissection.

Dissecting an animal in high school can also aid in a persons choice of a particular field in college. For example, if someone liked it when they were dissecting it might open up a new idea for then to think about when choosing a field of study in college. If a person did not like it, that would close a few options so that they do not waste their precious time and money studying medicine. Without dissection before college many medical students are going to get to their dissection lab and be grossed out by the fact that they are touching internal organs and removing them. By this time they have spent a whole lot of money and time on something that they found out they did not want to do. With this example, dissection has actually aided in a persons career choice by either ruling out a career in the medical field or giving a person the opportunity to experience it and like it, so the medical career could be a strong consideration. Computer simulations could not give a person the effect of seeing it in real life and making a decision if it interests the person or not. Because computer screens don't have juices flowing out, the smell, and the feel that the real thing has.

When dissecting in high school I was made to learn all the tools that were involved in doing the dissection before the dissection was ever in progress. Ms. Hess, my anatomy teacher, taught us the dangers, needs, and proper ways of usage for the scalpel, tongs, tweezers, and various other tools that aid in a successful dissection of a animal. A person is also getting the hands-on experience not only with the animal but with the tools also. For example, the scalpel is a knife that if used incorrectly could cause a person harm. If the person never picks up another scalpel again in their life they have at least learned how to cut something with a knife safely and properly without causing harm to themselves. Doing the dissection also can aid in a person using these various tools with precision and accuracy. It will show a person if they have the ability to hold the scalpel correctly and make the cut just deep enough to get to where they want to be without messing anything up. It will show them if they can perform under pressure, granted that doing a dissection is not like operating on someone, but it has some pressure involved for the grade that a person will receive at the end of the dissection.

Dissection can also grasp a persons attention more than a computer simulated dissection. Students will be more attentive just for the mere fact that dissection is not a every day activity and there is something real in front of them. A computer is nothing new to anyone today. Kids are starting off at very young ages learning how to use computers. For the fact that computers are in everyday life people are eventually going to get bored with it. The dissection will give the person a opportunity to experience something new and interesting. And when you're dealing with high school kids getting their attention can sometimes can be tough to do. I know that when I was in high school it was tough to get my attention for a full class.

Dissection has been a tool of learning for decades, maybe even hundreds of years. Without it we could be losing out on brilliant doctors due to the fact that they never realized that they were interested in it. With out it there will be a major loss of a great learning experience in our society today.

Editor's Note: Bill Berlow's article appears as a sidebar to "It's Time to Cut Out Dissections" in the same issue of the *Tallahassee Democrat*.

Sample 4
Paper 3: Speculating about Causes Essay
Final Draft

BACKGROUND

This is the final draft of the third paper in English 102, the second half of the first-year writing requirement. In the course, students are to write four essays employing the argument genres in *The St. Martin's Guide to Writing* (5th edition). The first assignment was an evaluation essay where students critiqued a sample argument. The second assignment asked students to argue a position on a subject. Now, in the third essay, students are to explore the causes of a selected problem and, in the last essay, propose solutions to the problem. Students are to create a rhetorical situation for the writing and then generate an argument appropriate to the situation, using several outside sources.

In preparation for this assignment, the class has continued to study logical reasoning, the use of emotional appeals, and methods of establishing one's credibility as a writer. Students have worked on invention and development activities in class workshops. They also have exchanged early drafts with two classmates who completed a two-page peer response sheet and discussed their suggestions with the writer.

Joe is a low-key yet friendly student. He has been having some difficulty with his work in the course, but he does not seem very anxious about his writing or overly concerned about his grades. You've been pushing him to put forth more effort in the class even as you've looked to recognize his successes. He seems to be quite knowedgeable about his subject for this paper, the prohibition against paying college athletes, but he is having problems developing his ideas; his invention materials and early drafts have been skimpy. When he came in for his scheduled conference to go over his second rough draft, you discussed some general strategies of development. The following paper is what he came up with in his revision.

Students are allowed to rewrite one of their papers after it is returned with a grade.

ASSIGNMENT

Following the instructions from the "Speculating about Causes" chapter of *The St. Martin's Guide for Writing*, write a causal argument about a college-related issue. Choose an argument with "surprising" or "disputed" causes or consequences. A topic like "second-hand smoke may cause cancer" is not arguable enough. Be creative in your topic choice.

Consider societal trends or political and economic changes, or consider more pragmatic topics like the causes of ADD/ADHD or causes of poor reading skills or school failure.

Causal Argument Checklist

1. Is this a causal argument? Do you argue about what caused something to happen or what the consequences will be from something happening? Your argument must involve "surprising" or "disputed" causes or consequences. Will other sensible people have objections to your ideas? Do you anticipate these objections? You want an *arguable* causal claim, not a proven fact.

2. Consider the organization of your essay, which might contain these four basic features: 1) a description of the subject, 2) a presentation of proposed causes and reasons for them, 3) a refutation of counterarguments, and 4) the consideration and rejection of alternative causes. Do you order your ideas effectively?

3. Is your position on the issue clearly stated and appropriately qualified?

4. Review revising and editing principles to make sure you anticipate your opposition and have a well-supported argument.

5. Remember that you are dealing with probabilities and not certainties, so claim that your explanation is plausible, not that you have the only answer.

6. Is there enough evidence to support your explanation of causes or effects? Do you cite specific cases? Personal observations? Statistics?

7. Have you presented the causes with more certainty than is actually the case? Have you oversimplified your case? Have you shown (or at least argued) that each of the causes actually did contribute to the phenomenon? Have you placed too much importance on only one cause?

8. Is your essay properly formatted? Four full pages long? APA or MLA documented? Titled? Paginated? Have you checked for sentence clarity? Does each sentence say what you intend it to say? Have you fully developed paragraphs? Transitions?

9. Don't forget to check for errors before turning in your paper.

—Sources: *The St. Martin's Guide to Writing*

Editor's Note: This classroom context and paper come from a writing class taught by Christine Helfers at Arizona State University.

Scoring Guide for "Speculating about Causes" Essay

The introduction is engaging and grabs the reader's attention.

Excellent   *Good*   *Average*   *Poor*

The claim is appropriate to the assignment because it is about "surprising" or "disputed" causes or effects.

Excellent   *Good*   *Average*   *Poor*

Support for the claim is effectively developed.

Excellent   *Good*   *Average*   *Poor*

Conditions of rebuttal are considered with appropriate depth.

Excellent   *Good*   *Average*   *Poor*

The essay is clearly organized, logically moving from one point to the next.

Excellent   *Good*   *Average*   *Poor*

The paragraphs are fully developed with supporting details, using topic and clincher sentences.

Excellent   *Good*   *Average*   *Poor*

Sentences are varied in length and style and grammatically correct.

Excellent   *Good*   *Average*   *Poor*

The language reflects Standard English and college-level prose, with word choices that are precise and appropriate to the writing task.

Excellent   *Good*   *Average*   *Poor*

There are no errors in grammar, spelling, punctuation and usage.

Excellent   *Good*   *Average*   *Poor*

Joe Dora
English 102
Paper 3

It's for a Good Cause

John Voss was an excellent football player, an above average student, and a devoted and caring father. Yet John Voss had a problem, John
could not afford to support his family and continue to play football. But
if John quit playing football he would loose his scholarship and his
dream of attaining his college degree. I believe that it is necessary to pay
college athletes money for participating in college athletics. I understand the causes for paying the student athlete are the time constraints
of the student athlete, the allowance the student athlete receives is unacceptable, and the background of the student athlete.

One of the greatest arguments against paying the student athlete is
that the student athlete is already granted a full ride scholarship, and that
the student athlete receives special preferences the normal student does
not receive. First of all, not all student athletes are on a full ride scholarship. Some student athletes are on partial scholarships or have no
scholarship at all. These student athletes are considered walk-ons. The
walk-on has to support them selves and pay for their tuition.
Furthermore the special preferences that are given to the student athlete;
i.e. early registration, extra days off of school, and special tutoring; are
due to the reality that the student athlete need these benefits because of
their commitment to their respective sports. These athletes have enough
time restraints to consider let alone waiting in the long lines that accom-
pany the registration process. Which leads to my first cause for paying
the student athlete.

Since a student athlete must be a full time student (12 semester
hours or more) to participate in college athletics, the student athlete has
few hours for anything else besides their sport and the academics. On
the average, a student spends three hours day in class, and four hours
studying. Now, the student athlete also spends three hours practicing,
and 2 hours working out. Take into account the film sessions, learning
the game plan and that might take another 2 hours a day. Don't forget

the normal everyday tasks such as showering, eating and other everyday events and that's about 14 or fifteen hours spent in a day. The only thing the student has time left for is sleep, or maybe an ocassional movie. So ask yourself, is it fare to ask the student athlete to pick up a side job just to cover their everyday expenses in day to day life? I don't see where the student athlete could possibly find the time for a part time job to make a little money.

The National Collegiate Athletic Association (NCAA), the governing body of college athletics in the United States of America, recently approved a measure in which "Division-I athletes that have been enrolled for one year will be able to hold a part-time job and will be able to earn up to $2,000 a year" (Associated Press 1998) Therefore at $2,000 a year divided by 9 months in a school year that equals out to about $222 a month, which is definitely not enough money to live on for a month. Yet the sports programs generate millions of dollars for the university and the NCAA will only allow the student athlete a pathetic $222 a month? That would be similar to paying an artist $100 for a masterpiece that will be sold for hundred of thousand of dollars. Jim Rhome, a highly respected syndicated sports radio personality, said "At the end of the month, college athletes are completely broke. They can't afford to do their laundry, make a phone call or go out to eat. College athletes need to be paid somewhere for their participation in college athletics." (Rhome 1998) Rhome brings up a very good point, but the NCAA regulates how much the student athlete can be paid, therefore it would be illegal for the student athlete to receive anymore money. I could not conjecture having to live on only $222 a month. Should the student athlete be penalized and be able to earn only $2,000 a year when he could make more money as just a student. As a student athlete I would most likely have to borrow some extra money to get by from month to month, hopefully from my parents, assuming they could afford it.

So do most college students have parents that can afford to send the extra income sometime needed? On the average most students do, therefore it would be possible to get by with a little help from their parents.

Pat Farrell, Head Football Coach at St. Mary's High School in Phoenix, Arizona states "most of the athletes at the university level are inner city kids, therefore these kids are not capable to afford the normal college life that most students enjoy. The inner city kids do not have the resources for income that most student families have. . ." (Farrell P. personal communication). Mr. Farrell is right in saying that the inner city kid would have a tough time finding the extra money for an enjoyable college experience. Could you imagine seeing normal college students living a comparative luxurious life style, while you. the student athlete can barely afford to eat Snack Ramens? Or how about the students that ride around in their expensive bikes when the student athlete can't afford to call home and say hello. The inner city kids are at a definite disadvantage when it comes to the college lifestyle. It's almost somewhat unjust to the student athlete not to pay the student athlete, and rather let the student athlete struggle financially.

Now, in a society in which student athletes were paid to participate in college athletics, student athletes would be at level "playing field" as normal collegiate student. Student athletes such as John Voss would have been given the chance to be great quarterback, an excellent student, and an even better father had he had been paid to play quarterback at the university level. Instead, in today's setup John decided to give up his dream of being the professional quarterback and took a job to support his family.

Samples 5, 6, 7, and 8

Papers 4 and 5: Personal Essays in a Sequence

Final Drafts

BACKGROUND

The next four papers were written in the same first-year-writing class that is under study in Chapter 4, as part of a sequence of seven personal essays on a common topic: achievement. The first two papers to come were written by the same student: the first in response to Assignment 4, the second in response to Assignment 5. The next two papers were composed by two other students in the class, in response to Assignment 5. All four are final drafts, but students may rewrite as much as they want any paper they want, to work on their writing and improve their grade.

By this point in the semester, after eight weeks, five exploratory writings, and three formal essays, Heather has emerged as one of the most consistent and competent writers in the course. The comments on her last paper looked to challenge her to step up the level of difficulty in what she was attempting in her writing and get even more to say, more fully.

Amy has been rather quiet in class discussions, but it is evident that she is involved in the class and interested both in working on her writing and doing the best she can do in the course. Her writing has not measured up to her expectations or yours, but, through frequent talks with you after class and in conference, she has inspired your confidence and encouraged you to give her as much help as you can. In commenting on her recent essays, you've tried to ride the line between calling on her to develop her content and guiding her to clarify her expression.

Kandi has been a ball of energy in the class. She is always among the first to jump into the conversation and seems intent on contributing to the work of the class. Her writing has this same exuberance, but she seems to have trouble containing and getting control over all she wants to say. Your comments have routinely asked her to try to make her voice simpler and more direct, less sophisticated and more conversational, even as they have called on her to develop her key claims.

Students will write two more essays on achievement and, now that it is just past the midpoint of the course, they will be expected to give greater and greater attention to the overall shape, style, and correctness of their writing.

ASSIGNMENT 4

Identify something in your past that you wanted to achieve and use this experience as an occasion or instance for explaining how you go about striving for a goal. You may address what frame of mind you adopt in striving for such a goal or examine how you actually go about pursuing it. On the basis of this experience, what can you say about how you look at, or how you go about, striving for goals?

As in our previous formal essays, use your writing to discover what you can add to our classroom conversation about achievement and share your thoughts with readers. But make an additional effort, as you are writing or as you go back over what you have already got down on the page, to form your paper into a unified essay, where each of the parts looks to achieve a certain purpose and contributes to the whole. (For more on this assignment, see p. 193)

ASSIGNMENT 5

Explore one idea or set of related ideas on the downside of striving for goals, being ambitious, or devoting oneself to a goal. We are told, for example, to give ourselves completely to our tasks. But we know we can't always give ourselves fully to our goals. What are we to do in the face of such conflicting demands? How do we decide to give ourselves to one thing or another? What are the gains and losses of a life given to constant striving? Given to a certain kind of striving?

Or examine a popular attitude, view, or saying about achievement and modify or work against the idea. Look at the claim in light of your own experience and test it, turn it over on itself, or qualify it in some way. Is there a better way to see achievement or ambition? Is there something more to see than our everyday views might lead us to see?

Use your writing as a means of discovery and pay attention to how you shape the writing so that you get at your ideas and share them with your audience, the members of this class. Look to form your paper into a unified essay, where each of the parts contributes to the effect of the whole. Construct the essay around a central issue or idea, be selective about your introductory and concluding paragraphs, and arrange your writing in a way that will best get at your views and enable your readers to understand them. (For more on this assignment, see p. 214.)

SAMPLE 5

Heather G.
ENC 1101
Writing 4

It's Okay to Fail

I was the best! No matter where I competed I was guaranteed first place. The judges were completely mesmerized as I balanced on the beam, twirled on the bars, sprang over the vault, and tumbled on the floor. Gymnastics was my life. Since the age of ten I have been a gymnast. My first three years I competed on a team out of Miami, Florida, and I did extremely well. I was ranked the number one level three gymnast in the state of Florida for my age group. At the age of thirteen my big chance came. I was invited to compete on a German international gymnastics team in Germany. What was to be the greatest experience became the biggest shock ever! I went from being the best to the worst.

One could imagine just how discouraging this was. All of the other girls were awesome, and I was just a mere peon. I was nothing compared to these powerful and graceful athletes. Until then I had never failed, and now I was the epitome of failure. These next five years would be hell. They were years of broken toes and wrists, cracked ribs, monster bruises, and floods of tears. I was an utter failure my first year on the team. I only placed once the whole year. That being a sixth place on the floor. You don't understand how degrading that was! My self-esteem was flushed down the toilet, What had happened to me?

I realized that I was going to have to work a whole lot harder. That summer I trained like I've never trained before. Instead of six hours a day, I trained for eight. Yet the satisfaction wasn't quite there yet. I guess it was obvious.

Out of all the people I knew, Tom Richmond stands out in my mind. He was another American gymnast. Tom could tell how flustered I was, and he was determined to help me. He kept telling me how good I was and what I still needed improvement on. I distinctly recall one instance when Tom came up to me and said "Heather, you have an awesome beam routine, but you need to improve your split leap. The judges really like a good split leap." So I hopped on the balance beam and began to leap. After doing a couple leaps, I decided to go for it. I did the perfect split leap, but as I landed, my foot slipped off the beam, and I ended up scraping the whole side of my right leg, Not a pretty sight. As I was lying on the floor absolutely stunned, Tom walks away saying "Good split leap . . . except for the fall."

That year, with the help of Tom I did exceptionally well. I ended up placing first in Europe on beam and floor, and received a second all round rank in Europe as a level two gymnast. Although it was not first place, I was satisfied with myself and determined to do better the next year.

I progressively got better. The next year I was ranked number one, and was moved up one level. I was now an elite gymnast (level one). I would now be competing against the likes of Brandy Johnson and Phoebe Mills. I owed it all to Tom. I really feel that if it was not for Tom, I would not have gone as far as I did. He inspired me to help others. Tell them that failure was okay. One can't always be the best, but they can try their best. That was what really counted. I told people this because I knew it was true.

Those five years made a definate impression on me. I realized that I must keep an open mind when it comes to striving after a goal. Before my move to Germany, failure was never a word in my vocabulary. Now when I have a set goal, I try my best knowing that I might possibly fail. If I do fall on my face, it may hurt, but it's okay. I'll survive. I can easily get back up on my feet and try again. Not only did I learn a lot of German, but I learned a whole new view of achievement.

SAMPLE 6

Heather G.
ENC 1101
Writing 5

Personalized View of Achievement

Big cars, a lot of money, or even a first place rank are typical views of achievement. So often achievement is popularized by big prizes such as these. "Champaign wishes and caviar dreams." To several people this is the height of achievement. To have such a tremendous lifestyle that some scrawny British man monopolizes good television time by showing it off to thousands of pathetic American viewers, is the peak on the mountain of achievement. This type of living has been played up so much in the United States that everyone wishes for their champaign and caviar in life. They view achievement only as great wealth and social status.

Others view achievement as winning big in a contest or accomplishing some great athletic feat. If I learned this anywhere, I learned it in this class. When told to talk about achievement, quite a few of us wrote about athletic accomplishments. I even did. There was a time in my life when my ultimate goal was to do well athletic wise. Because of my environment, I considered myself pond scum until I received that first-place rank.

People in today's society think of achievement only as having success. When I say success, I mean having good jobs, lots of money, social status, or an Olympic gold medal. These are big goals. Society gets so caught up in this view of achievement that they fail to think of the little goals. (Such as having a good family life or a good friendship.) They feel that if one doesn't achieve anything big, that that person is a loser and a failure,

I do not have these great achievements, nor do I plan on having them, but I do not consider myself failure. To me, achievement is all the goals that I have set for myself and accomplished. These goals offer me fulfillment and personal gratification.

I set little goals for myself, such as . . . say dieting. If I feel that I have accomplished this dreadful task, then I am happy. No one gave me a lot of money or a gold medal. I wasn't even crowned queen of the lose five pounds club. It was personal. I achieved something I set for myself.

The one person who made me realize this was my father. He grew up poor on a farm in Modesto, California. His family milked cows for a living. He and his brothers never had a Christmas. The only gifts they received were gifts they had made for each other. Because I was fortunate enough to grow up with a Christmas every year and plenty of presents, I pitied my father when he told me this story. He told me not to because he was happy. He had the family and that was all that he needed. He and his family were content.

Way too many people are narrow-minded when it comes to the subject of achievement. It is society's fault. Society programs these ideas in our head causing people to fail to break away from the norm. If it is what society believes, then it is what they should believe. This makes life more difficult for people such as myself. These people constantly nag and push this kind of achievement on us. So what if I don't have big goals for now! All I want is to be content with myself. The goals I have and succeed in are all I need for personal satisfaction.

Amy T.
ENC 1101
Writing 5

Take a Chance

"I want to have it all, nothing more and nothing less." Unfortunately this is the way many people choose to live their lives. Feeling timid, unsure and unaware of the outcome or the sacrifices to be made along the road is a part of taking risks. Many people are not willing to do this and do not excell towards their goals. In order to achieve a goal than risks have to be willing to be taken. Risks can simply be defined as a chance of loss but the definition in comparison to what we make a risk to be is dissimilar. The attitude that we adopt for ourselves has a great deal to do with whether or not we are going to be successful. As achievers we look at risks as a dead end and definite drawback. Apparently this is a negative way of thinking of a situation and therefore becomes a set back to achievement. To us, a risk may include failing completely, being shut off from our goals, loosing our sense of ambition and being called worthless. Vitally we must reconsider and reanalyze whether or not a risk is a negative thing that brings us further away from true fulfillment. It is important to work towards handling one goal at a time and one day at a time.

Significantly realize what a goal would entail without risk. Being able to take risks enlightens the reward of achieving standard goals. "Standard" goals includes any act that is deserving of our full attention and effort in order to attain. The consequences of what is referred to as a risk such as failing are not as great of a set back as they may seem. For example, failing may result in several things; it may cause a lesser sense of self worth, it may cause embarrassment, or it may cause a lower sense of activation or stimulation. However, failing could possible result in positive aspects such as making us try harder next time, make us evaluate the things we truly want from the rest and give us the advantage of experience.

Accepting the challenge of risk taking could be considered a drawback in itself yet it is impossible to avoid. Rejection in humans is
extremely difficult to accept and having anything imperfect scares people in general. Many people like myself already have a sense of perfectionism that places us at an even greater disadvantage. Because of the
way we visualize ourselves, we feel that if the results of a circumstance
is less than perfect then we are unsuccessful. Apparently this statement
is false because not every thing is capable of being done in a perfect
sense. Frequently the concept of perfectionism is simply something that
is a part of the unrealistic imagination. We are successful in that our
complete effort was put forth and we tried. Many times we set ourselves
up and don't leave room to take risks or make changes in everyday situations. For example, I feel incomplete unless I devise a daily tentative
schedule. I like to have everything I must do: errands, classes, study
hours, etcetera, listed and next to them the time I will do them. This
makes me feel more organized and prepared for each task because I
have something that is concrete and I can be aware of my plans. If by
chance my schedule does not always run on time or the way I planned,
I sometimes feel anxious. After careful thought, I later realize that by
setting myself up, I must allow room to take a chance.

Some risks are simple yet some are more complicated. An example
of a more complex risk was seen in Gatsby, by working towards achieving his goal, he constantly took risks. His major risk was his unthought-
ful planning. He never had a plan for his future with Daisy, only the act
of the catch. He disposed all of his dreams because he chose to handle
things in an aggressive yet impromtu way. I think that it is safe to say
that he may have never really felt confident enough with himself to
think he would succeed, therefore there was no reason for him to plan
ahead. In "Rick", Rick took a major risk as a coach. He had to always
live with the thought that several boys were continously watching him
to see what his next move would be.* He could never be positive that
his plan would have a significant effect on Brad or any other members
of the team. Luckily it did, however, there was that unpredictable risk

involved. The risk of not having the impact that he should have on the team members or the risk of loosing the respect of his eager members. Any of these things would cause the coach to loose his superiority over the boys.

Whether it be a daily goal or long-term goal, the chance of loosing something, risking, must always be kept in perspective. Being aware of risk and dealing with changes does not always have to be a drawback but rather can be considered a golden stepping stone to a new path. A path that is walked on with the chance of falling every so often and being able to pick right back up and continue walking. Without risks our goal could be considered lofty or without stride. Opening ourselves up to accept rejection can be considered a part of maturing and developing our own sense of self worth. A friend much deserving of my admiration once advised me that when in doubt, risk it.

Editor's Note: "Rick" is the title of a student essay that was assigned from Charles Cooper and Rise Axelrod's *Reading Critically, Writing Well* (St. Martin's).

Kandi S.
ENG 1101
Writing 5

I've Learned More From Failure

Did you ever notice that guy in high school who would always try out for the football team with no shot in hell of making it? Or that nerd from out of no where who decides to run for class president. Both these character types have something in common, their drive to achieve; they knew and felt that if they were willing to lose they could win. It seemed though as soon as they were defeated they got right back in line; the dimmer their future, the brighter they would shine. They have very much achieved in that they faced up with reality. I soon saw this phase of achievement once I got settled in to college.

You see I share the same situation with that guy who wants to play football and that nerd who wants to be class president. I was shot down immediately in college by not getting into the sorority of my choice. Yes, disappointment does sometimes occur, but I thought I was exactly what they wanted; the girl who had practically everything in high school. I went from head cheerleader, homecoming court member, and four year class officer to what I defined as a dud in matter of three months.

I thought sorority life was perfect for me, and I thought I was perfect for them. I wanted to be a Alpha Delta Pi. You see every girl in my high school who came to Florida State was a Alpha Delta Pi, from former cheerleaders, to old neighbors, to even old fellow Kiwanette members. I felt sure this was the home for me. I was aware of the so called "Rush Tragedies" in that many girls are left out, but I never expected this. During the entire rush week I was striving to become a Alpha Delta Pi, I felt like one, looked like one right down to the earrings I wore. I felt for sure on that last day of the rush process, that on bid day I would be right back at that Alpha Delta Pi house with all of the sisters and those older girls I had looked up to so much in high school.

That last night of rush I was so relieved to fill in their name. I knew for sure that my Rho Chi would not have to come and tell me the next morning that I did not get a bid. I went to church that following day and was home by noon. The Rho Chi had said that she would be stopping by the girls' rooms who did not get bids, but this possibility did not even occur to me. I was cooking my pizza for lunch when I heard that knock at my door. It was not until I opened it that I realized I had not received a bid. As I saw my Rho Chi's face, tears began to fall on mine, I felt like a total loser. Did those girls hate me? What happened? Was I black-balled? I felt betrayed, as if I had no friends on this earth, especially at FSU. I felt as if I would now never meet the girls that were to be my new best friends because they would be in sororities.

As the first week of school went on, I put to rest those sad feelings and concentrated on my classes. Though, as I walked through campus and saw many girls who seemed to be just like me, wearing those letters I still felt very empty inside. It was not until my best friend from high school, who goes to the University of Florida, came to visit me one weekend that I began to look upon the whole situation in a different light. She reminded me that sometimes you do lose but you just have to get right up again.

It was at this point in my life that I had achieved by losing. You see, we all can learn from those losers who get right back in line. Most girls that I know who are similar to me would have gone home after this dis-appointment to go to the local college there, but not me. I found out that those who try are achievers in themselves. If you do not try you'll never know. I really forgot what achievement was until I had failed. I found that you can give in, you can give out, but you don't give up, and I did just that. I have found things to keep me active with my free time and making friends has been easier than I thought. Next year I do plan to get right back in line and rush again, but this time I plan to look at other sororities and keep my options open. To me by rushing again I will truly achieve. I have found that success all the time is just not healthy and that one might learn more from a little failure now and then to keep them humble.

I was a lucky one with a perhaps good head on my shoulder to real-ize that my failure was not a loss but a gain. Others might have been torn apart by the powers of achievement that I once had. Achievement is almost like playing with the devil except that you always get something in the end, as I got the courage to actually become a regular college student without credits to my name and still be content.

My learning from failure will not be complete until I go home for my high school's homecoming. You see it will be my first time home since I got to college. I will be crowning the new homecoming queen, but I will also be being judged by many of my peers and I hope that I will be able to hold my head high without having a sorority to my name. I would like to show them that I could be and am content with just being Kandi, without that title of my achievement before or after my name. Then I will have achieved the ultimate by facing the fear of gossip.

> ## Samples 9 and 10
> ## Paper 7: Personal Essay in a Sequence
> ## Final Drafts

BACKGROUND

The next two papers were written by two of the case-study students—Rob and Cherri—whose work is examined in Chapter 4. They are the final drafts of Writing 7, the last assignment in the sequence of assignments on achievement. Students completed a rough draft at the end of week 11, received comments from their peers, and handed in the final draft in the middle of week 12. To get a sense of the students behind these texts and their work thus far in the course, see Chapter 4.

ASSIGNMENT

> A personal essay frequently is not autobiographical at all, but what it does keep in common with autobiography is that, through its tone and tumbling progression, it conveys the quality of the author's mind. Nothing gets in the way. Because essays are directly concerned with the mind and its idiosyncrasy, the very freedom the mind possesses is bestowed on this branch of literature that does honor to it, and the fascination of the mind is the fascination of the essay.
>
> Edward Hoagland
"What I Think, What I Am"

In this essay, this attempt to think through and come to terms with what you think, I'd like you to consider how your goals fit in with, grow out of, or depart from, your parents' or your close friends' goals or their sense of what it means to achieve. If you want, you can look at your goals in relation to what you see as our culture's views about achievement. What similarities or differences do you see, and how do you account for them?

I'd like you to focus your essay on why you are striving for the things you are and how these goals fit in with, or in some way contrast with, those of your parents or friends or culture. To what extent do you think your goals have been influenced by the setting you grew up in? To what extent have they been shaped by your reacting against others close to you or striving to be different from them? To what extent are your goals shaped or influenced by the attitudes and values of your town or by the larger culture, as reflected for example in the marketplace and media?

Again, you do not have to take up all of these issues. The questions are there to help you find something—some idea, some pattern or inconsistency, some puzzlement, some slant—that you might take up in this paper and, by writing about it, come to terms with it. Ultimately, your goal is to come to some understanding about the sources that influence your major goals and to share that understanding with the rest of us. By now it should be clear that the more your ideas or perspectives go somehow beyond the immediate and the obvious, somehow beyond what others in the class already know or could say, the more likely we will be interested in reading the essay and get something out of it. And, before that, the more you try to figure out something that is important to you, the more likely you will get involved in the writing and get something to say, first of all, for yourself, which you can then give to others.

Rob L.
ENC 1101
Writing 7

Under the Influence

Life is full of influences. Without them, we wouldn't have done some of the things we've done. Whether it was ten years ago or two hours ago, by family or friends, we were all influenced or pressured in one way or another. As we grow older and wiser, we will influence others just like it was done to us. (Though on the topic of influence, I'd rather use the word "push" instead.)

I can admit that I'm easily influenced, but only to a certain extent. When it comes to drugs, that's when I draw the line, but I believe that is a different type of influence. I feel that I was influenced in athletics the most of all. My parents pushed me, my father in particular, to do many things. They made school my first priority and wrestling my second. Notice that I said "they made." They both felt that school was most important and that wrestling was more important than "hangin' out" with my friends. I guess my need to make friends was a product of this. I suppose that my father wanted me to become a superb athlete, so he didn't want me conversing with anyone other than athletes. Since athletics has always been a part of my family, tradition in some ways, I was to follow the same trail as others before me. Sports wasn't exactly a necessity to be a part of the Langon family, but it was important to my father so I went along with it.

Numerous times during wrestling season my father would lecture me about what it takes to win and to be a champion. He told me that, like life, you need to make sacrifices in order to get something in return, in other words, you need to give a little to get a little. I was often reminded what would happen if I was to slack or miss practice. He would be disappointed and pissed off if he knew I had missed out on practice. I would never hear the end of it. My father made me feel like the scum of the earth whenever he would lecture me. All these lectures would push me further away from playing any sports, but there was some kind of connection that would pull me back. It's hard for me to explain this connection, but if you ask any true athlete he or she would understand what you were talking about.

With all the hassles there were good times to go along with them also. When my father would push me to work harder and harder, I would see results in a few days. He would push me to the point that I would break down and cry. All the pressure and stress would come out in an instant. But it made me strong beyond belief, it felt like no one could break me, and it made me feel good, real good. I loved working hard and winning, I felt like I was on top of the world. I had lost about twenty pounds since wrestling started, but it was twenty pounds below my natural weight. I was beating my opponents at these weights, but I often lost to wrestlers who were wrestling at there natural weight. The only reason I lost these matches was the reason that my strength wasn't at it's fullest potential. I was somewhat depressed about losing these matches, so I resorted to steroids to suppress my idea that I was weak. Even though this point of my life was down the tubes, I really didn't care what anyone thought about me "juicin", because I was satisfying my urge to become strong again, quickly. This episode in my life was short, very short, and also unimportant.

When I first moved to Florida, my family and I tried to find a school with a good reputation for having great athletics. It felt like athletics was taking a more important role than school, so I applied myself more to wrestling than my schoolwork. I still maintained a good GPA due to the fact that I wasn't going to make a career of wrestling. I knew that academics was more important than being an athlete, because an education was going to give me a future, not sports.

I found my life to be complex and controversial. I suppose a majority of my actions, throughout my life, were made out of influences. I haven't made any bad choices, nor was I led in the wrong direction, because I wouldn't be where I'm right now.

SAMPLE 10

Cherri S.
ENC 1101
Writing 7

My Own Goals

My out look on goals and goal seeking is very different from the world around me. My parents started off with nothing, and through a lot of hard work have acquired a rather stable amount of wealth. Because of this, my mother puts a high value on money and education, and she has tried to pass this on to me. I too value education, but money has always been something that isn't all that important to me. Of course, I want to earn enough money to be comfortable. I do not to want to have to worry where my next meal is coming from, or how I am going to pay the light bill, but more that any thing I want to be happy in my chosen profession. Whenever I talk about wanting to become a teacher my mother immediately mentions that there is not a lot of money in teaching, as if money were the only thing that is important.

I had the same conflict at school too. I went to a private junior high school, and if you didn't wear a certain type of clothes or act a certain way you were considered an outcast. I was miserable there because I wasn't willing to give up my individuality to be like every one else. When I started high school I went to public school for the first time in my life. Once I was there I had the chance to meet a lot more people than I had before. The rich kids all reminded me of a big flock of sheep. They all dressed and acted exactly alike. They talked about others behind their backs, and made fun of people who weren't just like them. Their idea of success was to drive a BMW, have a desk job, make a lot of money, and look good to the others within their little group. I was immediately turned off by them because of the way they treated people who were different. The poor kids, on the other hand seemed to except anyone. They stuck together and were very friendly. They weren't afraid to be different, and they didn't give a damn what others thought about them. Most of them were from unstable homes, and they had never had it easy. These people didn't care about social status, they cared about each other. For the first time I was making friends easily and really felt like I could be myself. My mother was not exactly thrilled with my new friends at first, but after she met them she really started to like them.

Of course, there are still people who only look at the outside of others instead of the inside. I remember having a teacher named Mrs. Larkin who constantly made fun of our little group that sat in front of the trophy cases in the morning. Yet, she praised the rest of the kids in our class and let them do anything they wanted. I had to practically beg her for a pass to go call my mom one day, and when I got out to the pay phone there were two of her favorite students who were suppose to be doing errands for her out on the phone making a drug deal for the week- end. I remember thinking, "I wish she could see her star students now". I wanted to tell her about that every time she made fun of us, but I never did.

We talk a lot about how we let television and the people around us influence our decisions in life, but I don't think we should allow these forces to think for us or make our important decisions. When I look at the goals in my life I see things that will make me happy. They aren't lofty aspirations that would impress others, or things that would even be important to others, but they are important to me. The friends I made in high school are some of the most influential people in my life because they showed me that it was possible to be happy without putting on a show for all the world to see and approve of. Now when I begin to seek a goal I think about whether or not I am striving for that goal to impress someone else, or if achieving it will help someone around me, and make me happy. Goal seeking and achieving should be based on your own personal outlook on life, not on some generic goal that you let others make up for you.

Appendix

RUBRIC FOR ANALYZING COMMENTS

Warnock

"Drugs Legal"

FOCUS	1	1a	2	2a	3	4	4a	5	5a	5b	6	7	8	9	10	11	11a	Total
Content	1	1	1	1	1	1		1	1	1	1	1	1		1	1	1	17
Organization		1		1	1		1		1		1		1			1	1	11
Style							1											5
Correctness																		
Context													1					1

MODE	1	1a	2	2a	3	4	4a	5	5a	5b	6	7	8	9	10	11	11a	Total
Corrective																		
Criticism																		
Qualified Criticism																		
Praise																		
Command																		
Advice		1							1									2
Closed Question																		
Open Question	1	1	1	1	1	1		1					1		1	1		10
Reflective	1				1	1		1			1			1				5

Peterson

"Drugs Legal"

comment no. →	1a	2	3	4	5	6	7	8	9	10	11	12/a	13	14	15	15a	16	16a	17	17a	Total
FOCUS																					
Content	||				|	|	|	|	|	|	|	|||	|	|							14
Organization		|													|	|					3
Style			|																		1
Correctness				|																	1
Context														|			|		|		3
MODE																					
Corrective																		|			1
Criticism		|														|					1
Qualified Criticism		|																			1
Praise				|										|							3
Command																					
Advice			|														|				2
Closed Question					|	|	|		|	|	|						|				8
Open Question	|							|				|									3
Reflective	|												|		|				|		4

Analysis of Teacher Comments

	Est'd Comp Scholars	New Comp Scholars	Both Groups
Focus			
Content	54	39	48
Organization	11	10	11
Style	13	23	17
Correctness	2	13	6
Context	20	15	18
Mode			
Corrective	1	10	5
Criticism	7	13	9
Qual Crit	7	4	6
Praise	12	15	13
Command	8	5	7
Advice	10	13	11
Closed Ques	6	4	5
Open Ques	13	10	12
Reflective	36	26	32

This table shows, in percentages, how the two groups of teachers whose responses are showcased in Chapters 1 and 3 distribute their comments across the various focuses and modes. The percentages of the nine established teacher-scholars are based on 13 sets of comments on three sample student essays. The percentages of the six new composition teacher-scholars are based on eight sets of comments—all in response to papers written by students in their own classes.

Analysis of My Comments in Chapter 4

Focus

Content	74
Organization	4
Style	6
Correctness	0
Context	16

Mode

Corrective	0
Criticism	4
Qual Crit	6
Praise	24
Command	1
Advice	4
Closed Ques	4
Open Ques	22
Reflective	35

This table shows, in percentages, an analysis of my own comments on the three case-study students' writing in Chapter 4. The analysis is based on the nine papers that are discussed in the chapter, three by each of the students. All three papers were written in the first nine weeks of the semester and were open to further revision.

Analysis of My Comments
to the Three-Case Study Students

	To Rob	To Chris	To Cherri
Focus			
Content	69	78	74
Organization	6	2	4
Style	1	0	16
Correctness	0	0	0
Context	24	20	6
Mode			
Corrective	0	0	0
Criticism	2	6	4
Qual Crit	4	13	4
Praise	33	20	19
Command	2	0	0
Advice	1	0	8
Closed Ques	2	6	3
Open Ques	14	20	31
Reflective	41	35	31

This table shows, in percentages, an analysis of my comments to each of the three case-study students in Chapter 4. In each case, the percentages are based on responses I made on three of their nine formal papers in the course: Writing 1, Writing 4, and Writing 5, all of which were written in the first nine weeks of the semester.

RUBRIC FOR ANALYZING COMMENTS

comment no. —>   Total

FOCUS

Content																			
Organization																			
Style																			
Correctness																			
Context																			

MODE

Corrective																			
Criticism																			
Qualified Criticism																			
Praise																			
Command																			
Advice																			
Closed Question																			
Open Question																			
Reflective																			

Contributors

Chris Anson, North Carolina State University

Simone Billings, Santa Clara University

Ron DePeter, James Madison University

Peter Elbow, University of Massachusetts–Amherst

Anne Ruggles Gere, University of Michigan

Christine Helfers, Arizona State University

Glynda Hull, University of California–Berkeley

Richard Larson, Lehman College, City University of New York

Margaret Lindgren, The University of Cincinnati

Ben McClelland, University of Mississippi

Frank O'Hare, Ohio State University

Peggy O'Neill, Georgia Southern University

Jane Peterson, Richland College

Summer Smith, Penn State University

Patricia Stock, National Council of Teachers of English

Tom Thompson, The Citadel

Edward White, California State University–San Bernardino

Tilly Warnock, University of Arizona

Index